Accelerating Sustainable Energy Transition(s) in Developing Countries

Accelerating sustainable energy transitions away from carbon-based fuel sources needs to be high on the agendas of developing countries. It is key in achieving their climate mitigation promises and sustainable energy development objectives. To bring about rapid transitions, simultaneous turns are imperative in hardware deployment, policy improvements, financing innovation, and institutional strengthening. These systematic turns, however, incur tensions when considering the multiple options available and the disruptions of entrenched power across pockets of transition innovations. These heterogeneous contradictions and their trade-offs, and uncertainties and risks, have to be systematically recognized, understood, and weighed when making decisions.

This book explores how the transitions occur in fourteen developing countries and broadly surveys their technological, policy, financing, and institutional capacities in response to the three key aspects of energy transitions: achieving universal energy access, harvesting energy efficiency, and deploying renewable energy. The book shows how fragmented these approaches are, how they occur across multiple levels of governance, and how policy, financing, and institutional turns could occur in these complex settings.

This book will be of interest to students and scholars of energy and climate policy, development studies, international relations, politics, strategic studies, and geography. It is also useful to policymakers and development practitioners.

Laurence L. Delina, a Rachel Carson Fellow, conducts research at the Frederick S. Pardee Center for the Study of the Longer-Range Future at Boston University, USA.

Routledge Studies in Energy Transitions
Series Editor: Dr. Kathleen Araújo
Stony Brook University, USA

Considerable interest exists today in energy transitions. Whether one looks at diverse efforts to decarbonize, or strategies to improve the access levels, security, and innovation in energy systems, one finds that change in energy systems is a prime priority.

Routledge Studies in Energy Transitions aims to advance the thinking which underlies these efforts. The series connects distinct lines of inquiry from planning and policy, engineering and the natural sciences, history of technology, STS, and management. In doing so, it provides primary references that function like a set of international, technical meetings. Single and co-authored monographs are welcome, as well as edited volumes relating to themes, like resilience and system risk.

Series Advisory Board

Morgan Bazilian, Columbia University, Center for Global Energy Policy (US)
Thomas Birkland, North Carolina State University (US)
Aleh Cherp, Central European University (CEU, Budapest) and Lund University (Sweden)
Mohamed El-Ashry, UN Foundation
Jose Goldemberg, Universidade de Sao Paolo (Brasil) and UN Development Program, World Energy Assessment
Michael Howlett, Simon Fraser University (Canada)
Jon Ingimarsson, Landsvirkjun, National Power Company (Iceland)
Michael Jefferson, ESCP Europe Business School
Jessica Jewell, IIASA (Austria)
Florian Kern, University of Sussex, Science Policy Research Unit and Sussex Energy Group (UK)
Derk Loorbach, DRIFT (Netherlands)
Jochen Markard, ETH (Switzerland)
Nabojsa Nakicenovic, IIASA (Austria)
Martin Pasqualetti, Arizona State University, School of Geographical Sciences and Urban Planning (US)
Mark Radka, UN Environment Programme, Energy, Climate, and Technology
Rob Raven, Utrecht University (Netherlands)
Roberto Schaeffer, Universidade Federal do Rio de Janeiro, Energy Planning Program, COPPE (Brasil)
Miranda Schreurs, Technische Universität München, Bavarian School of Public Policy (Germany)
Vaclav Smil, University of Manitoba and Royal Society of Canada (Canada)
Benjamin Sovacool, Science Policy Research Unit (SPRU), University of Sussex (UK)

Titles in This Series Include

Accelerating Sustainable Energy Transition(s) in Developing Countries
The challenges of climate change and sustainable development
Laurence L. Delina

'A thought-provoking volume that ties together the salient topic of energy transitions through a diverse array of lenses. Its engagement with institutional theory, technology studies, energy policy, and finance makes this a book to be reckoned with.'

– **Benjamin K. Sovacool,** *Professor of Energy Policy,*
University of Sussex, UK

'The hopes of the Paris Agreement in 2015 were quickly quelled by Trump's presidency and his climate change skepticism. Delina's book is extremely timely in this era of uncertainty and urgently calls for the acceleration of sustainable energy transitions in developing countries. This book makes a major contribution on how to evoke this change, focusing on the fields of hardware, financing and institution shift.'

– **May Tan-Mullins,** *Dean of Graduate Studies, and Director of Asia and*
Pacific Studies, University of Nottingham Ningbo China, China

'Current development pathways fail to propel the world toward a sustainable and more prosperous future for human society and the planet. The countries that need to develop the most are also those that stand to lose the most from climate-change-related impacts. The good news is there is a better future to be had. By achieving a sustainable energy system transition, we can take our global environment and development goals and "move the needle" toward making them a reality. This book accurately illuminates the indisputable linkages between energy access, poverty alleviation and sustainable development through achieving energy system transitions across the developing global south. By taking stock of the current capacities available for accelerating the transition, it provides a menu of solutions across policy, financing and governance to tackle the vast barriers presently preventing us from moving at the speed and scale required. There is no one silver bullet and the task ahead is immense. But as explained in this book, an energy system transition that is socially just offers us a better, more prosperous future for all.'

– **Andrew Steer,** *President and Chief Executive Officer,*
World Resources Institute, USA

'Laurence Delina's new book presents research findings that make a significant contribution to the current literature on sustainability and energy development. The analysis is novel and the book fills a vacuum for a better understanding of sustainable energy transitions from a developing country perspective. The author's key message is that the deployment of transition hardware to achieve sustainable energy development and climate change mitigation goals will require enabling and inclusive policy frameworks, appropriate and flexible financing mechanisms and, most importantly, institutional arrangements to channel energy transition.'

– **Debajit Palit,** *Associate Director, The Energy and*
Resources Institute, TERI, India

'Laurence Delina's book is a timely and significant contribution to a real discussion that policymakers in developing countries are already having. As a climate change negotiator for the Philippines and as a sustainable energy advocate, Delina presents comprehensive information on and analysis of our options. He grounds his analysis on the Sustainable Development Goals (SDG) and the Paris Agreement under the United Nations Framework Convention on Climate Change, both agreed to in 2015. The book also profiles fourteen developing countries: Bhutan, Brazil, Chile, China, El Salvador, India, Indonesia, Morocco, Nepal, Philippines, South Africa, Thailand, Vietnam, and Zambia. Given the diversity of these countries, geographically and in terms of state of development, the insights and lessons Delina extracts from these case studies will inform developing countries of any region, whether the country is middle income or less developed. The book reassures and gives practical guidance for all our countries to achieve an energy-secure future, one that guarantees access to affordable energy to the poor without sacrificing the environment and exacerbating climate change.'

– **Antonio La Viña,** *Executive Director, Manila Observatory,*
and Climate Change Lead Negotiator for the Philippines

'Laurence Delina's new book starts from the premise that "a global transition to socially inclusive and low carbon development that is responsive to poverty reduction has become indispensable." Founded firmly in the belief that such transitions are not only necessary but also achievable, *Accelerating Sustainable Energy Transition(s) in Developing Countries* makes a major contribution towards clarifying the choices that lay before key decision-makers when determining how such ambitious goals might best be operationalized at the national level.'

– **Ed Brown,** *Senior Lecturer in Human Geography,*
Loughborough University, UK, and National Co-Coordinator,
UK Low Carbon Energy for Development Network

'*Accelerating Sustainable Energy Transition(s) in Developing Countries* is rich in promise and possibilities. It puts forth evidence to demonstrate that such a transition is both possible and desirable in fourteen nations. Overall, this is a work of significant breadth exploring technologies, policy strategies, financial paths and institutional support mechanisms for supporting a global energy transition that requires expedience. It is a valuable gateway into what is perhaps the greatest challenge mankind has ever faced.'

– **Scott Victor Valentine,** *Assistant Dean (Research) and*
Associate Professor, Lee Kuan Yew School of Public Policy,
National University of Singapore, Singapore

Accelerating Sustainable Energy Transition(s) in Developing Countries

The Challenges of Climate Change and Sustainable Development

Laurence L. Delina

LONDON AND NEW YORK

from Routledge

First published 2018 by Routledge

2 Park Square, Milton Park, Abingdon, Oxfordshire OX14 4RN
52 Vanderbilt Avenue, New York, NY 10017

Routledge is an imprint of the Taylor & Francis Group, an informa business

First issued in paperback 2019

British Library Cataloguing-in-Publication Data
A catalogue record for this book is available from the British Library

Library of Congress Cataloging-in-Publication Data
Names: Delina, Laurence L., author.
Title: Accelerating sustainable energy transition(s) in developing countries :
   the challenges of climate change and sustainable development /
   Laurence L. Delina.
Description: Abingdon, Oxon ; New York, NY : Routledge, 2018. |
   Includes bibliographical references.
Identifiers: LCCN 2017026355 | ISBN 9781138741133 (hb) |
   ISBN 9781315182995 (ebook)
Subjects: LCSH: Power resources—Developing countries. | Energy
   development—Developing countries. | Sustainable development—
   Developing countries.
Classification: LCC TJ163.25.D44 D45 2018 | DDC 333.7909172/4—dc23
LC record available at https://lccn.loc.gov/2017026355

ISBN: 978-1-138-74113-3 (hbk)
ISBN: 978-0-367-24470-5 (pbk)

Typeset in Goudy
by Apex CoVantage, LLC

To my brothers, Michael and Rito Jr.

Contents

Figures

Tables

Foreword

The transition to a world where we have sustainable energy for all needs to be intensely driven and built as a movement. Laurence Delina's focus on accelerating the transition in developing countries should spur us on. It is an excellent addition to our understanding of what it will take.

Today, we risk breaking the promises we made in 2015 in Paris at the Climate Conference and in New York at the General Assembly's adoption of the Sustainable Development Goals. The latest data from the Global Tracking Framework produced by the organizations in the Sustainable Energy for All Knowledge Hub, led by the World Bank and the International Energy Agency, show that we are not on track to meet our climate and sustainable development ambitions. While many innovations are taking place and there are remarkable stories of progress all around the world, the transition lacks speed and scale.

To reach the ambition of the sustainable development goals within the targets agreed in the climate agreement, we need to build energy systems that for the first time in history provide everybody with clean, reliable, and affordable energy. It may seem audacious, but it is within our technical knowhow; it can be financed. But it will require a shift in mindset, new priorities, political leadership, and reoriented institutions.

It means rethinking our more than 100-year monolithic approach to centralized energy generation, distribution, and consumption predicated upon fossil fuels as the key source. Our focus will need to embrace more integrated energy systems, combining renewable energy with other sources in an increasingly clean mix, and combining centralized with distributed, or off-grid power sources.

Our approaches to regulation will need to keep pace with or open up space for new business models and for a world where energy comes from multiple sources and points in where energy is stored in buildings and cars and the landscape. The financial models will shift too, and our relationship to the energy system as consumers will shift as we contribute and consume.

This book enjoins us to rise to that challenge, to commit to greater action, to be bold, to do it quickly, and to do it together.

The timelines of our present challenge are tough: 2030 for the Sustainable Development Goals (SDGs), 2050 for the Paris Agreement. The future path looks steep, but all we need to do is look back at where we have come from to know that we can scale these new heights. In my years working for development and climate action, I have seen how we can make the impossible possible by daring to imagine what the future world will look like and how it will empower and improve life for everyone.

Putting our economy back in balance with the planet's chemistry calls us to a degree of focus, discipline, smart policy, inclusive partnerships, and political leadership that often eludes us. We will need to move to a world where decisions we make now that will benefit us, our children, and our grandchildren will carry the day in the ballot box, now. A revolution in energy productivity, tighter and tighter standards of efficiency for vehicles, buildings, appliances, mean cleaner air, and good local jobs, but are not the stuff of campaign promises yet.

Laurence Delina is right when he contends that we need a simultaneous turn in hardware deployment, policy, financing, and institutions to accelerate the transition.

Institutions are key. The SDGs were crowdsourced from countries, civil society, and businesses across the world. The Paris Agreement would have remained out of reach without the engagement of cities and businesses as well as civil society and governments, with their message that they needed and would welcome a bold outcome.

These changes in the way we arrive at agreements now needs to be mirrored in the way we secure action and implementation. Countries and cities across the world need to have access to evidence and data to make no-regrets long-term decisions. Global goals need to be translated into national and local plans and into policy reform priorities, structural changes, institution building, and a place where good long-term investments can be made, domestic and international, public and private.

Policy needs to be coherent. Prices need to be right, carbon prices need to be effective, finance needs to be able to flow. Harmful fossil fuel subsidies need to be eliminated, quickly. Often, good news travels more slowly – what works in one jurisdiction may not be known by neighbors struggling with the same set of problems. Cooperation and partnership are key.

The energy transition that is already under way is at the vanguard of the economic transformation that is called for by the boldness of global sustainable development goals in a world where warming should be limited to 'well below 2 degrees' as we said in Paris. This is the challenge of this generation. It is on our watch that we will build economies that are clean, attract new businesses into cities with clear air and efficient fast transport options, with digitalized energy grids that minimize use and where new generations of appliances bring everything to the fingertips of even the poorest among us. It is on our watch that we will support communities whose proud pasts were identified with the fossil fuels that gave us the wealth we have today to thrive through this transition, retraining and finding new ways to generate income and livelihoods. It's on our watch that the excitement of capturing energy around us, some of it not yet fully imagined, will offer us opportunities for more inclusive societies.

As Laurence Delina underscores, I believe we are not running away from an energy system that was polluting and served some but not all. We are running to a brightly imagined future. Sustainable energy for all is essential and achievable and ours to do.

Rachel Kyte
Chief Executive Officer of Sustainable Energy for All,
and Special Representative of the United Nations Secretary General
for Sustainable Energy for All
New York
26 June 2017

Preface

I began writing this book in 2015 when the world was starting to witness a number of tectonic shifts in the ways human societies are ordered (and, to a large extent, dis-ordered). It was during this period that the community of nations agreed in Paris to decarbonize their economies in response to global anthropogenic climate change. Three months before that, nations also agreed on a new development agenda that brings to fore the word 'sustainability.' In addition, societies are also politically changing, with democracy, science, and human dignity being challenged across the political spectrum. The impacts of climate change, meanwhile, continue to affect lives and livelihoods – with many of these largely felt in developing countries. Five-hundred-year storms become frequent; prolonged droughts are commonplace; record-breaking temperatures are the new norm. Truly, the year 2015 will remain in history as the beginning of the period of large-scale political, social, and, to a large extent, physical changes.

The ways in which humanity responds to these tectonic changes, however, remain tenuous. Fossil fuel combustion continues. The grip of powerful actors to maintain their incumbency in the energy sector has become tighter. Climate change denialism is strong in the highest echelon of governments. It seems now that meeting the ambitions of the Paris Agreement and the 2030 Agenda for Sustainable Development are in jeopardy. But, the transition to sustainable energy systems (the modus operandi by which the Agreement and Goal Numbers 7 and 13 of the 2030 Agenda are animated) is expected to proceed despite changes in politics. Sustainable energy transition (the changes in the technologies, structures, cultures, and practices in the extraction, production, delivery, and consumption of energy) is occurring across scales. The disruption of powerful energy monoliths is happening nonetheless – yet, not rapidly enough.

Rapid transition is vital if we are to meet the ambition of the Paris Agreement and the 2030 Agenda. This is a process imploring us to look at the many facets of energy transition as it is currently executed and, most importantly, in determining what needs to be done for the goal of accelerated transition to materialize in earnest. We, in the developing world, are already experiencing extreme weather events (such as super typhoons) and extended droughts. These events directly affect our lives and livelihoods. As climate change intensifies, we can only expect further challenges, from the availability of secure water and food supply to the stability of our communities, institutions, and governments. We, however, face not only the impacts of climate change; we also continue to battle lingering deprivation, hunger, and inequality. Most recently, as politics shift, our troubles also include those associated with the protection of our human rights and, at its core, our democracy. One also has to throw into that messy pot a number of other mega-changes that we, in the developing world, are experiencing: increasing population, rapid urbanization, and increasing consumption, among others. With a sense of foreboding, this array of challenges requires a systemic and urgent transition.

We do not necessarily know what the future can be, but we can at least prepare, mitigate, and adapt for some of its eventualities. I wrote this book with optimism, subscribing to the tenets of learning by example and learning by doing. Here, I offer a synthesis of how developing countries can work towards accelerating their energy transitions. I do not claim to provide a comprehensive bird's-eye view of the necessary turns in policy, financing, and institutions; rather, I concede that what I can offer instead is a humble toad's view – looking up from the ground.

I write this book as a contribution to the emerging literature of accelerated energy transitions while acknowledging my own normative positions in relation to it. I am a Filipino academic having grown up in a rural farming community in one of the southernmost parts of the Philippines, where energy poverty was the norm. I grew up studying with a kerosene lamp at night and gathering fuel wood for cooking. I spent extended periods of time living and working in the developing world. I was employed in a state-owned development banking institution in the Philippines and have worked as a resident research consultant at the United Nations in Thailand before deciding to take a life in academia. While most of my education was in the southern Philippines, I have also received graduate education and training in northern universities – in Auckland, New South Wales, Harvard, and Boston universities, respectively. In these great universities, I had the opportunity to learn from Macapado Muslim, Rufa Cagoco-Guiam, Yvonne Underhill-Sem, Ruth Frances Irwin, Mark Diesendorf, Sheila Jasanoff, and Anthony Janetos. My education and experiences influenced my normative commitments to climate change mitigation and sustainable development for all. I subscribe to the need to address climate change at its key source: anthropogenic emissions from fossil fuel combustion. Most importantly, I subscribe to the idea that accelerated transition to environmentally benign, perpetually available, and sustainably sourced energy systems is required to properly address climate change. This book, in many ways, reflects these framings.

During the last five years, I had the good fortune to be involved in a number of stimulating, provocative, and engaging classes, conversations, discussions, debates, workshops, seminars, and lectures. There are therefore so many people who have influenced my thinking that eventually led to this book, and I would like to mention them here. I hope, however, that those I have failed to acknowledge can forgive my frail memory.

Anthony Janetos, Director of the Frederick S. Pardee Center for the Study of the Longer-Range Future at Boston University, is the first person to suggest writing this book. Tony has always been a very supportive postdoc supervisor. He provided me great independence in steering a project on the future of energy in developing countries. Also at the Pardee Center, I thank Cynthia Barakatt, who read portions of this book and suggested improvements. Theresa White and John Prandato have also extended help in a number of ways.

This book, first conceived as a scoping report for my postdoc project, received thoughtful and helpful comments from experts who looked at parts of it before and during a workshop I convened in Boston in July 2016. I thank Debajit Palit, Ryan Hogarth, Marcio Giannini Pereira, Dawa Zangmo, Joni Jupesta, Tri Ratna Bajracharya, Hartley Walimwipi, Louise Tait, Thanh Nguyen Quang, Worajit Setthapun, and Bharath Jairaj for their thoughtful, sincere, and helpful comments.

The project on the future of energy in developing countries has also received inputs from a number of Boston University academics whose invaluable insights helped shaped the project even prior to my return to Boston in June 2015. I have to thank the groundwork collectively done by Kevin Gallagher, Les Kaufman, Robert Kaufmann, Nathan Philips, Suchi Gopal, and Julie Klinger, among many others who shared their precious time during those lunchtime discussions.

I completed the writing of this book as a Rachel Carson Fellow at Ludwig Maximilian University of Munich. I thank the Rachel Carson Center for the opportunity that enabled me some undistracted time to finish the book. I thank Christof Mauch, Helmuth Trischler, Arielle Helmick, Carmen Dines, our able assistants, and the rest of the 2017 Rachel Carson Fellows cohort.

I also had the opportunity to re-engage with the United Nations Economic and Social Commission for Asia and the Pacific when I was writing this book, during which I was commissioned to author chapters in its study on sustainable energy for development. At this engagement, I had thoughtful conversations with Hongpeng Liu and Kohji Iwakami. I thank them for the opportunity.

I also thank many friends for their support: Alma Redillas-Dolot, Ric Samanion, John Connors, Delia Catacutan, Charmae Andas-Kacir, Merlyn Jarrell, Cheryl Magbanua-Alolor, Ever Pinon-Simonsson, Aynee Triunfante, Remedios Pineda, Nixie Mabanag-Abarquez, Joannah Bahian, Rima Alfafara, Allan Lao, Andro Yumang, Doris Quidilla, Mary Ann Frugalidad-Latumbo, Jose Tenecio Jr., Erna Baylaran-Frias, Rufa Cagoco-Guiam, Maria Ivanova, George Manzano, Roditt Cruz-Delfino, Alfie Custodio, Franziska Mey, Nahid Sultana, Alicia Bergonia, Vipra Kumar, Sheila Siar, and Ivyjane Cortuna.

My greatest debt is to my family, my parents (Rito Sr and Lucy), my brothers (Michael and Rito Jr), my sisters-in-law (Brendaly and May), and my nephews and nieces (Matheo, Michaela, Sophia, Gabriel, and Lorraine) for supporting my calling that physically took me away from home.

Laurence Delina
Lisbon
29 May 2017

Abbreviations

5Ps	pro-poor public-private partnership
ADB	Asian Development Bank
AGF	High Level Advisory Group on Climate Change Financing
BRICS	Brazil, Russia, India, China, and South Africa
CDM	Clean Development Mechanism
CER	certificate of emissions reduction
CFL	compact fluorescent lamp
CHP	combined heat and power
CNG	compressed natural gas
CO_2	carbon dioxide
CO_2e	carbon dioxide equivalent
COP	Conference of Parties to the UNFCCC
CSP	concentrating solar power
CST	concentrating solar thermal
EEP	Energy and Environment Partnership
ESCAP	United Nations Economic and Social Commission for Asia and the Pacific
ESCO	energy service company
ETS	emissions trading scheme
FDI	foreign direct investments
FiT	feed-in tariff
GDP	gross domestic product
GHG	greenhouse gas
GNH	gross national happiness
HDI	human development index
HFO	heavy fuel oil
ICT	information and communication technology
IEA	International Energy Agency
IPCC	Intergovernmental Panel on Climate Change
IRENA	International Renewable Energy Agency
LACE	levelised avoided cost of electricity
LCOE	levelised cost of electricity

LED	light-emitting diode
LPG	liquefied petroleum gas
LULUCF	land use, land use change, and forestry
MDB	multilateral development bank
NDC	Nationally Determined Contributions
NGO	non-government organization
ODA	official development assistance
OECD	Organisation for Economic Co-operation and Development
O&M	operation and maintenance
PPA	power purchase agreement
PPP	purchasing power parity
PV	photovoltaic
REN21	Renewable Energy Network 21
SD	standard deviation
SDGs	Sustainable Development Goals
SDG7	Sustainable Development Goal 7
SE4All	Sustainable Energy for All
TFEC	total final energy consumption
TPES	total primary energy supply
UN	United Nations
UNDP	United Nations Development Program
UNEP	United Nations Environment Program
UNFCCC	United Nations Framework Convention on Climate Change
US EIA	United States Energy Information Agency
VRE	variable renewable energy
WRI	World Resources Institute

Units of measurement

EJ	Exajoule
GJ	Gigajoule
Gt	gigatonne
GW	gigawatt
GWh	gigawatt-hour
kW	kilowatt
kWh	kilowatt-hour
MJ	Megajoule
Mt	metric tonne
MW	megawatt
MWh	megawatt-hour
TWh	terawatt-hour
Wp	Watt-peak

Currencies

$	US dollar, unless specified
CNY	Chinese yuan
EUR	Euro
INR	Indian rupee
PHP	Philippine peso
RMB	Chinese renminbi
THB	Thai baht
VND	Vietnamese dong
ZAR	South African rand

1   Introduction

The year 2015 can be said to be the watershed year for an intensely globalized, yet sustainably fractured, world. For example, 2015 saw governments agreeing in New York and in Paris to two key documents that laid the foundations for the future of energy: an international agreement that would arrest the damages (and would-be damages) brought about by rapid climate change through a focus on transitioning away from an energy sector based on fossil fuel sources; and a new framework that would steer nations into an era of sustainable development for all, with energy access as a key goal.[1] This introductory chapter describes how energy is deeply intertwined with development and sustainability (1.1); how a change in the ways energy is generated, distributed, and used are essential when addressing both development and sustainability challenges in developing countries (1.2); and how developing countries can accelerate their progress in processing this change (1.3). At its core, therefore, this introduction chapter delves into the processes of a sustainable energy transition as a normative exercise that developing countries can use as a framework to simultaneously meet their development and sustainability ambitions. I also discuss key challenges and the promise of accelerating this important transitions. I then lay out the thrust of the book and the chapters ahead (1.4).

1.1.   Energy, development, and climate change

Energy and fossil fuels

Human population grew from 3.8 to 7.1 billion in less than 50 years, i.e. between 1972 and 2015. Annual energy use per capita also went up from 57 to 80 gigajoules (GJ).[2] Over this period, total energy consumption in the two biggest economies in the global south, India and China, grew 226 and 449 per cent respectively.[3] This energy consumption trend highlights the accelerating quest for mass consumption, and, following that, energy use in many developing economies. The modern global energy system has been fueling this route and spreading it far and wide.

However, the contemporary global energy system, although varied in type, is still almost homogeneously carbon-sourced. In 2015, humanity used about 0.55 exajoules (EJ) of energy – 81.7 per cent of which was produced using fossil fuel sources, a mere 10 per cent by biomass and biofuels, 4.8 per cent by nuclear, and 3.5 per cent by hydro and other renewable sources.[4] Fuel for energy was derived largely from oil (31.4 per cent), coal (29 per cent), and, increasingly, natural gas (21.3 per cent).[5]

Fossil fuels still dominate the contemporary global energy system by a large margin. Fossil fuels not only serve as material inputs for producing modern energy; they are also – and perhaps more importantly – a principal base that continues to trigger and drive modern industries including mining, shipping, railroads, and electricity generation, transmission, and distribution. Inarguably, the dominance of fossil fuels has historically defined the way human beings have ordered societies.

Regardless of whether one is in the industrialized north or in the developing south, human dependence on energy has expanded considerably. Many tangible benefits obtained from consuming energy, collectively called 'energy services,' include electricity for lighting, heating, cooking, communications, or mobility. Of these services, electricity has become so integral to our daily lives that we seem to forget that electricity powers our light bulbs, televisions, cooktops, refrigerators, mobile phones, and, increasingly, vehicles. For those who have reliable, steady, and affordable access to electricity, the ease of using it and its dependability and versatility make electricity a vital part of improved productivity and quality of life. However, not every person in the world has access to modern forms of energy. Energy poverty, indeed, remains a major international development challenge.

Energy and development

Acknowledging the persistent challenge of energy poverty, the United Nations declared (in 2011) the year 2012 as the international year of sustainable energy for all,[6] and in a subsequent document in 2013 it assigned the period 2014 to 2024 as the international decade of 'Sustainable Energy for All.'[7] Sustainable Energy for All has become the United Nations Secretary General's global initiative that would mobilize action from all sectors to support three interlinked objectives: providing universal access to modern energy services; doubling the global rate of improvement in energy efficiency; and doubling the share of renewable energy in the global energy mix.[8] Since its launch, the initiative has generated momentum, including partnerships with 106 countries and the European Union.

Further in the process of elevating the issue of sustainable energy access internationally, the United Nations General Assembly has – as it approved the Sustainable Development Goals (SDGs) in 2015 – included all three key components of the Secretary General's initiative. Goal No. 7 of the SDGs (SDG7) elevated the need for energy access in meeting sustainable development ends to ensure access to affordable, reliable, sustainable, and modern energy for all by 2030, while calling for a substantial increase in the share of renewable energy in the global energy mix and for doubling the global rate of improvement in energy efficiency. SDG7, therefore, provides a stronger foundation for acknowledging the key role of improved access to modern forms of energy and the services they provide in achieving and sustaining development.

When fully achieved, SDG7 can bring about substantial change in the lives of many.[9] Globally, 1.3 billion people lack access to electricity, which is equivalent to 17 per cent of the entire global population or about the entire population in the global north.[10] Some 2.85 billion people also lack access to clean and safe energy for household cooking, an essential aspect of daily life.[11] Of the world's energy poor people, two-thirds live in ten countries: four in Asia and six in sub-Saharan Africa.[12] Half of the people lacking clean cooking facilities live in only three countries: China, India, and Bangladesh.[13]

Meeting SGD7 offers a number of poverty reduction opportunities, which could lead to the development of capabilities necessary for a flourishing and high-quality life. The costs of lighting fuel in these poor households often represent over 10 per cent of their income. If this expenditure could be redirected to solar lanterns, electricity grid fees, or solar home systems, for example, it would lead to improved energy services and would save the household money.

Since energy has become a prerequisite for almost all economic activities of modern life, energy access reflects social and economic equity.[14] Ensuring and providing access to energy, thus, cuts across societal lines. For instance, a person's place in contemporary society seems to be defined by whether the person has access to energy. Modern computers and mobile technologies, and the energy system that powers them, for example, are only available to those who can afford them. An unequal distribution of energy services, therefore, only tends to exacerbate the difference between the haves and the have-nots.[15]

Health concerns related to energy poverty are also far reaching and include indoor air pollution, physical injury during fuel wood collection, and the consequences of a lack of refrigeration and health care services.[16] The health effects of burning solid fuel indoors are devastating. Acute respiratory infections, tuberculosis, chronic respiratory diseases, cardiovascular disease, lung cancer, asthma, low birth weights, diseases of the eye, and adverse pregnancy outcomes are among these many impacts.[17]

Energy poverty has also strong gender dimension. Many women and girls have to walk a round trip of far distances, several times a month, carrying heavy loads of firewood on the return journey. In addition to these long fuel-collection journeys, the activity also exposes women and children to physical and sexual violence.[18]

Little, however, has been done to improve access to energy in much of the global south.[19] Many in the developing world still face unreliable electricity, with shortages and blackouts being accepted as realities of life. In many countries, electricity remains so expensive that it is largely unaffordable to many.[20] With grid connection and other charges way beyond the price that poor people can afford to pay, tapping illegal electricity connections is common. Energy access, therefore, covers beyond the physical proximity to modern energy services. Access is also about the availability of affordable, improved, legal, and more efficient end-use energy devices such as improved cookstoves (those using traditional fuels but burning in a cleaner fashion, or cookstoves fueled by liquefied natural gas, electricity, or biogas), more efficient lights, water pumps, low-cost agricultural processing equipment,[21] as well as energy-efficient housing and transport options. Broadly, *energy access could refer to the affordable, stable, legal, and reliable services of cleaner energy options that ensure consistent quality.*

Delivering energy services to reduce poverty, however, implies more than just delivering energy to energy-poor households.[22] Invigorating sectors that create and sustain employment, business enterprises, and community services – by providing reliable electricity – are also part of this wider development picture. The sustainability of supply also matters, although, technically, 'access' can be achieved with unsustainable sources – at least according the to the IEA and SE4All definitions. Following the fossil-fuel-based development tracks of many countries in the global north no longer makes sense when a sustainable future for all is at stake, especially with the impacts of anthropogenic climate change.

Energy and climate change

The Intergovernmental Panel on Climate Change (IPCC) defines climate change as 'a change in the state of the climate that can be identified, e.g. using statistical tests, by changes in the mean temperature and/or the variability of its properties, and that persists for an extended period, typically decades or longer.'[23] It refers to any change in climate over time, whether due to natural variability or as a result of human activity.' Parties to the Paris Agreement – the latest mechanism of the global convention to address climate change – have acknowledged that 'climate change is a common concern of humankind' and have recognized 'the need for an effective and progressive response to the urgent threat of climate change.'[24]

A progressive response is needed to avoid the dangerous impact of climate change; that means limiting global average temperature increase to, at most, 2°C above preindustrial levels. This temperature target necessitates stabilizing atmospheric greenhouse gas (GHG) concentrations below 450 parts per million.[25] While these numbers provide some quantifiable targets, a progressive climate response entails transforming the global economy away from dependence on carbon-based energy sources. Science has already determined that curtailing future emissions from the energy sector, which constitute the most important source of GHG emissions responsible for anthropogenic climate change, is necessary in the decarbonization agenda.

The IPCC reports that 'CO_2 emissions from fossil fuel combustion and industrial processes contributed about 78 per cent of the total GHG emission increase from 1970 to 2010.'[26] From 15,633 metric tons (Mt) of CO_2 in 1973, energy-based emissions rose to 31,734 Mt of CO_2 in 2015 – a doubling in less than 50 years.[27] In 2015, coal burning contributed 44 per cent of CO_2 emissions, oil 35 per cent, and natural gas 20 per cent.[28] Emissions from energy sector were at 72 per cent of this total coal combustion.[29]

The consequences of increasing GHG concentration in the atmosphere and its direct contributions to rising global mean temperature have already been causing alarm. With warming, the natural world is subjected to intense pressure through changes in weather systems, shifting climate zones, melting of ice sheets, and sea level rise.[30] These repercussions to the natural environment have direct implications to societies in the form of reduced food availability, constrained water resources, forced migration, impacts to health, and civil unrest, among others.[31] Many developing countries are expected to bear most of these climate-related impacts, despite climate change being largely a legacy of highly industrialized countries. Many of these developing countries are already sites of entrenched poverty and underdevelopment; now, they are also poised to become the most vulnerable places on the planet to the burden of climate change.

Still, countries in the global south can contribute significantly to curtailing future emissions. One estimate shows that developing countries collectively have the most mitigation potentials: of the 17 billion tons of emission reductions required in 2020, 70 per cent of the most cost-effective options are achievable in developing countries.[32] Obviously, it is impossible and unfair to ask developing countries to deliberately halt their own development, all in the name of emissions reduction. It is, however, vital that they at least slow the rate at which their carbon emissions grow. The only strategy that would address this is for developing countries to deliberately choose sustainable energy transition pathways.

1.2. A new global agenda

Linking sustainable development and climate change mitigation through energy transitions

The ongoing search for development pathways that will replace fossil fuel energy systems with ones that are completely reliant on sustainable forms of energy fuel must be infused with urgency in addressing the overlapping goals of sustainable development and climate change response. This means that the transitions need to also overcome social injustice and the conditions of inequality that continue to entrench poverty and reproduce underdevelopment.[33] From a policy and moral perspective, it would be realistic to support the transition only if the basic needs of poor people are also satisfied.[34] While some see this as a dilemma, the international community, through the United Nations, has produced two important multilateral documents to serve as a foundation for a new architecture that attempts at integrating them.

Three months after the community of nations collectively endorsed the SDGs in New York, they also forged, in Paris, a new climate agreement. Through the Paris Agreement, Parties to the United Nations Framework Convention on Climate Change (UNFCCC) recognize the need to accelerate decarbonization,[35] while agreeing 'to pursue efforts to limit the temperature increase to 1.5°C above preindustrial levels, recognizing that this would significantly reduce the risks and impacts of climate change.'[36] The Agreement also strongly recognized climate action 'in the context of sustainable development and efforts to eradicate poverty.'[37] The need for accelerating climate mitigation is also made explicit with Parties aiming 'to reach global peaking of greenhouse gas emissions as soon as possible' while also 'recognizing that peaking will take longer for developing country Parties.'[38] Varied development circumstances are also acknowledged as the Parties decide to continue upholding 'equity and the principle of common but differentiated responsibilities and respective capabilities, in the light of different national circumstances'[39] in implementing the Agreement.

Another key development aspect of the Agreement pertains to the issue of finance. Parties acknowledged that UNFCCC has to be implemented by 'making financial flows consistent with a pathway towards low greenhouse gas emissions.'[40] More explicit is the agreement that 'developed country Parties shall provide financial resources to assist developing country Parties with respect to both mitigation and adaptation'[41] and that 'as part of a global effort, developed country Parties should continue to take the lead in mobilizing climate finance from a wide variety of sources, instruments and channels, noting the significant role of public funds . . . [with] such mobilization of climate finance should represent a progression beyond previous efforts.'[42]

Climate mitigation through decarbonization (the central aim of the Paris Agreement) and universal energy access with substantial increase in energy efficiency and renewable energy (the thrust of SDG7) are complementary and could be achieved simultaneously through sustainable energy transitions.[43] Energy transition, as a concept, has no standard or commonly accepted definition. Broadly, *sustainable energy transitions can refer to the processes involving a change in an energy system,*[44] *and the structures (e.g. organizations, institutions), cultures (including norms, behavior), and practices (e.g. routine, skills) in the extraction, production, delivery, and consumption of energy.*[45] In the context of both SDG7 and the Paris Agreement, supporting a global transition to socially inclusive and low carbon development that is responsive to poverty reduction has become indispensable. There are multiple terms used to describe this concept, with some equating the word 'transition' with 'revolution' or 'transformation.'[46] The most obvious aspect of transitions, however, is its temporal dimension, meaning it can be technologically 'measured' from the moment when an energy system either grows or shrinks, in terms of its share in the energy mix.[47]

Sustainable energy transitions, however, are not only processes of changing energy systems – from polluting to environmentally benign technologies and sustainable, efficient, and superabundant energy systems. They also imply the reconfigurations of physical structures – the landscapes, communities,[48] cities, coasts, and agricultural lands – that the energy choices of the past had shaped. They also entail changes in policy, institutional arrangements, and consumer behaviors.[49] Social structures, thus, need to be simultaneously revised to reflect the changes on the existing and enduring heterogeneities and diversities of cultures, norms, spaces, places, histories, and connectedness. They will most likely require changing social infrastructures, transforming established patterns of life in these spaces, and allocating benefits and harms.[50] Sustainable energy transitions, thus, are multifaceted, complex, and messy exercises and processes.

By virtue of this complexity, the transitions could be best conceptualized as transitions of sociotechnical systems. As a sociotechnical transition, these processes will comprise both technological and non-technological elements, including aspects regarding capacity, implementation, and regulation; and relevant actors and institutions that make decisions through policy and regulations; agencies that manage and administer the system; and energy service consumers including households and enterprises. This multidimensional aspect opens up the idea that sustainable energy transition governance will occur as combination of technical, scientific, and social endeavors.

In many developing countries, sustainable energy transitions require development interventions in terms of resources (i.e. the technology for generation, integration, transmission and distribution, and the necessary financing); capacity (i.e. skills and knowledge transfer to individual and institutional actors); implementation (i.e. the administration and management of new sociotechnical systems, including ensuring their integration and sustainability); and regulatory approaches (i.e. the policy required in facilitating the intervention). These, however, do not come as a given; other drivers are necessary to push developing countries towards adopting the transition agenda. This means activating the strongest political will or, in the absence of one, engaging the public with the need for it, which entails activism and social action.[51]

The case for the transitions: their benefits

Broadly, the transitions deliver both climate and development dividends. Energy-based emissions are reduced, thereby offering a strong contribution to the global climate mitigation agenda.[52] There are also other environmental benefits in relation to air quality and pollution, including the reduction of particulates, low-level ozone, sulfur, and nitrogen oxides. Over the longer-range future when renewable electricity penetrates other form of energy services (transport in particular), local pollution from road transport would also be minimized, if not totally eliminated.

In many developing countries, one particular benefit can occur with the transition away from traditional use of biomass for heat and cooking into improved cook stoves and, in the longer-future, cleaner fuels such as renewable electricity for cooking. Forests, which remain the major source of livelihoods and fuel for energy needs, especially heating and cooking, for many of the world's poor people, will be protected. If people in countries where forests remain the important source of cooking fuel do not transition towards cleaner cooking fuel and improved cookstoves, loss of forests could threaten these poor people's very livelihoods, while, at the same time, destroying important biodiversity, and removing carbon sinks. The transition away from biomass combustion can also have significant impact on indoor air quality and, therefore, on human health.[53]

Improvements in air quality are indeed directly correlated with improved health as energy systems are transformed into cleaner sources.[54] This can have substantial social and economic value, especially in developing countries where public health expenditures are the highest. According to one study, for instance, about $8 billion of air-pollution-associated cost is incurred in the city of Mumbai, India.[55] The World Health Organisation, in their 2014 report, found that six of the ten most polluted cities in the world in terms of air quality are in India – and these are largely due to coal-fired power generation.[56] With transition, a significant portion of this cost can be avoided. Another co-benefit can immediately be realized through cost savings in the required air pollution control equipment.[57]

The transition – especially with its access component – also has direct impacts to modern health services, the facilities to provide them, and the professional and health sector workers who deliver them. While health costs are the highest in developing countries, public expenditure on health care provision have typically been low, especially in rural areas, which also happen to be the spaces where access to energy is direly needed. Although energy access provision may not totally eradicate rural health challenges, the quality of health service delivery can be vastly improved with this intervention. It is also key to note that the quality of medical care available in a health care institution is directly related to its access to energy services, electricity in particular. Examples of these services include illumination, communication, refrigeration for vaccines and medicines, power for diagnostic machines, hot water, sterilization processes to maintain sanitary conditions, space heating, and cooking. Indirectly, electricity access also helps attract medical personnel to work in rural areas. Availability of health workers helps avoid needless maternal deaths, particularly those associated with pregnancy complications.

Since energy is required as an input in the production process, there is also a close link between energy and the development objectives of achieving full and productive employment and decent work for all,[58] including for women.[59] Affordable and reliable energy supply has significant impacts on job creation and security. At the macro level, reliable and sustainable energy supply has significant impact on productivity. On its own, the presence of electricity does not guarantee full employment or enough value-adding jobs to ensure decent work and poverty elimination; but it can expand the range of employment opportunities, especially in rural areas.[60]

With affordable energy, poor people are enabled to allocate their limited, yet much needed, financial resources to meet their most essential needs, including improved diet and amount of food intake as well as ability to afford better education and better health access. Additional savings can also be used in value-adding and income-generating activities, which can facilitate access to better social services and improved housing conditions that in turn could enable them to gradually escape their poverty, thus improving well-being and quality of life.[61]

Key challenges of energy transitions

In many developing countries, energy transitions need to focus on energy access provision to meet SDG7, while looking at and developing new opportunities for contributing widely to climate change mitigation. The access component of the transition has been addressed extensively in the literature. The efficiency and renewable energy components as developing country response to climate mitigation are also well covered. However, the transition processes in the context of climate change and the time boundaries of the SDGs and the

Paris Agreement need serious attention from analysts and policymakers. The only demonstrated and verified option for accelerating energy transitions, thus far, in developing countries, is large-scale harvesting of energy efficiency potentials across sectors and a staged, systematic, and structured decommissioning of fossil-based energy systems and their replacement with renewable energy technologies.

Accelerating energy transitions is the next stage and the most essential in these processes since many developing countries already have commitments to simultaneously address energy poverty, maximize energy efficiency gains, and increase their shares of renewables. The barriers to achieve this new ambition, however, are numerous and complicated to address with a single policy or by a mere commitment. These limitations broadly include lack of political will to institutionalize the need for accelerating transitions, many policy uncertainties, institutional limitations, market barriers, financial challenges, infrastructure issues, lack of skilled workforce, and weak public engagement, among others.

Many developing countries also have varying priorities and concerns. These variations are evident across different economic stages. For example, fast-developing economies may have the following energy sector policies: stockpiling, diversification, increasing the share of renewable energy in their mix, improving energy efficiency and demand management, reformation and/or creation of new markets, and investments in infrastructure including generation capacity and transmission. Low-income developing countries, particularly those who are highly dependent on energy imports, have priorities such as addressing energy poverty by closing gaps between energy demand and supply and by enhancing universal energy access efforts, and securing capital and financing for investment in energy infrastructure including new generation capacity and transmission. Most developing countries also look at how to improve energy governance,[62] to increase the use of locally available renewable energy resources, and to ensure the stability of international support through development aid financing.[63]

The most important limitation preventing a transition that effectively responds to the need for deep decarbonization, however, pertains to perception. Many developing countries perceive that the risks of going the low-carbon development pathway are just too significant; hence, the transition is often taken as an exercise involving huge trade-offs. The pressure points, for instance, between sustainable energy policy, climate policy, and economic policy are perceived to be very high. For many policymakers in developing countries, energy transitions decrease their economic competitiveness, result in job losses, and impinge on their very right to development itself. Addressing this perception challenge requires a clear appreciation of reality. When real world development is carefully examined, for instance, a favorable picture supporting the case of the transition emerges.

The renewable energy sector, for example, is already seeing faster growth especially in terms of installed capacity. In 2015, this capacity grew by 8.3 per cent, such that by the end of 2015, global renewable energy capacity has reached 1,985 gigawatts (GW).[64] The amount of generating capacity added in wind and solar photovoltaics, the most mature renewable energy technologies other than hydro in 2015, came to 118 GW, surpassing the 94 GW installed capacity in 2014.[65]

Excluding hydro, renewables made up 53.6 per cent of total new installed capacity of all technologies, including conventional ones in 2015. For the first time, renewables took the lion's share of new installations. These figures offer some optimism for the transitions – although it is important to note here that the contribution of renewable energy as a fuel supply to the global primary energy supply remains very low.[66] Bringing the share of renewable energy closer to 100 per cent – while displacing all fossil fuels – and electrifying all energy services need to become the ultimate aim of energy transitions. Although it seemed impossible in the past, this has already been modeled as plausible futures.

1.3.   Energy futures

A 100 per cent renewable electricity scenario

The past ten years show a preponderance of scenarios and models suggesting that renewable energy can provide all energy services we need.[67] The key focus of these studies is twofold: eradicating emissions from the energy sector and moving all energy services over to renewable electricity. This has direct implications not only for renewable energy deployment but also for energy access and energy efficiency, two other key components of energy transitions in developing countries. It has strong access implications because when modern access is provided and scaled up, this not only closes energy poverty gaps but also magnifies other key development benefits.[68] The relationship with efficiency is one of complementary policy: demand-side management and supply balancing can be accomplished only when efficiency is brought to the core of transition strategies.

Researchers from Stanford University developed one of the oft-cited papers in this corpus.[69] In this scenario, the authors suggest that sustainable energy transitions can be fully achieved by utilizing wind, water, and sunlight sources alone, without new hydro installations, and without tapping energy sources from bioenergy, nuclear energy, and combustion with carbon capture. Existing hydropower dams are assumed to run more efficiently for producing peak power. Countries with geothermal and ocean energy are assumed to exhaust their full potential. Tidal and wave energy technologies are also tapped, but their shares in the mix are expected to be tiny.

Most of the technologies needed for the full transition to sustainable energy systems are already available in the market. The choice of technology, however, varies according to a number of criteria. In the Stanford study, these criteria include the maturity of the technology, and the relative abundance and viability of renewable energy resources. Key, however, in realizing a 100 per cent renewable energy future is to balance what has been called variable renewable energy (VRE) or those that are produced by renewable sources such as wind and sun but are intermittent in their ability to provide a reliable supply stream. Balancing would require, in many developing countries, options such as large fleets of natural gas plus existing hydropower and nuclear energy capacity – both of which need to be retired in the long term. Also required is grid expansion with new transmission lines to connect new VRE plants and thus reduce its variability. This also entails the provision of ancillary services such as for voltage control and frequency regulation. Most importantly, however, is the need for storage systems. But, these are only the technical aspects of the transition; equally important is to look at the non-technical issues that need to be resolved.

In many developing countries, the challenges to transition towards a 100 per cent renewable electricity are significant. Aside from the technical barriers, these transitions also entail major, if not tectonic, changes in the market, financing, regulatory, policy, institutional, and consumer environments. Addressing these aspects simultaneously requires that strategies to overcome political and social barriers related to public acceptance, political will, and business preparedness also be hurdled. This multifaceted challenge to transition is further complicated when the need to accelerate the required change is included in the picture.

Full throttle: accelerating the transition

Given the normative international ambitions to provide full access by 2030 as set in SDG7 and to peak emissions as soon as possible as set in the Paris Agreement, the most pressing challenge for developing countries, as with those in the global north, is this: how to achieve the transition at its required pace.[70] The speed at which the transition can take place is vital for a number of reasons. For its access component, accelerating the transition also means accelerating development-related benefits accruing to its end users. The bigger picture, however, is that if the transition does not occur quickly, it may be too late, especially in the context of climate impacts.[71] However, achieving successful transitions will defy a number of current contexts.

The first context is the historical understanding that energy transitions are generational exercises. Grubler's work on the history of European energy transitions, for instance, highlights this traditional view.[72] To illustrate, Grubler shows that the time that coal took to takeover biomass had ranged from 96 to 160 years. Hughes similarly argues that the electricity utility system, being a large technical system, took a significant amount of time to establish a stronghold.[73] This process, according to Hughes, involves decades to complete and follows a predictable pathway. Along the way, as a new energy system establishes its incumbency, lock-in and inertia are created.[74] Vaclav Smil[75] also argues along the same lines:

> There can be no rapid transition either to new sources of primary energy or to new materials: inertia of existing complex systems, their expensive capitalization, scale of the needed replacements and many inherent problems with alternative conversions and materials make any rapid shifts (that is changes that could be accomplished in less than several decades, or on the order of two generations) impossible.[76]

One of the foci of the transition agenda is to alter path dependency, lock-in, and inertia of the fossil-fuel incumbency. To accelerate the transition, therefore, every level of the energy sociotechnical system must also be quickly altered: the technologies, policy, regulations, price signals, and social behaviors. Given these complexities, one can easily assume that a full transition will indeed take a longer time to eventuate.[77] However, some preliminary empirical studies suggest that, given certain conditions, energy transitions can occur rather quickly.

Benjamin Sovacool presents one of these studies. In his study of ten cases of energy transitions, Sovacool shows that expedited transitions are possible. Briefly, he demonstrates how, for instance, the province of Ontario in managed to transition its electricity sector from 25 per cent fueled by coal in 2003 to zero coal in 2014 – a clear illustration of a shorter transition: 11 years, not a generation.[78] In 2003, the provincial government of Ontario committed to phasing out all its coal-fired electricity generation by 2007, primarily for health reasons. Coal generation subsequently declined to 15 per cent in 2008, 3 per cent in 2011, and eventually to zero in 2014, seven years behind schedule.[79] The province achieved this transition through investments in wind, hydroelectricity, solar, and nuclear power, as well as in grid upgrades and improvements in energy efficiency.[80] It is key, however, to mention that this speed was realized also partly because of the age of the coal plants being replaced. Ontario's coal plants were nearing retirement when the provincial government decided they did not want any coal replacement.

The age of coal-fired power plants appears to be a key condition in the Ontario transition. In many developing countries, however, the case is different: new coal-fired power plants are either being planned or built. This has serious consequences in the transition agenda since these plants have lives of at least half a century, which means that developing countries with investments in new coal-fired power plants can easily be locked into these assets. Unless they are stranded, which is an expensive option, building or even considering a new coal-fired power plant in developing countries is a proposition that runs counter to the purposes of the transition. The same can be said with other fossil-fired installations such as natural gas-fired systems.

Benjamin Sovacool has also cited in his paper an example related to transition to achieve universal energy access. His study of the Indonesian transition from kerosene stoves to liquefied petroleum gas (LPG) stoves in urban and rural households offers a new way to envisage how transition in terms of access can proceed quickly.[81] This transition, Sovacool demonstrates, occurred in three years, between 2007 and 2010. To achieve this, the Indonesian national government lowered kerosene subsidies, thus increasing its price, and constructed new LPG terminals to act as national distribution hubs. In addition, households were offered the right to receive packages of a 3 kg LPG cylinder, a one-burner stove, a hose, and a regulator. Affected businesses were also supported as they shifted from selling kerosene to LPG. By 2009, there were 43.3 million LPG stoves in Indonesia, up from a mere 3 million in 2007. While the story offers us a glimpse that the transition in the cooking service can be accelerated, it is key to note that the Indonesian case represents only a first stage in the transition process. Eventually, the country needs to move away from LPG, a fossil fuel, towards renewable electricity for cooking, in the long term.

What the Ontario and Indonesian case studies illustrate is that given the right policy support, new technologies could quickly overturn locked-in technologies. These illustrations partly dispel the argument that energy transitions require generational timescales. However, Sovacool himself puts a number of caveats in this claim.[82] First, the aspects of the energy sector are variegated such that, for instance, household electricity and household cooking imply a very different transition timeframe as illustrated by the Indonesian case compared to the energy supply of a city, region, or nation. Second, the subjective and ambiguous nature of 'speed' also entails difficulties of assigning dates to moments of change, especially since energy transitions are irreducible to a single factor or cause. Given the attributes of complexity, timing, and causality of energy transitions, the full transition to sustainable energy in developing countries would, therefore, be processed according to the contextual specificities of the locations of new deployment, points of energy efficiency improvements, and spaces for closing access gaps.

This chapter illustrates how energy is deeply entrenched with development and sustainability. The global push for climate mitigation and universal energy access brought about a new development agenda that is largely animated by sustainable energy transitions. These transitions are expected to change not only the hardware aspects of energy generation but also its complementary social and political components across the supply and demand chain. Considering that these technologies are never politically neutral, the transitions to a sustainable future – those aimed at ensuring universal energy access while rapidly reducing emissions in the energy sector through improved energy efficiency and renewable energy deployment – are expected to be navigated in multiple ways. In developing countries, these entail the understanding and appreciation of the benefits of the transitions, as well as their risks and trade-offs. Although it could never be claimed that the transitions would solve poverty and global climate change, they have substantial role in improving well-being and the overall quality of life. Compared to doing nothing and to letting the transitions progress in business-as-usual fashion, the balance is tilted towards more benefits accruing from such large-scale change, especially if it is accelerated at the pace required to prevent further climate impacts. This book offers broad strokes on how rapid sustainable energy transitions could be achieved in developing countries, taking stock of their existing capacities in terms of hardware, policy, financing, and institutions, as well as in normatively pushing for significant turns in these areas.

1.4.   This book

Why take stock

This book is borne out of recognition that the transitions have to be a function of rigorous – yet structured, systematic, reflexive, and inclusive – processes. Taking stock of the capacities available for processing the transitions in developing countries comes at an auspicious time. This book corresponds within a historical period where the community of nations multilaterally approved two key documents: the

SDGs and Paris Agreement. Taking stock – understanding and recognizing what can be done and how it can be done – is a first step in the achievement of these new highly ambitious, yet interrelated, goals. Providing broad strokes on how to accelerate energy transitions could never be more urgent.

The book attempts to hurdle two related barriers that hinder effective decision-making towards achieving accelerated energy transitions. First, energy policy debates are subject to deep divisions over what constitutes and what could be the best way forward for the future of energy, in general, and of sustainable energy, in particular. Even with the focus on the transitions, many decision-makers in developing countries are still presented with a variety of technology options, policy and funding options, and institutional designs to achieve their desired sustainable futures. Selecting what could work for their contexts, thus, could mean navigating complicated processes in the absence of some guide that enables a structured and systematic decision-making. Second, substantial uncertainties surround the nature of environmental problems, especially concerning climate change, the direction of markets, the strength of policy, the sustainability of financing, and the quality of public engagement. These uncertainties will make significant action and allocation of limited resources challenging to justify.[83]

As these divisions are shattered, as risks are understood, and as their trade-offs are analyzed, decision-making for energy futures, particularly towards an accelerated transition, becomes more systematic and structured, thus reducing ambiguities and closing some key gaps. A diagnosis that takes stock of the current capacities available for accelerating the transition, therefore, injects more impartiality in energy and climate policy debates, lessens disagreement on the extent of the challenges, and concentrates more on the solutions. When decision-makers use better modes and systematic methodologies to reduce uncertainties and risks, they, too, can advance coherent policy objectives and design stronger institutional arrangements based on more than educated guesses or mere hunches. At times when decision-makers need to allocate scarce resources more efficiently, access to these methods provides them a key advantage.

Taking stock also matters because it highlights the gaps in our collective and current knowledge. This is important in the case of many developing countries where data-driven and science-based decisions remain a key challenge simply because of the absence of coherent and reliable data. The prospect for a more sustainable energy future would be more realistic and achievable only if decision-makers are provided with some lenses through which they can see these current realities, compare extant tools, understand their own capacity gaps, and locate the dilemmas and trade-offs when making key decisions.[84]

Against this backdrop, this book aims to provide some practical frames by which decision-makers can understand the wide range of challenges. This book is meant to serve as a foundation upon which to make sense of the complexities and nuances of transitions, especially beyond its technical and economic dimensions. By decision-makers, I mean a number of actors with key roles in the transitions. They include development practitioners whose focus is on energy transitions for addressing its three complementary agendas (access, efficiency, and renewable energy) and whose work is situated across multiple levels of governance. Practitioners can be either state or non-state actors and institutions. State actors and institutions are members of the public sector or government in local, provincial, national, regional, and international levels of governance. They include state development banks, multilateral development banks, regulators, and policymakers. Non-state actors are also working across these multiple levels and comprise private firms, small and medium-size enterprises, private banks and financiers, civil society, NGOs, and activists. However, it is key to recognize that decisions are no longer siloed within a single actor arrangement; rather, contemporary solutions benefit from partnerships, cooperation, and coalitions that bring together multiple and heterogeneous actors.[85]

The stance of the book, although it is normatively triggered by the desired climate-and-development trajectories, is rather descriptive and diagnostic. I do not claim to have been able to comprehensively parse out everything related to sustainable energy. That would be impossible. The book is more of a narrative survey of the nuances across a heterogeneous cohort of policy, financing, and governance options. As a menu of options, this book does not, however, promise a comprehensive assessment; rather it offers a broad overview and stocktaking. It only attempts to provide wider, but not necessarily deeper, qualitative, and some comparative looks and insights into the key aspects and processes of sustainable energy transitions in the global south.

I acknowledge the import of framings including my own normative position in relation to this book and my personal and professional perspectives more broadly. I am a Filipino male academic having grown up and been educated in the global south but also educated and now mostly working in northern universities. I spent extended periods of time living and working in two Southeast Asian countries: Philippines and Thailand. In the Philippines, I worked as a development banker assisting farmers, fisherfolk, cooperatives, small and medium enterprises, and rural banks in their financing needs. I have also worked as a resident research consultant at the United Nations Economic and Social Commission for Asia and the Pacific headquartered in Bangkok, which gave me some intimate knowledge of energy issues in the Asia-Pacific region more broadly. I continue to consult for the United Nations, engaging, from time to time, with national and international policymakers on sustainable development, climate change, and energy policy. My normative commitment to universal energy access is largely due to my own experience as a child living in energy poverty in rural Philippines. My normative commitment to climate change mitigation and sustainable development for all naturally progressed from that experience and our projected vulnerabilities to climate change.

The chapters ahead

In scoping the three aspects of energy transitions in the global south – access, efficiency, and renewables – I look at some examples from some countries. In Chapter 2, I introduce my study countries and how heterogeneous they are in terms of their development and sustainability profiles. It is key to note that this chapter is not about showing a bird's-eye view 'about' these countries; rather, it is more aptly a toad's view, a perspective emanating from below. While never comprehensive in details, the chapter is broad enough to give the reader some descriptions of the countries under study. This book profiles fourteen developing countries: Bhutan, Brazil, Chile, China, El Salvador, India, Indonesia, Morocco, Nepal, Philippines, South Africa, Thailand, Vietnam, and Zambia.

In Chapter 3, I survey the first capacity required in the transition: the hardware. I discuss the viability and potentials, current usage and market penetrations, and production costs and implementation issues of the many technologies for achieving energy access, expanding efficiency gains, and deploying renewable energy. Key trade-offs from every technology are also described. In Chapter 4, I then present the options for scaling up the deployment of this hardware. Two scales of deployments are explored – utility scale and distributed scale – as well as their potential trade-offs. Acknowledging that the transition is going to be produced from multiple directions, the chapter puts forward options for integrating 'big' and 'small' systems, and it describes how integration can be effectively supported in developing countries.

Following the chapters on the technological options, the next three chapters deal with the necessary turns in the non-technological aspects to accelerate the transition: policy, finance, and institutions. In Chapter 5, I present key examples of how a policy turn can occur, highlighting the need to mainstream new development pathways that are aligned with the aspirations of the SDGs and the Paris Agreement. This would require periodic reviews and staged improvements regarding target setting, policy design, and implementation. In Chapter 6, I survey the available multi-level funding sources and mechanisms for supporting the transition. Funding mechanisms developed endogenously, such as through carbon pricing, are discussed, alongside funding support brought about by external actors, such as those from bilateral and multilateral arrangements, as well as from non-state sources. The varieties of exogenous support, flowing both from north-to-south and from south-to-south, are also explored in some details. Central in the chapter's discussion is the role of various actors and institutions in a fragmented climate-and-development finance system, and the implications of these multiple forces to the collective vision for facilitating a financing turn required in accelerating the transition. In Chapter 7, I describe how developing countries can initiate an institutional turn, which is key, yet it is the most challenging to perform in developing countries owing to their relatively weak and fragmented institutional designs. The chapter nudges countries to develop and strengthen institutional infrastructures that seek to encompass the crosscutting elements of knowledge-making, capacity-building, institutional-strengthening, and decision-making necessary for accelerating the transitions. The imperative of building working coalitions and linking polycentric approaches to transitions is also tackled in this chapter.

Notes

1 These are the 2030 Agenda for Sustainable Development (see United Nations General Assembly 2015, *Transforming Our World: The 2030 Agenda for Sustainable Development*, A/RES/70/1, www.un.org/ga/search/view_doc.asp?symbol=A/RES/70/1&Lang=E, accessed 10 May 2016) and the Paris Agreement (see United Nations Framework Convention on Climate Change 2015, *Paris Agreement*, FCCC/CP/2015/L.9).

2 Computed from World Bank 2017, 'World development indicators,' http://databank.worldbank.org/data/reports.aspx?source=world-development-indicators, accessed January to May 2016 and May 2017.

3 Ibid.

4 International Energy Agency 2014, *Energy Efficiency Market Report 2014, Executive Summary*, IEA: Paris, France.

5 Ibid.

6 United Nations General Assembly 2011, *Resolution Adopted by the General Assembly, 65/151: International Year of Sustainable Energy for All*, A/RES/65/151.

7 United Nations General Assembly 2013, *Resolution Adopted by the General Assembly, 67/215: Promotion of New and Renewable Sources of Energy*, A/RES/67/215.

8 Ibid.

9 It can indeed be argued, for example, that SDG7 not only is a goal itself but can also be considered as a means to achieving other SDGs. I thank Bharath Jairaj for this insight.

10 World Bank 2017, 'World development indicators,' http://databank.worldbank.org/data/reports.aspx?source=world-development-indicators, accessed January to May 2016 and May 2017.

11 Ibid.

12 International Energy Agency 2015, *Key World Energy Statistics*, IEA: Paris, France.

13 Ibid.

14 Sovacool, B, et al. 2012, 'What moves and works: Broadening the consideration of energy poverty,' *Energy Policy*, vol. 42, pp. 715–719.

15 Myers, N & Kent, J 2003, 'New consumers: The influence of affluence on the environment,' *PNAS*, vol. 100, pp. 4963–4968.

16 International Energy Agency 2016, *Energy and Air Pollution: World Energy Outlook Special Report*, IEA: Paris, France.

17 Downward, GS, et al. 2015, 'Outdoor, indoor, and personal black carbon exposure from cookstoves burning solid fuels,' *Indoor Air*, vol. 26, pp. 784–795.

18 Clancy, JS, et al. 2015, 'The predicament of women,' in L Garuswamy (Ed.), *International Energy and Poverty: The Emerging Contours*, Routledge: Abingdon, Oxon, UK, pp. 24–38.

19 Sovacool, B 2012, 'The political economy of energy poverty: A review of key challenges,' *Energy for Sustainable Development*, vol. 16, pp. 272–282.

20 Winkler, H, et al. 2011, 'Access and affordability of electricity in developing countries,' *World Development*, vol. 39, pp. 1037–1050.

21 Burney, J, et al. 2010, 'Solar-powered drip irrigation enhances food security in the Sudano-Sahel,' *PNAS*, vol. 107, pp. 1848–1853.

22 Bazilian, M & Pielke, R Jr. 2013, 'Making energy access meaningful,' *Issues in Science and Technology*, vol. 29, pp. 74–78.

23 Intergovernmental Panel on Climate Change 2007, *Fourth Assessment Report*, IPCC, p. 30.

24 United Nations Framework Convention on Climate Change 2015, *Paris Agreement*, FCCC/CP/2015/L.9, accessed May 2016.

25 IPCC 2007, *Fourth Assessment Report*.

26 IPCC 2014, *Climate Change 2014: Synthesis Report Summary for Policymakers*.

27 Ibid.

28 World Resources Institute 2016, *Climate Data Explorer*, WRI, accessed January to May 2016, https://cait.wri.org.
29 Ibid.
30 IPCC 2014, *Climate Change 2014: Synthesis Report Summary for Policymakers*, IPCC: Geneva, Switzerland.
31 Ibid.; also see World Bank 2012, *Turn Down the Heat: Why a 4C Warmer World Must Be Avoided*, World Bank: Washington, DC.
32 Project Catalyst 2009, *Scaling Up Climate Finance*, Climate Works & European Climate Foundation: San Francisco, California.
33 See for example Altieri, K, et al. 2016, 'Achieving development and mitigation objectives through a decarbonization development pathway in South Africa,' *Climate Policy*, vol. 16, S78–S91.
34 Casillas, C & Kammen D 2010, 'The energy-poverty-climate nexus,' *Science*, vol. 330, pp. 1181–1182; Zerriffi, H & Wilson, E 2010, 'Leapfrogging over development? Promoting rural renewables for climate change mitigation,' *Energy Policy*, vol. 38, pp. 1689–1700.
35 UNFCCC 2015, *Paris Agreement*.
36 Ibid., Article 2.1.a.
37 Ibid., Article 2.1.
38 Ibid., Article 4.1.
39 Ibid., Article 2.2.
40 Ibid., Article 2.1.c.
41 Ibid., Article 9.1.
42 Ibid., Article 9.3.
43 cf. Sokona, Y, Mulugetta, Y & Gujba, H 2012, 'Widening energy access in Africa: Towards energy transition,' *Energy Policy*, vol. 47, pp. 3–10.
44 Smil, V 2010, *Energy Myths and Realities: Bringing Science to the Energy Policy Debate*, Rowman and Littlefield: Washington, DC.
45 Loorbach, D & Rotmans, J 2010, 'The practice of transition management: Examples and lessons from four distinct cases,' *Futures*, vol. 42, pp. 237–246; German Advisory Council on Global Change 2011, *World in Transition: A Social Contract for Sustainability*, WBGU: Berlin, Germany; Miller, CA, Iles, A & Jones, CF 2013, 'The social dimensions of energy transitions,' *Science as Culture*, vol. 22, pp. 135–148.
46 Miller, CA, Iles, A & Jones, CF 2013, 'The social dimensions of energy transitions,' *Science as Culture*, vol. 22, pp. 135–148.
47 Smil, V 2010, *Energy Myths and Realities: Bringing Science to the Energy Policy Debate*, Rowman and Littlefield: Washington, DC.
48 Van der Schoor, T, et al. 2016, 'Challenging obduracy: How local communities transform the energy system,' *Energy Research & Social Science*, vol. 13, pp. 94–105.
49 Allcott, H & Mullainathan, S 2010, 'Behavior and energy policy,' *Science*, vol. 327, pp. 1204–1205.
50 Stirling, A 2014, 'Transforming power: Social science and the politics of energy choices,' *Energy Research and Social Science*, vol. 1, pp. 83–95.
51 Delina, L & Diesendorf, M 2016, 'Strengthening the climate action movement: Strategies from contemporary social action,' *Carbon Management*, vol. 5, pp. 397–409; Delina, L, Diesendorf, M & Merson, J 2014, 'Strengthening the climate action movement: Strategies from contemporary social action campaigns,' *Interface: A Journal for and about Social Movements*, vol. 8, pp. 117–141.
52 Casillas, C & Kammen D 2010, 'The energy-poverty-climate nexus,' *Science*, vol. 330, pp. 1181–1182; also see Sovacool, B 2012, 'Deploying off-grid technology to eradicate energy poverty,' *Science*, vol. 338, pp. 47–48.
53 Ezzati, M & Kammen, D 2001, 'Indoor air pollution from biomass combustion and acute respiratory infections in Kenya: An exposure-response study,' *The Lancet*, vol. 358, pp. 619–624.

54 Bailis, R, et al. 2005, 'Mortality and greenhouse gas impacts of biomass and petro-leum energy futures in Africa,' *Science*, vol. 308, pp. 98–103; Buonocore, J, et al. 2015, 'Health and climate benefit of different energy-efficiency and renewable energy choices,' *Nature Climate Change*, vol. 6, pp. 100–105.

55 Kumar, A, et al. 2016, 'Air quality mapping using GIS and economic evaluation of health impact for Mumbai City, India,' *Journal of the Air & Waste Management Association*, vol. 66, pp. 470–481.

56 Ramsay, L 2015, 'These 10 cities have the worst air pollution in the world, and it is up to 15 times dirtier than what is considered healthy,' *Briefing, Business Insider Australia*, 21 September, www.businessinsider.com.au/these-are-the-cities-with-the-worst-air-pollution-in-the-world-2015-9, accessed 19 May 2017.

57 International Energy Agency 2016, *Energy and Air Pollution: World Energy Outlook Special Report*, IEA: Paris, France.

58 Bazilian, M & Pielke, R Jr. 2013, 'Making energy access meaningful,' *Issues in Science and Technology*, vol. 29, pp. 70–79.

59 Sovacool, B, et al. 2013, 'The energy-enterprise-gender nexus: Lessons from the Multifunctional Platform (MFP) in Mali,' *Renewable Energy*, vol. 50, pp. 115–125.

60 Barnes, DF, et al. 2010, 'Energy access, efficiency and poverty: How many households are energy poor in Bangladesh?,' *Policy Research Working Paper No. 5332*, World Bank: Washington, DC.

61 United Nations Development Program 2006, *Energizing Poverty Reduction: A Review of Energy-Poverty Nexus in Poverty Reduction Strategy Papers*, UNDP: New York.

62 Delina, L 2012, 'Coherence in energy efficiency governance,' *Energy for Sustainable Development*, vol. 16, pp. 493–499.

63 Sarkar, A & Singh, J 2010, 'Financing energy efficiency in developing countries-lessons learned and remaining challenges,' *Energy Policy*, vol. 38, pp. 5560–5571; Delina, L 2017, 'Multilateral development banking in a fragmented climate finance system: Shifting priorities in energy finance at the Asian Development Bank,' *International Environmental Agreements: Politics, Law and Economics*, vol. 17, pp. 73–88.

64 International Renewable Energy Agency 2016, 'Renewable capacity highlights,' 6 April, IRENA, www.irena.org/DocumentDownloads/Publications/RE_stats_highlights_2016.pdf, accessed May 2016.

65 Frankfurt School-UNEP Collaborating Centre for Climate and Sustainability Energy Finance 2016, *Global Trends in Renewable Energy Investment 2016*, UNEP & Bloomberg New Energy Finance: Frankfurt, Germany.

66 In 2014, only 9.5 per cent of the total primary energy supply was attributed to renewable sources, with contributions from solar, wind, heat, and geothermal at a measly 1.7 per cent; see International Energy Agency 2015, *Key World Energy Statistics*, IEA: Paris, France.

67 For the list of these studies, see Delina, L 2016, *Strategies for Rapid Climate Mitigation: Wartime Mobilisation as a Model for Action?*, Routledge-Earthscan: Abingdon, Oxon, UK, pp. 43–49. Of course the 100 per cent renewable energy future is a nuanced scenario with its underlying complexities and debates; see, for example, Renewable Energy Network 21 2017, *Renewables Global Futures Report: Great Debates toward 100% Renewable Energy*, REN21 Secretariat: Paris, France; Smil, V 2016, 'Examining energy transitions: A dozen insights based on performance,' *Energy Research & Social Science*, vol. 22, pp. 194–197; Kern, F & Rogge, K 2016, 'The pace of governed energy transitions: Agency, international dynamics and the global Paris Agreement accelerating decarbonisation processes?,' *Energy Research & Social Science*, vol. 22, pp. 13–17.

68 Sovacool, B 2015, 'Scaling and commercializing mobile biogas systems in Kenya: A qualitative pilot study,' *Renewable Energy*, vol. 76, pp. 115–125.

69 Jacobson, M, et al. 2015, '100% wind-water-sunlight energy for all countries, excel spreadsheet,' http://web.stanford.edu/group/efmh/jacobson/Articles/I/AllCountries.xlsx, accessed January to May 2016.

70 There are a number of suggested pathways aimed at emissions to approach zero soon; see, for example: Rockstrom, J, et al. 2017, 'A roadmap for rapid decarbonization,' *Science*, vol. 355, pp. 1269–1271; Delina, L 2016, *Strategies for Rapid Climate Mitigation: Wartime Mobilisation as a Model for Action?*, Routledge-Earthscan: Abingdon, Oxon, UK.

71 Zhang, D, et al. 2011, 'The causality analysis of climate change and large-scale human crisis,' *PNAS*, vol. 108, pp. 17296–17301; Giddens, A 2009, *The Politics of Climate Change*, Polity: New York; for a review of the relationships between climate impacts and low-ambition climate action, see Delina, L 2017, *Strategies for Rapid Climate Mitigation: Wartime Mobilisation as a Model of Climate Action*, Routledge-Earthscan: Abingdon, Oxon, UK, pp. 27–33.

72 Grubler, A 2012, 'Energy transitions research insights and cautionary tales,' *Energy Policy*, vol. 50, pp. 8–18.

73 Hughes, TP 1983, *Networks of Power: Electrification in Western Society 1880–1930*, Johns Hopkins University Press: Baltimore, MD, USA.

74 Unruh, GC 2000, 'Understanding carbon lock-in,' *Energy Policy*, vol. 28, pp. 817–830.

75 Smil, V 2010, *Energy Myths and Realities: Bringing Science to the Energy Policy Debate*, Rowman and Littlefield: Washington, DC.

76 Smil, V, 16 November 2012, email to the author, used with permission.

77 For example, Global Environmental Assessment 2012, *Global Energy Assessment: Toward a Sustainable Future*, Cambridge University Press and the International Institute for Applied Systems Analysis: Cambridge, UK & New York, USA & Laxenburg, Austria.

78 Sovacool, B 2016, 'How long will it take? Conceptualizing the temporal dynamics of energy transitions,' *Energy Research & Social Science*, vol. 13, pp. 202–215.

79 Ibid.

80 Government of Ontario 2013, *Achieving Balance: Ontario's Long-Term Energy Plan 2013*, www.energy.gov.on.ca/en/ltep/achieving-balance-ontarios-long-term-energy-plan/.

81 Sovacool, B 2016, 'How long will it take? Conceptualizing the temporal dynamics of energy transitions,' *Energy Research & Social Science*, vol. 13, pp. 202–215.

82 Ibid.

83 See Oreskes, N 2015, 'The fact of uncertainty, the uncertainty of facts and the cultural resonance of doubt,' *Philosophical Transactions of the Royal Society* A, vol. 373: 20140455; Lewandowsk, S, Ballard, T & Pancost, R 2015, 'Uncertainty as knowledge,' *Philosophical Transactions of the Royal Society* A, vol. 373: 20140462.

84 Wong-Parodi, G, et al. 2016, 'A decision science approach for integrating social science in climate and energy solutions,' *Nature Climate Change*, vol. 6, pp. 563–569; Stern, P, Sovacool, B & Dietz, T 2016, 'Towards a science of climate and energy choices,' *Nature Climate Change*, vol. 6, pp. 547–555.

85 Kyte, R 2016, *Science and Democracy Lecture: Looking Up: How Coalitions of Bottom-Up Organizations are Driving Action for Sustainable Development*, Harvard University, Cambridge, MA, USA, 18 October, recording available at https://vimeo.com/189929317, accessed 12 May 2017; Sovacool, B 2013, 'Expanding renewable energy access with pro-poor public private partnerships in the developing world,' *Energy Strategy Reviews*, vol. 1, pp. 181–192; Yadoo, A & Cruickshank, H 2010, 'The value of cooperatives in rural electrification,' *Energy Policy*, vol. 38, pp. 2941–2947; Jordan, A, et al. 2015, 'Emergence of polycentric climate governance and its future prospects,' *Nature Climate Change*, vol. 5, pp. 977–982; Cole, D 2015, 'Advantages of a polycentric approach to climate change policy,' *Nature Climate Change*, vol. 5, pp. 114–118.

2   Study countries

This chapter shows an attempt to include, consider, and study a constellation of countries that consider varieties, multiplicities, and pluralities in terms of their geography, natural endowments, political systems, emission profiles, institutional capacities, and development stages. This book profiles fourteen developing countries. In South Asia, India, Nepal, and Bhutan are considered. Morocco, Zambia, and South Africa are studied in the African region. Chile, Brazil, and El Salvador are chosen for the Latin American region. From Southeast Asia, Indonesia, the Philippines, Thailand, and Vietnam are included. China is also studied. This chapter broadly shows the profiles of these countries, including their broader development, energy access, efficiency improvements, and emissions profiles, and their official commitments towards the transition as registered in their targets to improve access, efficiency, and renewable deployment. I have to highlight that these study countries are not representative of *all* countries in the global south. While ensuring heterogeneity is a key aspect in the selection process, I also used the following criteria: the availability of narratives and case studies reported in the secondary literature and the availability of statistics and policy profiles.

I concede selection bias is one of the limitations of the book. However, it is vital to note that the book does not attempt to provide an encyclopedic and comprehensive scoping study of transitions in countries in the global south – although, of course, it would be ideal. Rather, its aim is to present what some countries have been doing so that others can take a look at them and hopefully appreciate these data as they understand what their options are and the risks and trade-offs of those options so that they can ultimately move forward with accelerating their own sustainable energy transitions. I can only hope that this modest attempt can broadly show how countries could move towards that direction – and, most importantly, nudge them towards intensifying their transition ambitions.

It is also important to note at the outset that despite the preponderance of narratives and statistics from these countries, the lack of reliable data, both qualitative and quantitative, remains an important challenge in these countries. While the book uses the best sources possible, it should be noted that the countries we are looking at admittedly have relatively weak local and national level institutions. Studies done about energy transitions in these countries are also fragmented. In case these transitions are reported, they exist in various types of literature:

mostly grey ones. These limitations, however, while important to mention, do not hamper the overall purpose of the book, i.e. to present, in broad strokes, how developing countries can accelerate their transitions by gazing at what others have done and been doing. To counter this challenge but not necessarily to fill the gaps, I try to triangulate the data I found with primary information mostly gathered from my professional network as an academic and as a development practitioner.

2.1.   Country profiles

This section offers a broad picture of the development profiles of the study countries, looking specifically at the statistical data on the trend of their human development indices, national and per capita income, some poverty data, as well as their energy access, energy efficiency, and carbon emission profiles. Most of the statistics presented here are aggregated national-level data. While these numbers provide broad views of what these countries 'look' like, it is key to note that statistics are but one representation of the inarguably complex and multidimensional conditions of people living in developing countries. The big rural-urban divide, for example, in terms of the impacts of access or *in*access to basic social services, including energy, to people's lives could not be fully captured in these numerical data. These stories of human development are not easily quantifiable – hence, obviously missing. One example of data that could not be gleaned from numerical or index characteristics is the resulting social benefits such as cohesion brought about by community-oriented renewable energy programs to neighbors. While numbers speak broadly about country conditions, a deeper assessment of development on the ground as they impact quality of lives and communities is required to fully appreciate the trends and evolution of development in these settings.

Human development

Development is a multifaceted concept. The United Nations Development Program (UNDP), the foremost global institution on development, emphasizes in their assessments of development that people and their capabilities should be the ultimate criteria. Thus far, UNDP uses the human development index (HDI), a summary measure of average achievement in three key dimensions of human development – health, education, and income – as its key barometer for measuring development. Using this metric, the HDIs in the study countries have shown improvements (see Table 2.1). Amongst them, Chile is ranked as having very high human development in 2016. Three of these countries are ranked on the high human development category: Brazil, China, and Thailand. The rest are in the medium category.[1]

 The HDI, despite its extensive use, remains an incomplete abstraction of a country's development. HDI neither captures nor reflects aspects of development such as human security, empowerment, and other forms of inequalities. It is also

Table 2.1 Human Development Indices of the study countries

	1990	2000	2010	2015	Rank in the 2016 HDI
Bhutan	No data	No data	0.573	0.607	132
Brazil	0.611	0.685	0.724	0.754	79
Chile	0.700	0.761	0.820	0.847	38
China	0.499	0.592	0.700	0.738	90
El Salvador	0.529	0.615	0.666	0.680	117
India	0.428	0.494	0.580	0.624	131
Indonesia	0.528	0.606	0.662	0.689	113
Morocco	0.458	0.530	0.612	0.647	123
Nepal	0.378	0.446	0.529	0.558	144
Philippines	0.586	0.622	0.669	0.682	116
South Africa	0.621	0.629	0.638	0.666	119
Thailand	0.574	0.649	0.720	0.740	87
Vietnam	0.477	0.576	0.655	0.683	115
Zambia	0.398	0.424	0.543	0.579	139

Source: extracted by the author from United Nations Development Program 2017, 'Trend in the Human Development Index, 1990–2016,' http://hdr.undp.org/en/composite/trends.

critiqued on other grounds. For instance, its focus on the income-health-education trifecta means that it excludes other facets of a multifaceted development. In appreciating sustainable energy transition, for instance, the HDI does not necessarily include aspects such as ecology, justice, and democracy. While the HDI can never be an accurate and comprehensive picture of how development can be defined in its most complex meaning, other alternatives have been suggested, including, for example, the Bhutanese index: the Gross National Happiness (GNH) Index.

The Fourth King of Bhutan, Jigme Singye Wangchuck, in the 1970s coined the term GNH to suggest that sustainable development should take a holistic approach towards notions of progress and give equal importance to non-economic aspects of well-being.[2] GNH has four pillars: good governance, sustainable socioeconomic development, cultural preservation, and environmental conservation. These pillars have been further classified into nine domains in order to reflect the holistic range of GNH values: psychological well-being, health, education, time use, cultural diversity and resilience, good governance, community vitality, ecological diversity and resilience, and living standards. These domains represent each of the components of Bhutanese well-being. Under the nine domains are 33 indicators where the GNH, a single number index, is developed. Based on compiled indicators in 2015, the GNH index suggests that 91.2 per cent of Bhutanese were narrowly, extensively, or deeply happy. Of this proportion, 43.4 per cent reported to be extensively or deeply happy.[3]

In the year 2016, there were 3.572 billion people living in the study countries. This population represents about five in ten people in the world, and about six of ten people in all countries in the global south. Two of the world's most populous countries, China and India, are represented. Heterogeneity can be observed across the study countries. A broader picture of the development condition of people living in the study countries is shown in Table 2.2. While close to half the population living in the study countries are, on average, urban dwellers, the majority of the population in these countries – with the exception of Brazil and Chile – are living in rural areas.[4] Variances and differences are also observed in other key indicators. Income per person varies as well as income disparities. While a Chilean, for example, earns, on average, $21,665 annually in 2016, a Nepali earns only a tenth of it. Disparities in terms of poverty, when measured in terms of the number of people living below the $1.90 per day poverty line, are also evident. According to this metric, 64 per cent of Zambians are poor, while no Thai can be considered poor.

Table 2.2 Development snapshot of the study countries, 2016

	Population, in millions	Urban population, in per cent of total	Population living below income poverty line, PPP $1.90 a day, in per cent	Inequality-adjusted HDI	Gross national income per capita PPP$_{2011}$ $	Life expectancy at birth, years	Expected years of schooling, years
Bhutan	0.8	38.6	2.2	0.428	7,081	69.9	12.5
Brazil	207.8	85.7	3.7	0.561	14,145	74.7	15.2
Chile	17.9	89.5	0.9	0.692	21,665	82	16.3
China	1,376	55.6	1.9	n.a.	13,345	76	13.5
El Salvador	6.1	66.7	3	0.529	7,732	73.3	13.2
India	1,311.1	32.7	21.2	0.454	5,663	68.3	11.7
Indonesia	257.6	53.7	8.3	0.563	10,053	69.1	12.9
Morocco	34.4	60.2	3.1	0.456	7,195	74.3	12.1
Nepal	28.5	18.6	15	0.407	2,337	70	12.2
Philippines	100.1	44.4	13.1	0.556	8,395	68.3	11.7
South Africa	54.5	64.8	16.6	0.435	12,087	57.7	13
Thailand	68	50.4	0	0.586	14,519	74.6	13.6
Vietnam	93.4	33.6	3.1	0.562	5,335	75.9	12.6
Zambia	16.2	40.9	64.4	0.373	3,464	60.8	12.5

Source: extracted by the author from United Nations Development Program 2017, 'HDR Country Profiles,' http://hdr.undp.org/en/countries/profiles. Note: inequality-adjusted HDI adjusts the HDI for inequality in each of the distribution across the population. The IHDI equals the HDI when there is no inequality across people but falls below the HDI as inequality rises.

Energy access

Access to energy remains central among the development needs of many developing countries. Closing this gap has a number of positive impacts in terms of development benefits. Evidently, millions of people in the study countries are still in dire energy poverty. Many still lack access to basic lighting, to clean energy to cook their food, and to heat or cool their homes. For many people in the global south, energy supply also remains unreliable and, in most cases, unaffordable. Take, for example, electricity, a modern energy service: across the study countries, the number of people with and without access to electricity varies (see Table 2.3). Only China and Morocco have claimed to reach universal electrification. Thailand, although it reported full access to electricity in its urban areas, has a remaining 71,600 rural-area dwellers yet to be provided with electricity.[5] Vietnam and Brazil also reported full electrification in their urban areas; however, more than 9 million Brazilians and 1.4 million Vietnamese living in rural areas are still underserved. Overall, there are about 312 million people who have no electricity access in the study countries. The majority of them, except in Zambia, are living in rural areas. About 262 million rural-dwelling Indians comprise the majority of these people. Altogether, Zambia has the highest number of people without electricity access: 78 per cent of all Zambians. The

Table 2.3 Access to electricity profiles of the study countries, 2012

	Population with access, per cent of total	*Urban population with access, per cent of total*	*Rural population with access, per cent of total*	*Rural population without access*
Bhutan	75.6	100.0	52.8	223,368
Brazil	99.5	100.0	97.0	9,007,818
Chile	99.6	100.0	97.0	56,375
China	100.0	100.0	100.0	0
El Salvador	93.7	98.0	85.7	291,514
India	78.7	98.2	69.7	261,762,791
Indonesia	96.0	99.1	92.9	8,543,297
Morocco	100.0	100.0	100.0	0
Nepal	76.3	97.0	71.6	6,441,965
Philippines	87.5	93.7	81.5	9,803,513
South Africa	85.4	96.6	66.9	6,363,163
Thailand	100.0	100.0	99.8	71,621
Vietnam	99.0	100.0	97.7	1,395,187
Zambia	22.1	46.9	5.8	8,471,422

Source: extracted by the author from United Nations Sustainable Energy for All 2017, 'SE4All database,' from the World Bank database, databank.worldbank.org.

Table 2.4 Solid fuels for cooking profiles, 2017

	Per cent of population using solid fuels for cooking	Number of people affected by household air pollution	Number of deaths per year from household air pollution	Per cent of urban population using solid fuels	Per cent of rural population using solid fuels
Bhutan	37	274,474	285	<5	71.6
Brazil	6	11,919,361	21,350	<5	39.6
China	45	607,812,000	1,039,000	22.8	71.3
El Salvador	21	1,322,453	342,784	51.4	21.8
India	64	800,000,000	1,000,000	26.0	86.0
Indonesia	47	116,026,170	164,651	22.9	79.6
Nepal	80	21,979,502	19,533	36.3	91.4
Philippines	49	47,386,314	48,221	26.5	70.5
South Africa	13	6,654,610	7,623	6.9	41.2
Thailand	24	16,028,400	24,520	11.3	47.3
Vietnam	51	45,275,505	45,502	20.2	72.1
Zambia	83	11,682,332	8,629	62.4	>95

Note: data was from Global Alliance for Clean Cookstoves, 2017, country profiles.

contrast between urban-dwelling Zambians with access and rural dwellers is also striking: while half of urban Zambians have access, only six of 100 rural-dwelling Zambians had.

Access to modern electricity for all, especially if this is met by renewable sources, is essential in meeting both Sustainable Development Goal (SDG) 7 and in contributing to nationally determined contributions (NDCs) on climate mitigation. While the provision of electricity is essential in the transition agenda, positive changes in the lives of many people in developing countries can quickly occur when interventions to address basic needs for access to clean cooking, for example, are scaled up. In many developing countries, addressing this need is instrumental in securing life-saving reductions in particulate emissions. Where a large number of the population in these places still rely on solid fuels for cooking, ensuring access to affordable, reliable, efficient, and clean energy such as those provided by clean cookstoves matters a lot (see Table 2.4).

Energy intensity

The most economical option for many developing countries to ensure energy security, which although a concept defying definition could simply mean affordability and reliability of supply in many developing countries, is ensuring the efficient use of energy. Energy efficiency is also a key aspect of the transition since it reduces consumption. In countries where energy supply is dominated by fossil fuel sources, achieving greater efficiency in energy consumption means a reduction in emissions – which has direct implication to climate change mitigation. The levels of energy intensity and how they improved over time provide a proxy to measure progress in energy efficiency. Energy intensity is defined as the amount of energy required in producing a unit of economic output, and is measured in primary energy terms (TPES) per unit of national income, usually in terms of gross domestic product (GDP). Table 2.5 shows the trends in the level of energy intensity in the study countries.

Global energy intensity levels have been declining overall.[6] This implies that energy use, in the aggregate, is decoupling from economic growth. Between 1995 and 2014, for instance, energy intensities in all study countries decreased, except in Thailand where it increased. Plateauing can also be observed in many of the study countries. While energy intensity provides one way to measure improvements in energy efficiency, this proxy fails to account for the multi-dimensional nature of energy efficiency. For instance, it does not paint the extent by which mandates, obligations, voluntary approaches, nudges, and behavioral changes have directly influenced efficient behaviors. Also, the numbers only show commercial energy without due consideration of the contribution of the traditional use of biomass, which does not directly contribute to GDP yet continues to be a substantial energy resource in many developing countries.[7] Additionally, improvements in energy intensity levels could be a bit misleading to be attributed

Table 2.5 Energy intensity levels, TPES/GDP in MJ/$\$_{2011}$PPP

	1995	2000	2005	2010	2014
Bhutan	26.38	21.91	16.26	12.57	n.d.
Brazil	3.76	3.95	3.92	3.89	4.06
Chile	4.22	4.67	4.28	3.92	3.88
China	14.23	10.23	10.28	8.68	7.43
El Salvador	4.38	4.45	4.50	3.95	3.52
India	7.86	6.95	5.88	5.34	4.94
Indonesia	4.62	5.31	4.86	4.34	3.70
Morocco	3.65	3.53	3.74	3.37	3.22
Nepal	9.72	9.29	8.85	7.97	7.67
Philippines	5.09	5.08	3.95	3.22	3.03
South Africa	11.39	10.45	10.19	9.67	9.16
Thailand	4.64	5.23	5.50	5.45	5.56
Vietnam	6.23	5.85	6.05	6.32	5.72
Zambia	13.16	11.98	10.37	7.77	7.40

Source: World Bank 2017, 'World Development Indicators,' http://databank.worldbank.org/data/reports.aspx?source=world-development-indicators.

exclusively to energy efficiency policies. Most likely, these levels have been changing due to other drivers such as electricity supply crises, rising electricity prices, and economic slowdown.[8]

Carbon emissions

The relationship between economic growth and growth in emissions has already been studied and carefully established.[9] While developing countries are not historically major contributors to global greenhouse gas (GHG) emissions, many fast-growing economies in the global south have become principal emitters, especially during the last five years or so (see Table 2.6). Global energy-related carbon dioxide (CO_2) emissions in 2013 jumped to their highest-ever levels since recordkeeping begun, rising faster than their average growth rate since 1990.[10] Although emissions growth in 2014 had roughly halted, a first in 40 years outside of economic recession, economic growth in developing countries is still driving emissions profiles upward, especially in the energy sector.[11]

While global emissions were reduced in the 2000 level compared to 1990 by 7 per cent, all study countries, but Zambia, have increased their emissions. During this ten-year period, 1990 to 2000, Nepal registered the most increase at 59 per cent, followed by Vietnam and El Salvador at 56 per cent. Thailand increased its emissions by 48 per cent, the Philippines 42 per cent, Indonesia 40 per cent, India 38 per cent, Brazil and Chile 35 per cent respectively, and China 30 per cent. Increasing emissions are again evident in the succeeding

Table 2.6 Energy sector emissions, $MtCO_2e$

	1990	2000	2010	2013
Brazil	204.76	312.68	400.36	481.27
Chile	34.21	52.29	72.89	86.59
China	2,327.24	3,335.22	8,138.05	9,430.23
El Salvador	2.74	6.24	7.03	6.99
India	635.30	1,019.63	1,758.88	2,027.86
Indonesia	199.69	333.94	455.22	489.11
Morocco	22.02	32.01	48.88	53.51
Nepal	3.61	8.78	10.72	11.86
Philippines	42.20	73.29	82.85	95.92
South Africa	254.70	293.97	422.06	439.12
Thailand	85.51	163.38	239.32	264.64
Vietnam	25.74	58.58	149.35	153.74
Zambia	20.35	15.39	21.91	24.24

Source: World Resources Institute 2017, 'CAIT Data explorer,' http://cait.wri.org.

decade, 2000 to 2010. Vietnam again leads as its emissions rose by 61 per cent. China trails closely at 59 per cent and India at 42 per cent. Compared to the emissions of China and India, emissions in El Salvador, Nepal, and Zambia are almost negligible in 2013. During this year, the combined emissions of these three countries represent a miniscule 0.49 per cent of China's and 2.25 per cent of India's.

If we consider only electricity-based emissions – the energy service comprising 33 per cent of global emissions in 2013 – all study countries have registered increases (see Table 2.7). Between 1990 and 2000, emissions from combustion-based electricity generation have also risen. All study countries – except El Salvador, Nepal, and Zambia, which had almost negligible emissions – have registered an increase in their electricity-sector emission levels. Vietnam had the most increase at 58 per cent. The Philippines also experienced a similar surge. China and India have also more than doubled their emissions. During the next decade, 2000 to 2010, electricity- and heat-sector emissions have all risen. Vietnam, among the study countries, continued to rank the highest in terms of increased rates of emissions – at 72 per cent. China has also increased its emissions by 60 per cent during this period.

Looking at emissions per capita in 2016, one can also see the variations across the study countries (see Figure 2.1). A wide divide between the emissions of a Nepali or a Zambian compared to that of a South African or a Chinese is apparent. This implies, among other things, that even across countries in the global south, emissions on a per capita basis are also widely heterogeneous.

Table 2.7 Emissions from electricity and heat, $MtCO_2$

	1990	*2000*	*2010*	*2013*
Brazil	28.00	50.03	69.12	105.98
Chile	10.61	16.55	27.46	38.45
China	725.34	1,575.15	3,974.39	4,773.36
El Salvador	0.17	1.16	1.37	1.63
India	232.04	491.65	821.09	969.17
Indonesia	47.73	89.33	151.94	168.14
Morocco	7.92	11.24	17.77	19.12
Nepal	0	0.02	0	0.01
Philippines	10.65	25.51	34.83	44.58
South Africa	145.83	191.94	286.28	281.39
Thailand	30.76	64.28	98.06	114.79
Vietnam	4.88	11.49	41.49	44.45
Zambia	0.16	0.08	0.07	0.07

Source: World Resources Institute 2017, 'CAIT Data explorer,' http://cait.wri.org.

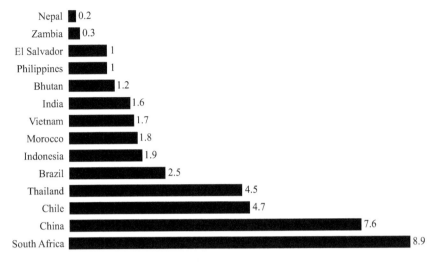

Figure 2.1 CO$_2$ emissions per capita, in tonnes, 2016

Source: extracted and drawn by the author from data in United Nations Development Program 2017, 'HDR Country Profiles,' http://hdr.undp.org/en/countries/profiles.

Since countries have already agreed to pursue reductions in emissions, bringing down these numbers as fast as they can needs to be set high in their agendas. Scaling up and focusing on the timing of the transitions towards that state, however, remains far from ideal, as will be discussed next.

2.2.   Transition commitments

In developing countries, sustainable energy transitions can be conceptualized as the simultaneous process of transitioning towards sustainable energy systems to meet three key development objectives: universal energy access, improved energy efficiency, and renewable energy deployment. Sustainable energy transitions, thus, given this context, can be assigned the role of primary mechanisms for meeting the SDGs – especially SDG 7 and others – and for contributing towards achieving their NDCs. This section describes how the study countries position and commit themselves towards meeting these normative ideals.

Universal energy access

Universal energy access has already become a key goal in the SDGs or the 2030 Agenda for Sustainable Development. Goal No. 7 explicitly stipulates this global objective. Improving access to modern fuels – the principal thrust of SDG7 – has, in many ways, already been registered as a key policy agenda in many countries in the global south. The focus on increasing access to cleaner cooking fuels, for example, has been an ongoing development imperative in the study countries, albeit it is also clear that the gap remains wide (see Table 2.8). Of the study countries for example, only Brazil, Chile, El Salvador, South Africa, and Morocco are close to achieving a full transition to cleaner cooking fuel where about eight of ten people living in these countries can now access these technologies. The challenge remains high in countries such as Nepal and India, where only two Nepalis and three Indians in ten have access to such cleaner cooking fuel.

While improving the cooking conditions in developing countries remains a key development imperative, the challenge of energy access also pertains to closing the gap on electricity service. This entails beyond mere provisioning of new generation systems – as a distributed, off-grid facility or on-grid – to include an assurance on the reliability and affordability of these systems and the electricity supply they provide. Ensuring reliability is key in development particularly since many developing countries are still having persistent blackouts, which have direct impact to economic competitiveness, access to better education and information and communication technologies, health provision, and other social services. Affordability of the service is also a key challenge in many developing countries, where the price of electricity often takes more than half a poor household's income. Reducing the price of electricity in many developing countries is a complex issue, but committing towards making electricity affordable for all has direct

Table 2.8 Per cent of population with access to clean cooking fuel and technologies

	2000	2005	2010	2014
Bhutan	38.03	49.00	59.59	68.14
Brazil	86.48	89.11	91.36	93.14
Chile	86.35	90.25	93.79	96.59
China	46.15	50.34	54.17	57.21
El Salvador	60.32	68.54	76.38	82.63
India	24.47	28.17	31.51	34.16
Indonesia	2.43	18.20	39.57	56.64
Morocco	90.40	93.90	97.00	99.40
Nepal	6.90	14.00	20.70	26.10
Philippines	38.70	41.20	43.20	44.80
South Africa	56.20	65.60	74.60	81.80
Thailand	60.30	66.10	71.50	75.90
Vietnam	23.60	33.60	43.20	50.90
Zambia	12.90	14.30	15.30	16.10

Source: extracted by the author from Sustainable Energy for All 2017, 'SE4All database,' accessible in the World Bank database, databank.worldbank.org.

development impacts that contribute to better quality of life for everyone. In many urban areas in the global south, where illegal access to electricity is prevalent, energy access provision also needs to include interventions on making these connections legal. Further down the access continuum is the provision of access for enhancing productive energy, especially in terms of new energy systems, that results in the generation of new or increased income in economically impoverished communities, such as improvements in irrigation, food processing, and product transport. All these energy development interventions need to be, in the long run, sustainably produced and efficiently consumed to have full impact to sustainable energy transition.

Increasing efficiency

Energy efficiency, for all of its direct impacts to improving energy reliability and affordability as well as for its contribution to emissions reduction, remains a key mechanism for accelerating energy transitions in developing countries. Already, many governments have made the pursuit of energy efficiency central in their energy and climate policy, and made it explicit in their policy documents. For instance, all study countries, except Indonesia, have mentioned either energy savings or energy efficiency in their NDCs (see Table 2.9).[12] Quantifying 'how much' energy efficiency these countries wish to achieve at some period in time is critical for monitoring purposes and most especially for determining opportunities for improving commitments and targets to accelerate the transition. However, only Brazil, India, Morocco, and Thailand, thus far, have quantified efficiency targets and explicitly mentioned the role of energy efficiency in their NDCs.

For energy efficiency improvements to be fully supportive of the accelerated transition agenda, countries need to regularly improve their targets, expand sectoral coverage (e.g. from residential to industrial and agricultural to transport and commercial sectors), and make it an essential component in the integration agenda.

Increasing renewables

The third component of the sustainable energy transition trifecta in developing countries is to increase the share of renewable energy, ideally replacing all current fossil-based generation systems in these countries with 100 per cent renewable energy systems for all kinds of energy services. In 2016, the share of renewable energy consumption vis-à-vis total final energy consumption in the study countries has been heterogeneous (see Figure 2.2). India, South Africa, and Nepal have the largest share of renewables in their energy consumption. The sources of renewable energy in these countries, however, are mostly from biomass and large hydropower, which are two of the most contentious forms of renewable energy.[13]

Table 2.9 Summary of NDCs from energy efficiency improvements in the study countries

Country	Energy efficiency targets
Bhutan	No numerical target but mentions proposed efforts to improve efficiency in freight transport, existing vehicles through standards and capacity building, appliances, buildings, and industrial processes and technologies. (The Department of Renewable Energy, as of July 2015, is drafting an energy efficiency policy that will cover sectors including building and appliances, industry, and transport. This can be reflected in amendments to Bhutan's NDCs in the future.)
Brazil	Achieving 10 per cent efficiency gains in the electricity sector by 2030 through enhanced energy efficiency measures in industry and transport sectors.
Chile	Mentions a 20 per cent reduction in energy consumption forecast by 2025.
China	No numerical target but mentions efforts to improve efficiency through increased share of concentrated and highly efficient electricity generation from coal and nuclear power and energy conservation and efficiency improvement in industries and buildings.
El Salvador	No numerical target but mentions the promotion of energy efficiency and the creation of incentives to reduce the high cost of efficiency improvements.
India	Upscale efforts to unlock the market for energy efficiency and help achieve total avoided capacity addition of 19,598 MW and fuel savings of around 23 million tons per year through a series of activities under its National Mission for Enhanced Energy Efficiency in electricity and heat generation, industry, buildings, appliance, and transport.
Indonesia	No mention of energy efficiency or energy savings.
Morocco	Achieve 12 per cent energy savings by 2020 and 15 per cent by 2030, compared to current trends; reduce energy consumption in buildings, industry, and transport by 2020 and 15 per cent by 2030. The breakdown of expected savings per sector is 48 per cent for industry, 23 per cent for transport, 19 per cent for residential, and 10 per cent for services.
Nepal	No numerical target but broadly mentions the promotion of energy efficient technologies.
Philippines	No numerical target but mentions grid efficiency improvement.
South Africa	No numerical target but mentions the rolling out of programs to increase efficiency of its coal-fired power plants, as well as of energy efficient technologies including energy efficient lighting and appliances.
Thailand	Its Energy Efficiency Plan for 2015 to 2036 aims to reduce the country's energy intensity by 30 per cent below the 2010 level in 2036.
Vietnam	Mentions energy efficiency and reducing consumption as measures to achieve NDC targets; mentions the government's policies on energy savings and efficiency such as the 'National Target Program on Energy Efficiency 2006' and the law on 'Economical and Efficient Use of Energy 2010'; also mentions the application of energy savings and efficiency programs in the residential sector, in trade and services, as well as in transport and in electricity generation; also mentions labeling of energy-saving equipment and the issuance of national standards for the quality of equipment.
Zambia	Broadly mentions energy efficiency.

Source: author's summary from UNFCCC 2017, *NDCs as communicated by Parties*, www4.unfccc.int/submissions/indc/Submission%20Pages/submissions.aspx.

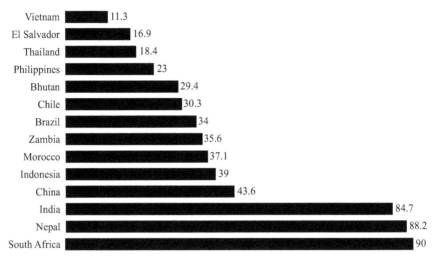

Figure 2.2 Renewable energy consumption, in per cent of total final energy consumption, 2016

Source: extracted and drawn by the author from data in United Nations Development Program 2017, 'HDR Country Profiles,' http://hdr.undp.org/en/countries/profiles. Note: most of the renewable energy consumed in developing countries is from either hydropower sources or biomass, which are both contentious in many respects.

The NDCs are, thus far, the best proxies for country commitments towards sustainable energy transition (see Table 2.10). All study countries are signatories of the United Nations Framework Convention on Climate Change (UNFCCC), which brought about the Paris Agreement. All governments of the study countries have already ratified the convention and also signed this Agreement.

On the lead to the Paris climate summit, Climate Action Tracker, a consortium of four research organizations – namely, Climate Analytics, Ecofys, New-Climate Institute, and Potsdam Institute for Climate Impact Research – independently tracked some of the major NDCs. The Tracker conducted 'fair share' calculations[14] of submissions from 32 countries, which represent about 80 per cent of global emissions. The Tracker then rated them according to four categories: role model (when emissions targets are more ambitious than the 2°C range); sufficient (when pledges are in the more stringent part of the 2°C range, where warming would be limited below 2°C with a likely probability); medium (when pledges are in least stringent part of the 2°C range and warming would likely exceed 2°C); and inadequate (when emissions targets are less ambitious than the 2°C range, where warming would likely exceed 3°C to 4°C). The Tracker had rated all but five of the study countries' INDCs (see Table 2.11).

Table 2.10 Summary of study countries' NDCs

Study country	NDC targets
Bhutan	To remain carbon neutral, by ensuring that GHG emissions will not exceed the sink capacity of its forests
Brazil	To unconditionally reduce net GHG emissions, including land use, land use change, and forestry (LULUCF), by 37 per cent below 2005 levels by 2025, with 'subsequent indicative contribution' to reduce emissions by 43 per cent below 2005 levels, including LULUCF by 2030, through a series of measures, including reaching a share of 45 per cent renewable energy in the energy mix by 2030.
Chile	To unconditionally reduce GHG emissions-intensity of GDP below 2007 levels by 30 per cent, which is equivalent to 222 per cent above 1990 and 75 per cent above 2010 GHG emissions levels, excluding LULUCF, by 2030. To reduce GHG emissions-intensity of GDP compared to 2007 by 2030 by 35 to 45 per cent, which is equivalent to 154 to 198 per cent above 1990 and to 38 to 62 per cent above 2010 GHG emissions levels, excluding LULUCF, conditional on international financial support in the form of grants.
China	To peak CO_2 emissions by 2030 at the latest; to increase the share of non-fossil energy carriers of total primary energy supply (TPES) to around 20 per cent by 2030; to lower the carbon intensity of GDP by 60 to 65 per cent below 2005 levels by 2030; and to increase forest stock volume by 4.5 billion cubic meters, compared to 2005 levels
El Salvador	To increase renewable energy by 2025 at no less than 12 per cent with respect to 2014.
India	To reduce the emissions intensity of GDP by 20 to 25 per cent by 2020 below 2005 levels; to lower the emissions intensity of GDP by 33 to 35 per cent by 2030 below 2005 levels; to increase the share of non-fossil-based power generation capacity to 40 per cent of installed electric power capacity by 2030 (equivalent to 26 to 30 per cent of generation in 2030); and to create an additional (cumulative) carbon sink of 2.5 to 3 GtCO2e through additional forest and tree cover by 2030.
Indonesia	To unconditionally reduce 2030 GHG emissions, including LULUCF, to 29 per cent below business-as-usual (BAU); to reduce 2030 emissions to 41 per cent below BAU with sufficient international support. (The INDC does not elaborate as to which sectors it intends to reduce emissions to achieve its targets.)
Morocco	To unconditionally reduce 2030 GHG emissions, including LULUCF, by 13 per cent below BAU; can be increased to 32 per cent with international support.
Nepal	No emissions reduction commitments; its own emissions make up less than 0.1 per cent of global emissions.
Philippines	To reduce 2030 GHG emissions from all sectors, including LULUCF, to 70 per cent below BAU levels, conditional on 'the extent of financial resources, including technology development and transfer, and capacity building.'
South Africa	To reduce GHG emissions between 398 and 614 MtCO2e, including LULUCF, over the period 2025–2030

(*Continued*)

Table 2.10 (Continued)

Study country	NDC targets
Thailand	To reduce emissions by 20 per cent from the projected BAU level by 2030; subject to adequate and enhanced access to technology development and transfer, financial resources, and capacity-building support, the level of contribution could increase up to 25 per cent.
Vietnam	With domestic resources, to reduce 2030 GHG emissions by 8 per cent compared to BAU; to reduce emission intensity per unit of GDP by 20 per cent compared to the 2010 levels; to increase forest cover to the level of 45 per cent; if international support is received through bilateral and multilateral cooperation, as well as through the implementation of new mechanisms under the Global Climate Agreement, to reduce 2030 GHG emissions by 30 per cent compared to 2010 levels.
Zambia	Partially conditional on international support, to reduce emissions by 47 per cent below 2010 level through sustainable forest management, sustainable agriculture (with biogas and biomass components), and renewable energy and energy efficiency

Source: author's summary from UNFCCC 2017, *NDCs as communicated by Parties*, www4.unfccc.int/submissions/indc/Submission%20Pages/submissions.aspx.

Table 2.11 NDCs 'fair share' ratings, according to Climate Action Tracker, 2017

	Fair share rating
Bhutan	Sufficient
Brazil	Medium
Chile	Inadequate
China	Medium
El Salvador	Not rated
India	Medium
Indonesia	Medium
Morocco	Sufficient
Nepal	Not rated
Philippines	Medium
South Africa	Inadequate
Thailand	Not rated
Vietnam	Not rated
Zambia	Not rated

Source: Climate Action Tracker 2017, *Tracking NDCs*, www.climateactiontracker.org.

The Tracker rates Bhutan's NDC as sufficient in-line with their 'fair share' of global efforts to hold warming below 2°C. If Bhutan does not implement any policies to arrest the emissions trend from energy, industry, and agriculture (which are of the same magnitude as its carbon sink), however, this rating could change to medium. In 2025 and 2030, the emissions level in the country is projected to increase because of industrial development and the implementation of the '2005 Rural Electrification Master Plan' aimed at achieving 100 per cent electrification rate. Although Bhutan's high reliance on hydroelectricity means that current power sector emissions are negligible, further extension of existing capacity using fossil fuel-based power generation would lead to higher emissions. In that regard, the Tracker is poised to reduce Bhutan's rating to medium.

Brazil puts forward an absolute target – a target relative to emissions in a historical year as opposed to reductions below BAU, thus adding more certainty to the system. The Tracker, however, had rated Brazil's submission as medium, indicating that their climate plans are at the least ambitious end. Instead of curbing emissions, Brazil's commitment will instead, according to the Tracker's calculations, result in increased emissions in 2025 by about 36 per cent above 2005 levels. Using the country's climate policies, the Tracker finds Brazil to be very close in meeting its NDC targets, especially given that Brazil had already achieved 41 per cent reduction in its emissions below 2005 levels in 2012 because of a significant decrease in land use, land use change, and forestry (LULUCF) emissions. The country's NDC target to reduce emissions by 37 per cent below 2005 by 2025, therefore, has effectively allowed Brazil to increase its emissions by 4 per cent.

Chile's NDC is rated inadequate. Chile, according to the Tracker, is on track to meet its unconditional target; however, it needs to implement additional policies to reach its 2020 pledge and 2030 target.

China's NDC is rated medium. Taken in isolation, the Tracker notes that emissions resulting from China's 2030 carbon intensity targets are significantly higher. This would lead to 'inadequate' rating. Considering this, the Tracker gives China's NDC a hybrid rating of 'medium with inadequate carbon intensity targets,' which means that the NDC alongside China's national climate activities are inconsistent with limiting warming to below 2°C. If the carbon intensity target dominates other elements of China's NDC, the Tracker suggests higher 2030 emission levels for China.

Most of the climate policies that China listed in its NDC are already being implemented. With full implementation of these policies alone, the Tracker calculates that China's emissions are likely to peak around 2025, with ongoing coal restrictions, according to the assessment, playing a large role. China's contribution to the 2°C pathway, however, can be accelerated, according to the Tracker, by adopting a 2020 instead of a 2030 target year. Full implementation of current Chinese climate policies, nevertheless, will still lead to emissions increase. The Tracker calculates a 22 per cent rise above 2010 levels by 2020 and 33 to 44 per cent by 2030. Thus, although China will meet its 2020 NDC pledge, it will still be a substantial emissions contributor. Much of the increase in emissions, according to the Tracker's projection, will emerge not from coal consumption but from non-CO_2 GHGs, where policy is currently lacking.

The Tracker rates India's NDC as medium, placing it at the same league with Brazil and China. With current climate policies, India, according to the Tracker, will achieve an emissions intensity reduction of around 41.5 per cent below 2005 levels by 2030. In 2030, the Tracker also projects, given current Indian transition policies, a 39 per cent contribution by renewable energy to the mix, corresponding to a 24 per cent share of electricity generation. If it is able to achieve its 40 per cent renewable energy target, India could also exceed its intensity target by up to 42 per cent below 2005 levels. The growing Indian demand for electricity, however, is most likely not able to be met by India's renewable energy target, according to the Tracker. The Tracker has warned that India can still be locked into a high-carbon development pathway, given the significantly larger absolute growth in coal-powered electric generating capacity vis-à-vis renewable capacity. With current policies alone, the Tracker suggests that India can achieve its NDC target.

The Tracker rates Indonesia's NDC as 'inadequate' in its fair share of meeting the 2°C target. However, the Tracker suggests that Indonesia, with full implementation of current policies alone, will likely overachieve its 2030 pledge. Given the continuing trend of deforestation in the country, however, Indonesia, according to the Tracker, can become the only principal deforestation emitter globally. Unaddressed, Indonesia's deforestation trends would likely result in a loss of 25 per cent of the current forest area by 2030. This could result in a potentially strong increase in the Indonesian 2030 emissions profile.

The Philippine NDC has been rated medium, but it could have been raised to 'sufficient' if it was partly unconditional. To meet its conditional target, however, the Tracker suggests that the Philippines will need to implement more policies than it currently has.

The Tracker rates South Africa's NDC as 'inadequate' and has even suggested that the country needs additional policies to achieve its targets. Under current South African policies, emissions can increase by 110 per cent in 2020 and 141 per cent in 2025, on 1990 levels, excluding LULUCF.

Morocco's NDC has been rated sufficient. Bhutan and Morocco, among the study countries, are the only countries to have received this rating from the Tracker.

Considering all NDCs, the Tracker has warned that the pledges, on condition that all the promises are delivered, will still bring warming at 2.7°C above pre-industrial levels in 2100. This implies a huge task ahead. For countries in the global south, their future NDCs have to be reflective of the imperative for accelerating implementation, regular monitoring, and improving targets. It is also important to highlight that their transition is a process involving actions in three key areas: access, efficiency, and renewables.

2.3. Conclusion

This chapter shows how heterogeneous, in many aspects, developing countries are. Their development trajectories are as plural as their demography and national income profiles. The extent by which energy has been made accessible to the population also varies. While the human condition appears to be improving in these countries, at least according to the HDIs, the magnitude and intensities of carbon emitted, in particular from the energy sector, are rising. Emission profiles have longer-range implications in the futures of these countries as these provide proxies as to whether they are meeting their emissions reduction objectives – a key goal of the sustainable energy transitions agenda.

Countries, including developing ones, have already acknowledged the need to reduce emissions, especially in the context of climate change. Their commitments to transition their economies towards low-carbon pathways in the context of safer climate, however, are still informally instituted. The NDCs (which, at present, represent a collection of these normative commitments) remain, in general, lacking of ambition. Future NDCs, therefore, have to contain improved commitments and to include contributions from local governments and non-state actors, which are conspicuously absent in present documents. An NDC also needs to be reflective of the country's sustainable development agenda. This means that NDCs have to integrate energy access goals, for example.

Along the same vein, the HDI, which is currently the 'best' development index we have, needs to be inclusive of other contemporary aspects of development, especially those related to the climate mitigation agenda, such as ecology, justice, and democracy. In the longer term, it may be best to develop an index that not only quantitatively assesses but also qualitatively appreciates sustainable development and climate change mitigation efforts simultaneously. Such index also needs to include a metric that places a premium over how countries temporally and spatially accelerate their respective sustainable energy transitions.

Notes

1 United Nations Development Program 2017, 'Trends in the Human Development Index, 1990–2015,' http://hdr.undp.org/en/composite/trends.
2 Bhutan Gross National Happiness 2016, www.grossnationalhappiness.com/articles/.
3 Bhutan Gross National Happiness 2015, www.grossnationalhappiness.com/SurveyFindings/Summaryof2015GNHIndex.pdf.
4 Note that there are varying definitions of and nuances about what constitutes an urban area.
5 Note that an electricity grid is not permitted access in forest reserves or protected areas where these populations live. I thank Worajit Setthapun for this point.
6 See World Bank 2017, 'World development indicators,' http://databank.worldbank.org/data/reports.aspx?source=world-development-indicators.
7 I thank Tri Ratna Bajracharya for this point.
8 I thank Louise Tait for this point.
9 Delina, LL 2011, 'Mitigating climate change via clean energy financing: An assessment of the Asian Development Bank's mitigation efforts in Southeast Asia,' in WL

Filho (Ed.), *The Economic, Social and Political Elements of Climate Change*, Springer: Berlin & Heidelberg, Germany, pp. 51–68.

10 International Energy Agency 2015, *Key World Energy Statistics*, IEA: Paris, France, p. 3.

11 Ibid.

12 United Nations Framework Convention on Climate Change 2017, *INDCs as Communicated by Parties*, www4.unfccc.int/submissions/indc/Submission%20Pages/submissions.aspx.

13 The business-as-usual condition in these countries – an energy mix that is hydropower-reliant – needs to be critically assessed in the context of sustainable energy transitions. What could 'transition' meant for these countries? I thank Bharath Jairaj for posing this critical question.

14 The methodology, including the assumptions made, for the Climate Action Tracker's INDC ratings is discussed in http://climateactiontracker.org/methodology. The rating focuses on CO_2 and other GHG emissions from fossil fuel combustion, industry, agriculture, and waste sources, which account for 93 per cent of global GHG emissions in 2010. The Tracker estimates and reports both historical and likely future emissions from broad sources of emissions.

3   Transition hardware

Although energy services are largely ignorant of the resource that supplies them, the fuel, infrastructure, and technological hardware in the production, delivery, and consumption chain are highly dependent on the particular type of energy resource. Identifying an energy resource and the technology and system that capture and distribute this energy, thus, is the first step in sustainable energy transitions. In developing countries, sustainable energy transitions will be processed in three key areas: closing access gaps, harvesting energy efficiency, and deploying renewable energy. These three complement each other to displace fossil fuels in current energy mixes.

Addressing universal energy access requires the deployment of hardware for cleaner cooking, efficient lighting, and productive energy, which, as much as possible, should be sourced from renewables (3.1). Harvesting energy efficiency requires technologies that ensure conservation and/or avoidance of energy use both at source and at points of consumption (3.2). Renewable energy deployment needs technologies that would replace existing polluting systems with a new hardware portfolio powered by environmentally benign, perpetually available, and sustainably sourced renewable energy (3.3). This chapter surveys these various commercially available technical hardware options and discusses their viability and potentials, their current usage and market penetrations, their trade-offs and benefits, and their production costs and implementation issues.

3.1.   Energy access

Energy access is often associated with the inverse of energy poverty. Energy poverty, alongside other terminologies in the energy literature, is a contested term, which could mean a number of things.[1] In one framing, the idea of energy ladder illustrates energy poverty.[2] This idea implies that primary types of energy in developing countries can be arranged on a ladder with the simplest or the most traditional fuels and sources at the bottom rung (e.g. candles, wood, and animal power) and the more advanced or modern fuels at the top rung (e.g. electricity). In this conceptualization, improved energy access is achieved as energy technologies become modern or as they become more efficient.

Benjamin Sovacool and Ira Martina Drupady neatly summarized the hardware component of improved energy access based on a sporadic literature on energy ladder.[3] They have organized the hardware component by sector across energy services and income profiles in developing countries. An example of the hardware for improving energy access at the household sector focusing on two basic energy services, cooking and lighting, is presented in Table 3.1.

The concept of energy ladder illustrates and, in some ways, provides a measurement of improved energy access in developing countries. With it, one can vividly see 'improvements' in access. It also provides a picture of the social and economic gaps and inequalities between the poorest and the richest consumers of energy. Evidently, those who use traditional fuels and hardware consume the least energy compared to those who have modern hardware. More often, the poor also pay more for their energy compared to richer energy consumers. When health impacts are accounted for on those who use traditional fuels, the inequality becomes more pronounced with the energy poor being the most affected.

Sustainable energy transitions require that energy-poor people be provided with reliable, affordable, modern, legal, and sustainable energy to replace conventional, traditional, and polluting energy hardware. Doing so could result in new opportunities that would not only meet their most basic needs for lighting, heating or cooling, and cooking but also strengthen their productive capabilities to improve the quality of their lives. In terms of sustainable development for all, an urgent focus on three energy services, hence, is imperative: lighting, heating and cooking, and mechanical power.[4] The hardware components for these three services can be summarized as processes of transition described in Table 3.2.

Sustainable energy transitions that address energy poverty provides a number of co-benefits. In terms of the three basic energy services mentioned above, the co-benefits of the transition are far-reaching.[5] A transition in lighting hardware brings about reduced cost for illumination since compact fluorescent lamps (CFLs) and light-emitting diodes (LEDs) cost less than kerosene lamps.[6] The system necessary to provide power for these bulbs obviously entails a separate cost, which is balanced in the long-term by other benefits. Lighting transition also reduced incidents of respiratory problems and infections, severe burns, and accidental fires. It also reduces emissions from fossil-based lighting, which has climate mitigation implications. Moreover, lighting transition improves opportunities for children

Table 3.1 Hardware for improving energy access at the household level

Energy service	Traditional hardware	Modern hardware
Cooking	Three-stone fire stoves fuelled by wood, charcoal, agricultural residues, and/or dung	Stoves fuelled by kerosene, biogas, liquefied petroleum gas, natural gas, or electricity
Lighting	Nothing Kerosene lanterns Candles	Compact fluorescent light (CFL) bulbs powered by distributed renewable electricity system such as a solar home panel

Table 3.2 Sustainable energy transition to improve energy access

Energy service	Transition from	Transition towards	Modern, renewable energy system
Lighting	Kerosene lamps and paraffin wax candles	CFLs and white light emitting diodes (LEDs)	Distributed systems such as solar home panels, micro-hydro, and microgrid
Heating and cooking	Traditional three-stone open fires, and brick-and-mortar models that emit significant amount of smoke	Improved cookstoves that improved energy efficiency, removed indoor air pollution, and reduced the need to physically gather solid fuels	Improved cookstoves, and bio-digesters
Mechanical power	Physical and manual labor, or diesel-powered energy systems	Distributed renewable energy systems such as solar-powered irrigation pumps	Small-scale, distributed systems such as micro-hydro and microgrid

studying during the night. The transition in heating and cooking hardware offers benefits in terms of reduction in the incidents of respiratory illnesses due to indoor air pollution, the strain to forest resources, and emissions from the burning of biomass. At the same time, such improvements increase productivity gains and time savings, especially for those who harvest fuel-wood. The transition in mechanical power has two key benefits. It improves the efficiency and effectiveness of productive activities for pumping, transporting, and lifting power, irrigating fields, processing crops, and small-scale or cottage manufacturing. In the long-term, the transition raises household and community incomes, which lead to further development-related dividends.

Despite their established benefits, energy access provision in developing countries faces challenges. Sovacool and Drupady in their study of ten projects for energy access in ten developing countries identify these common barriers as follows.[7] The technical challenges comprise availability of the hardware in domestic markets, standardization of the hardware, weak after-sales maintenance, poor operational performance, logistical challenges, and inconsistent fuel supply. The financing challenges include high upfront costs, difficulty in attracting financing, difficulty in collecting revenues and in ensuring profitability, market saturation, and bankruptcies. Institutional challenges are comprised of constrained institutional capacity, commitment of governments to perpetuating fossil fuels with uneven subsidies and other fossil fuel policy support, commitment of governments to grid electrification, instead of distributed systems, fragmentation in energy decision-making, and aid and grant dependency. The social challenges include low consumer awareness, unrealistic expectations, lack of familiarity with the hardware, and opposition and community disagreements.

3.2. Energy efficiency

The potential for harvesting energy efficiency as a component of energy transitions is universal. It remains and continues to be the logical first step for accelerating the transitions. Energy efficiency has been considered the 'low hanging fruit' in ensuring reliable and affordable energy supply as well as for climate mitigation and, therefore, has been advanced as a key energy and climate policy. The effects of energy efficiency to emission profiles, especially from energy end-use sectors, are made through direct reductions of the volume of fossil fuel combusted. Avoided electricity consumption, particularly if the sources are fossil fuels, indirectly leads to emissions reduction. When it comes to climate change, energy efficiency, thus, offers the least expensive contribution to rapid mitigation. In developing countries, therefore, energy efficiency is a critical and necessary part for accelerating sustainable energy transitions. Getting 'more' from current energy supply remains a vital option that should be carefully examined and integrated into public policy before considering any other technological options, particularly the installations of new power plants, whose costs are increasing and whose prospect for becoming stranded assets is almost assured.

Energy efficiency refers to using less energy input to deliver the same service or, similarly, using the same amount of energy input to deliver more service. Indeed, better and larger output from the same input is the key benefit when exploiting energy efficiency at its highest potential. In developing countries, where securing reliable and affordable energy supply remains a major goal in energy policy, domestically produced energy efficiency results in virtual power plants that enable countries to avoid primary energy imports. This has a number of macro benefits: improved country trade balances, increased trade surplus, and reduced trade deficit. In addition, improvements in energy efficiency have direct benefits to the climate due to avoided greenhouse gas emissions, hence essential in meeting nationally determined contributions (NDCs) to the Paris Agreement.

Harvesting the potential of energy efficiency includes efforts and activities to improve supply-side and end-use electricity efficiency. Broadly, these activities include improvements in buildings and appliances; electricity generation rehabilitation; loss reduction in improved transmission and distribution; and improvements in the efficiency of heating and cooling systems. In developing countries, the potential for tapping efficiency in the electricity sector remains of great import. The lighting sector, for instance, has the enormous potential for energy savings through the use of CFLs and LEDs. The potential is high, given the increasing demand for electric lighting, as a function of increasing population, rising income, and rapid urbanization in developing countries. Additionally, efficiency can also be potentially harvested at points of production (such as in productive opportunities in agriculture and enterprises) and consumption where consumers reduce their use of energy through behavioral changes and nudges that lead them to make environmentally conscious decisions, including in better fuel efficiency vehicles. The opportunities for harvesting energy efficiency across various sectors are shown in Table 3.3.

Table 3.3 Some energy efficiency opportunities in some key sectors in developing countries

Sector	Energy efficiency improvement opportunities
Households	Improved cookstoves; efficient lighting; efficient water heating; and efficient appliances especially fans and air conditioning systems.
Rural agriculture	Efficient irrigation pumps.
Small and medium-size enterprises	New technologies and systems for productive energy use (e.g. efficient kilns, mills, etc.).
Buildings	Integrated building design; better insulation; advanced windows; energy-efficient lighting; space conditioning; water heating; and refrigeration technologies.
Cities and municipalities	District heating and cooling systems; combined heat and power; efficient street lighting; efficient water supply, pumping, and sewage removal systems.
Transport	Better fuel efficiency vehicles; shift from roadways to railways to waterways.
Industry	Industrial processes; cogeneration and tri-generation; waste heat recovery; preheating; and efficient motors, pumps, and compressors.
Power supply	Reduced transmission and distribution losses through high-voltage lines, better-insulated conductors, capacitors, efficient and low-loss transformers, and improved metering systems.

The potential for exploiting energy efficiency in developing countries remains high. The International Energy Agency (IEA) projects that 'the energy efficiency market will continue to evolve as new cycles of stimulating and stalling forces influence economics and investments' and expects this market 'to grow in size, visibility and importance over the next several years.'[8] In spite of numerous studies suggesting the economic potential of energy efficiency through improved reliability of energy supply and its potential for emissions reduction through avoided combustion and consumption, it appears, however, that developing countries are yet to fully maximize the full use of this potential, and formally and explicitly reflect it in their policy and programs.

The impacts of avoided energy use on emission profiles, however, are fast becoming evident. China's wide-ranging energy efficiency policies as laid out in the 11th Five Year Plan (2006–2010) – but was not explicitly mentioned in their NDC – have contributed to the avoidance of 760 $MtCO_2e$.[9] These emissions savings, however, resulted beyond efficiency improvements in households and buildings, and mostly from avoided coal consumption.

In developing countries, much of the opportunity for harvesting further efficiency improvements can be generated from new building construction.[10] This potential is expected to remain high, given increasing population growth, economic development, and heightened urbanization in these countries. In China, for instance, the IEA reports that investment in building energy efficiency is already growing.[11] Of the $18 billion worth of building energy efficiency investment in 2014, China spent more than $11 billion in improving efficiency in residential buildings.[12] Over 70 per cent of this new spending was made in new building construction.

As developing countries grow their economy, electricity demand is also expected to rise. One clear indication of this will be from increased ownership of appliances, particularly air conditioners, refrigerators, and microwaves. India, for example, has already seen rapidly increasing ownership rates of air conditioners with annual sales rising by about 20 per cent.[13] As urbanization further intensifies, electricity demand for air conditioners is also likely to increase as has been demonstrated by the 250 per cent increase in India's energy consumption for appliances since 2002.[14] Efficiency improvements of appliances, therefore, continue to offer new opportunities for harvesting benefits from energy efficiency. It is key to note that India has already been implementing a star-rating program for appliances such that many appliances nowadays can be sold only if they were rated. This eliminated non-star-rated inefficient systems from the market.

Despite its promised climate and development gains, exploiting the many opportunities presented by energy efficiency, however, is not free of challenges.[15] Some of these technical challenges are availability of the hardware in domestic markets, particularly for building, industrial and commercial energy efficiency improvements; standardization of the hardware; and logistical challenges. There also remain key financing challenges, including high upfront costs, especially when replacement equipment and technologies are involved, and the difficulty in attracting financing. Generally, creditors and project funders still see cost-saving measures as less creditworthy. Banks continue to view these activities as not a core target business for lending. Institutional challenges are also prevalent. These include incoherent, weak, or absent legislative basis, national strategies, and plans; constrained institutional capacity; fragmented, weak, or insufficient organization and coordination among institutions; insufficient or absent capacity of human resources; and fragmented energy efficiency decision-making. There are also persistent social challenges, including rebound effects, low consumer awareness of efficiency programs, and unrealistic expectations. Addressing these barriers often requires government and policy interventions to make labeling mandatory, setting sectoral and national targets, and establishing institutions and legal frameworks for enforcing mandates.

3.3. Renewable energy

There are many definitions of what constitutes renewable energy, but, broadly, it can refer to 'any form of energy from solar, geophysical, or biological sources that is replenished by natural processes at a rate that equals or exceeds its rate of use.'[16] In the context of the transitions, renewable energy may refer to biomass energy, hydro energy, solar energy, wind energy, geothermal energy, and, in some instances, ocean energy. Renewable energy technologies may refer to the demonstrated and commercially available technologies that harness these types of energy and convert them into electricity. These renewable energy systems, nonetheless, are not free of contestations. Solar and wind energy, for example, are often tied with issues regarding community acceptance, land availability, land use, and aesthetics. Of the renewable energies mentioned, two are highly contested: hydropower and biomass. These contestations are explored below.

One proxy for looking at improvements in sustainable energy transitions is by peering how, through time, the share of renewable energy versus total final energy consumption (TFEC) has changed. Increasing shares over time provides a rough lens by which we can see how the transition is under way. TFEC includes the total combustible and non-combustible electricity use, all energy carriers as fuel for the transport sector, and heat generation for the industry and building sectors. Table 3.4 shows the evolution of the share of renewable energy in the TFEC, computed as the sum of all renewables use from all renewable sources divided by TFEC, in the study countries, since 1990.

As of 2014, Bhutan, Nepal, and Zambia appear to be close to achieving full transition. It is, however, apparent that other developing economies and high-emission countries such as China, India, and South Africa, in particular, have a long way to go in transitioning their respective energy consumption profiles. The same observation can be said for the rest of the study countries. These figures, nonetheless, as with other numbers presented in this book, have to be appreciated for their relative nuances. For instance, the numbers for the leading three countries – Bhutan, Nepal, and Zambia – are largely due to these countries' treatment of biomass energy as renewable energy. Biomass energy, in some contexts, can only

Table 3.4 Share of renewable energy to total final energy consumption, in per cent

	1990	1995	2000	2005	2010	2012	2014
Bhutan	95.90	94.37	91.40	91.66	90.89	87.85	n.d.
Brazil	49.86	46.13	42.80	46.35	47.01	43.62	41.81
Chile	34.03	34.17	31.36	32.26	27.03	30.33	26.42
China	33.08	29.47	30.25	20.78	17.41	16.83	17.10
El Salvador	67.14	54.75	50.86	47.19	34.30	27.26	28.17
India	58.65	54.48	51.58	48.58	39.48	38.39	36.54
Indonesia	58.60	50.10	45.58	41.78	38.38	39.10	38.07
Morocco	19.48	17.16	15.26	20.76	14.50	11.47	11.78
Nepal	95.12	91.73	88.28	89.52	87.29	84.70	84.38
Philippines	50.95	38.94	34.85	31.43	28.81	30.22	28.72
South Africa	16.63	18.11	18.51	16.27	17.09	16.64	16.59
Thailand	33.64	22.70	21.99	20.25	22.65	23.29	23.59
Vietnam	76.08	65.13	57.96	44.36	34.80	38.11	36.20
Zambia	82.98	87.11	89.99	89.00	92.10	88.63	88.09

Source: extracted by the author from World Bank 2017, 'World Development Indicators.'

be considered renewable if they are sustainably harvested and efficiently used. Also, both Bhutan and Zambia have large hydropower plants that contribute to this 'impressive' statistic. As discussed below, there are issues related to how biomass resources are harvested and are combusted in these countries and how hydropower is impacting on societies and the environment – aspects that are not fully captured by these statistics. It is also key to note some foreseeable changes in the energy mixes of these countries. Zambia, for instance, may well drop the contribution of renewable energy to TFEC with the introduction of a 300 MW coal-fired power plant in 2016 and more fossil-fuel-fired power plants.[17]

Looking exclusively at the electricity sector, the share of electricity generated using renewable sources – biomass combustion and hydropower included – versus the share of total electricity output in the study countries is presented in Table 3.5. Again, there are nuances in these statistics. For instance, the numbers do not capture electricity generation from isolated, small-scale, fossil-fueled energy generators such as captive diesel generation sets, which, in developing countries, are far common, especially in off-grid communities.

Bhutan, Brazil, Nepal, and Zambia are the top countries among the study countries with most renewable electricity. In the far end of this spectrum are Morocco, Thailand, and South Africa, which have consumed the least renewable energy among these countries. It is key to note again that these numbers are nuanced. The top renewable electricity producing and consuming countries, for example, are also countries that are heavily hydro-dependent. These statistics also do not necessarily capture the rapidly growing renewable energy deployments especially for systems that commenced deployment post-2014.

Table 3.5 Share of renewable electricity to total electricity output, in per cent

	1990	1995	2000	2005	2010	2014
Bhutan	99.55	100.00	100.00	99.94	84.72	99.99
Brazil	94.50	94.16	89.49	87.12	84.72	73.08
Chile	53.84	72.41	48.55	53.88	40.20	41.18
China	20.41	19.21	16.64	16.18	18.62	22.61
El Salvador	93.19	57.82	58.07	68.24	65.04	59.70
India	24.49	17.26	13.59	16.62	16.04	15.41
Indonesia	20.92	16.46	15.96	13.61	15.85	11.44
Morocco	12.67	5.05	6.08	6.14	17.43	12.39
Nepal	99.89	96.91	98.37	99.37	99.91	99.97
Philippines	45.42	36.84	42.89	32.37	26.30	25.60
South Africa	0.61	0.29	0.68	0.66	0.95	1.39
Thailand	11.26	8.74	6.81	5.54	5.61	9.08
Vietnam	61.85	72.24	54.78	31.67	29.14	41.65
Zambia	99.23	99.33	99.38	99.41	99.88	97.16

Source: extracted by the author from World Bank 2017, 'World Development Indicators.'

The next sub-sections review the contributions of each known type of renewable energy sources and the technologies to harness them in the study countries. Their inherent tensions are also discussed.

Hydropower

Hydropower, which exploits the energy of flowing or falling water by converting it into electricity, remains the most technologically developed and mature renewable energy. On one hand, the World Summit on Sustainable Development in Johannesburg, South Africa, in 2002 and the International Renewable Energies Conference in Bonn, Germany, in 2004 both considered hydropower, of all sizes and configurations, to be renewable. On the other hand, it has to be acknowledged that there are oppositions regarding this consideration.

Hydropower projects can be classified by either storage capacity or by purpose, although these classifications are not mutually exclusive. They are often categorized according to how they harness water to generate power. Reservoir-type projects involve damming water and creating reservoirs with significant storage capacity, which allows for the regulation of water flow and electricity production. This category is the most common in many developing countries. Run-of-river hydro projects, which have limited storage capacity, generate electricity according to the site's available hydrological fluctuations. Recently, this category of hydropower has received attention in many developing countries for their potential in community energy to address access challenges. Pumped storage projects pump water from a lower level to a reservoir at a higher elevation for storage, which are then released at times of higher demand.

Hydropower resources may be designed for electricity generation alone or for multiple resources. In most cases, multipurpose dam projects are typical in developing countries where their significant reservoir capacities also provide services such as irrigation, freshwater supply, flood control, and recreation. Given their unique abilities to store energy and move quickly to full capacity, pumped hydro projects can provide efficient storage of energy that can be used to address intermittency of variable renewable energy (VRE) resources.[18]

Pumped-hydro is not a totally new technology in developing countries. In Brazil, for instance, a pumped-storage hydro facility at 142 GW enhances security of supply.[19] The technology is growing the fastest in China, where a new pumped hydro station comes online every several months.[20] The 3.6 GW Fengneng Pumped Storage Power Station, in Hebei Province, is expected to be the world's largest when it comes online in 2022. The facility will be connected to the Beijing–Tianjin–North Hebei grid specifically for ensuring a reliable and flexible system, including as an emergency backup for wind and solar energy generation facility in northern Hebei.[21] South Africa also installed the 1.3 GW pumped Ingula storage facility that went online in 2016.[22]

The potential development benefits of pumped-hydro, like many natural resource projects, however, poses risks. One of the key risks is related to the rapid fluctuations in reservoir water levels as the system switches between pumping water from dam reservoirs to elevated storage reservoirs, and then lowering those upper reservoirs during electricity generation. These fluctuations can easily result to artificial flood for a few hours, then an artificial drought for about 20 hours, then another artificial flood. These fluctuations can severely affect terrestrial and freshwater ecosystems. Another risk is related to huge upfront capital cost, long construction times, and market structures. Extreme weather events, particularly reduced precipitation, could also significantly impact the future potential of this resource.

Globally, hydropower potential is estimated at around 15,000 TWh.[23] While most of these viable potential are already being exploited in most developed countries, the potential in developing countries remains largely untapped. At about 92 per cent, Africa is the region with the most untapped potential.[24] The Renewable Energy Network 21 (REN21) estimates that the global installed capacity for hydropower had reached 1,055 GW in 2014.[25] Of this capacity, 27 per cent was installed in China, 8.5 per cent in Brazil, and 4.3 per cent in India. Three of the world's largest hydropower plants are in China and Brazil: China's Three Gorges, Brazil's Itaipu, and China's Xiluodo. Table 3.6 shows the share of hydro energy in the energy consumption profiles of the study countries, along with their installed capacity in 2014.

Table 3.6 Hydroelectric profiles

	Electricity production from hydroelectric sources, in per cent of total in 2014	*Installed hydropower capacity, in MW in 2015*	*Hydropower generation, in GWh in 2015*
Bhutan	n.d.	1,615	7,780
Brazil	63.23	91,801	328,058
Chile	31.33	6,000 (2013 data)	19,400 (2013 data)
China	18.55	319,370, including 23,060 MW pumped storage	1,126,000
El Salvador	27.61	n.d.	n.d.
India	10.23	n.d.	n.d
Indonesia	6.63	5,258	13,741
Morocco	5.69	n.d.	n.d.
Nepal	99.79	753	3,635
Philippines	11.83	n.d.	n.d.
South Africa	0.39	n.d.	n.d.
Thailand	3.19	n.d.	n.d.
Vietnam	41.55	14,300 (2013 data)	52,800 (2013 data)
Zambia	97.16	2,257 (2014 data)	11,620 (2014 data)

Sources: data for electricity production from hydroelectric sources are extracted from World Bank 2017, 'World Development Indicators'; data for installed capacity and generation are from the International Hydropower Association 2017, 'Country Profiles,' from www.hydropower.org/country-profiles); n.d. stands for 'no data.'

Interestingly, energy provided by hydropower plants have registered minimal shares of energy consumed in the study countries (see Table 3.11). In 2012, for instance, Bhutan, Brazil, and Zambia are the three countries with the highest consumption of hydro energy; yet, the use of energy from this resource remains relatively low in these countries. At 280 GW, China has the highest installed hydropower capacity in 2014; however, only 3.9 per cent of its total final energy consumption was hydropower-supplied.

Often operating in isolation, hydropower plants provide electricity either for the grid or for communal use in off-grid systems. The maximum output of individual plants ranges from 0.1 kW to 852 MW. Amongst the large hydropower plants ever built, China's Three Gorges power station produces around 84 TWh per year at 22.5 GW capacity. Brazil's Itaipu, on the border of Paraguay and Brazil, generated a record 95 TWh in 2008 with an installed capacity of 14 GW.

Hydropower projects tend to have long lives. Its civil works, for instance, may last up to 100 years, while its electro-mechanical equipment may last for 40 years. This makes their economic lifecycles different from other energy options. Their high investment costs, however, make them high-risk investments. Lock-in potential is simply big. The cost of a hydropower project is very site-specific, making it extremely difficult to predict. This is despite hydropower being a mature technology. Typically, hydropower projects have high upfront capital cost, mostly due to their higher risk profiles. Once constructed, however, hydropower plants tend to have low operation and maintenance costs. Capital costs for less than 20 MW grid-based plants range from $750 to $2,500 per kW installed capacity, and up to $4,000 per kW for greater than 20 MW plants.[26] Transmission and distribution costs have to be included in the costs, especially since these plants are usually sited far from consumers.

An essential consideration when making investment decisions towards hydropower is the social costs to populations that need to be relocated.[27] A possible extensive relocation of communities to make way for these projects entails strong public resistance. If resettlement is required, the high costs and uncertainties make decision-making quite difficult. China's Three Gorges dam provides an illustration.[28] For quite some time, China has been building small and medium-sized dams without greater environmental and social impact. Its large-scale dam projects, however, have been controversial. The Three Gorges Dam project provides the most vivid example. Completed in 2008, the dam is expected to produce 84.7 billion kWh of electricity, or about a tenth of China's projected electricity consumption. Critics of the dam have alleged that the project could damage local environments, cultures, and historical resources. By changing the course of the Yangtze River, water quality, local biodiversity, and local climate have indeed been affected. The construction of the dam, however, had the most impact and repercussions to two million people who were forced away from their homes.[29]

In projects involving trans-boundary river basins, there are also international or regional challenges that need to be addressed, particularly to populations and communities in downstream areas. Absent institutional arrangements and mechanisms, conflicts over water are most likely to ensue in these situations.[30]

Yet another serious consideration is the environmental costs to ecosystems that will be seriously affected.[31] Hydropower development poses challenges about water availability, and changes in habitat, loss of biodiversity, fish stocks, and other species. Sedimentation and the consequent methane build-up, which can be released to the atmosphere and thus exacerbate climate change, is another serious environmental consequence of building gigantic dams.

Climate change will also potentially impact investment appetites for hydropower projects, a challenge that also extends to existing hydropower plants. Although uncertain as to the scale and scope of impacts, it seems clear that climate change will alter hydrologic cycles at the river basin level. Climate change does not change the volume of water in the global hydrologic cycle, but some changes can be anticipated in the location and timing of precipitation and glacial discharge. These changes could affect hydropower availability, particularly if reservoir storage is managed poorly, or if there is limited storage capacity as in the case of run-of-the-river devices. Another risk area is decreasing precipitation and prolonged droughts as climate change exacerbates. This can become an increasingly serious issue into the future of large hydropower plants since the 'fuel' – in this case, water – needs to be available for the longer-term viability of hydropower installations.

It can be misleading, however, to make broad conclusions since hydropower plants vary greatly and thus raise different environmental issues. Hence, they have to be considered on a project-to-project basis. Dams, for example, may be needed especially as climate change affects precipitation patterns. In some regions where water cycle can intensify and lead to a higher probability of flooding, more flood impact mitigation infrastructure, such as dams, will be needed. In regions where precipitation becomes less, the construction of new reservoirs may also be necessary for climate adaptation where dams can provide additional storage needs, especially for irrigation purposes as rain-fed agriculture may become less reliable.

Biomass energy

Biomass as an energy resource is derived from a wide variety of feedstock including agricultural crops and forestry residues, forest products, wood waste, aquatic plants, crop residues, animal manures, and wastes, such as municipal solid waste, wastewater, and food processing residues. Biomass accounts for about 10 per cent or about 51 exajoule (EJ) of global primary energy consumption.[32] In 2014, REN21 estimates that biomass energy capacity had reached 93 GW.[33] In many households in developing countries, biomass combustion is traditionally used for cooking, lighting, and space heating. Table 3.7 shows the share of solid biofuels for both traditional and modern uses in the total final energy consumption of the study countries in 1990, 2000, and 2012, respectively.

In 2012, biomass remains the dominant source of energy in Bhutan, Nepal, and Zambia, where their share in final consumption contributes more than 65 per cent. The dominant rural population in these three countries reflects biomass use

Table 3.7 Solid biofuels share of TFEC, in per cent

	Traditional uses				Modern uses			
	1990	2000	2010	2012	1990	2000	2010	2012
Bhutan	91.35	91.37	80.59	77.74	0.79	0.36	0.41	0.43
Brazil	8.44	5.00	4.01	3.34	19.16	16.37	20.30	19.41
Chile	n.d.	n.d.	n.d.	n.d.	27.67	23.24	19.44	23.68
China	32.25	26.69	13.70	12.13	0	0.05	0.14	0.17
El Salvador	44.80	34.65	16.14	15.53	14.94	11.05	7.68	8.38
India	44.96	40.20	30.20	28.72	11.52	10.66	8.26	7.93
Indonesia	47.85	36.25	31.66	31.24	10.09	7.92	4.63	4.31
Morocco	8.85	6.79	4.93	4.61	9.04	7.73	5.61	5.21
Nepal	93.16	85.51	83.22	79.33	1.01	1.05	1.03	1.03
Philippines	40.51	23.79	15.15	14.20	6.32	5.36	7.49	7.97
South Africa	13.51	15.17	13.65	13.70	2.96	3.18	2.89	2.90
Thailand	22.14	11.28	10.17	8.73	10.19	9.65	10.94	11.23
Vietnam	56.44	40.88	24.43	22.40	17.59	12.85	5.63	5.17
Zambia	60.54	67.51	69.05	66.42	10.78	11.90	12.16	11.70

Source: extracted by the author from the Sustainable Energy for All Database 2017, available from the World Bank Database.

for energy, particularly fuel-wood and charcoal for cooking. It is essential to note here, however, that unless there is evidence that this traditional biomass is being harvested, used sustainably (i.e. it is not depleting forests, and is used with efficient appliances), and combusted inefficiently, this energy source has to be considered unsustainable.[34]

In terms of modern biomass energy, Brazil, among the study countries, is consuming close to 20 per cent of its TFES from this source. Brazil's biomass electricity production primarily uses sugarcane bagasse and black liquor. Brazil also supports a program on biodiesel from soy and other sources.[35] The predominant technology for generating megawatt levels of electricity from biomass is the steam-Rankine cycle, with modest efficiencies, often under 20 per cent. Biomass systems rely largely on captive, low-value biomass, primarily from agricultural and forest-product-industry residues. Most steam cycle power plants are located at industrial sites, where they are configured for combined heat and power production.

Harvesting biogas – a resulting gas from anaerobic digestion of some biomass feedstock at the household or village level for small-scale generation, and in landfills for large-scale operations, which consists mainly of methane and carbon dioxide – is another modern use of biomass energy. Small-scale biogas systems can be used for cooking needs. This is their most pronounced use in many developing countries. To some extent, these systems, using a generator set, can also be tapped for lighting purposes. Large-scale installations use this energy source, after clean up, in internal combustion engines, micro turbines, gas turbines, fuel cells, and

Table 3.8 Biogas share, per cent of TFEC

	1990	2000	2012
Brazil			0.01
China		0.2	0.5
India			0.01
Nepal	0.1	0.4	1.6
Thailand			0.7

Source: extracted by the author from Sustainable Energy for All Database 2017, available from the World Bank Database. Note: Bhutan, while it does not have a numerical figure versus TFEC, has about 2,849 biogas plants as of 2016, according to Dawa Zangmo.

Stirling engines to generate electricity, as in the case of Brazil and Thailand. Biogas can also be purified to bio-methane for vehicle fuel. Biogas plants, nonetheless, also perform multiple other functions, including sustainable waste management and compost fertilizer production.

In terms of the share of biogas to TFEC, Table 3.8 shows that only Brazil, China, India, Nepal, and Thailand have been using this resource. The proportions, however, remain very low.

The relative small sizes of biogas digesters – about 1 to 10 cubic meters for household use in cooking and about 60 cubic meters for village electricity – provides one reason for these low numbers. In 2012, China has about 30 million small-scale digesters; India has about 3.8 million; and Nepal has more than 2.6 million biogas plants.[36] In 2014, China increased its biomass capacity to about 100,000 large-scale modern biogas plants and 45 million residential-scale digesters.[37] In 2016, India has also increased its capacity further to 4.83 million small-scale digesters.[38]

In terms of cost, residential scale, brick-made, underground-pit-type digesters cost around $85 in China.[39] In Thailand, some rural application uses improvised plastic material, thus bringing the cost further down.[40] A 75 kW to 20 MW biogas digester costs between $500 and $6,500 per kW, while a landfill gas operation costs between $1,900 and $2,200 per kW. A 0.5 MW to 200 MW biomass combustion plant costs up to $1,000 per kW in China and India.[41]

In developing countries, the availability and price of feedstock poses essential supply-side challenges for exploiting the full potential of bio-power harvesting for electricity and cooking purposes. In addition, drought, floods, fire, pests, and insect attacks also pose supply challenges. For modern biomass energy, land demand for food production, urban and infrastructure areas, biodiversity conservation, and the need to maintain forest areas hamper its full potential. Its interaction with other sectors, however, particularly in food and forestry, is its most important challenge. It is key, therefore, to distinguish first-generation biofuels, i.e. those crops developed for biofuel purposes with second-generation biofuels, i.e. feedstock for bioenergy derived from crop residues or non-crop plants. First-generation biofuels have

more significant land and food security concerns, whereas second-generation biofuels, with suitable sustainability safeguards, might pose lesser issues.[42]

First-generation bioenergy can have both positive and negative environmental
and social impacts. On one hand, it creates new income streams in the agricultural
sector, especially when demand for agricultural products increases. Demand for
bioenergy crops, on the other hand, may lead to rising agricultural prices, which
can reduce access to affordable food supply, particularly to poor people. Bioenergy
can also help in emissions reduction, but when emissions from direct and indirect
land-use changes, such as deforestation, are included, bioenergy emissions can be
large, indeed even higher than those of fossil-fuel-based alternatives.[43] When first-
generation bioenergy is considered in the energy mix, decision-making has to
clearly establish how much bioenergy can be produced without harming the environment, and without adverse social and economic impacts undermining potential gains. This process requires a systems approach that takes into account the
relevant interactions between various land uses and socioeconomic functions of
biomass. Some aspects of bioenergy production to be considered include:

- Plant species: perennial grasses such as switchgrass (*Panicum virgatum*), mis-
  canthus, and short-rotation coppice are ecologically less demanding than
  food crops in terms of their impacts on soils, soil erosion, biodiversity, nutrient leaching, and pesticide application.[44]
- Sites and land use: the conversion of forests or grasslands for bioenergy production causes dire ecological consequences,[45] including loss of soil organic
  matter,[46] and global terrestrial ecosystems and biodiversity.[47]
- Emissions: the production and use of fertilizers, pesticides, and other activities in the bioenergy chain result to emissions.
- Water demand: the water needs of bioenergy crops may cause environmental
  and social problems since they use 70 to 400 times more water per unit of
  energy than other primary energy carriers, excluding hydropower.

In many developing countries, bioenergy production from second-generation
biofuels – particularly from agricultural by-products, residues, and wastes – is
beneficial for a number of reasons.[48] It requires no land-use change or additional
land. It does not compete with food or fiber production. It does not require large
amounts of additional scarce inputs such as freshwater. In addition, agricultural
by-products-to-energy systems help in alleviating energy shortages, reducing
landfill requirements, and creating employment opportunities. In terms of animal manures as energy sources, well-managed biogas production can have significant positive environmental impacts, in terms of methane emission reductions.
Health and environmental co-benefits are also possible, primarily due to the transition from traditional biomass fuel. Bioenergy production from agricultural by-
products, however, is not free of negative effects. One key trade-off occurs when
feedstock is removed from the land, a process that could affect soil fertility.[49] If
feedstock is sourced from forests, forest ecosystems and forest conservation objectives can also be affected.

Wind energy

Wind energy is broadly available but diffused. Although wind resource quality varies according to location, there is sufficient potential to support high levels of wind energy generation in developing countries. REN21 estimates that 370 GW wind power capacity has been installed by 2014.[50] China, Brazil, and India are among the top five countries with net capacity wind energy additions in 2014; the other two are Germany and the USA. Globally, China leads the world in terms of total wind power capacity.[51] Table 3.9 shows the wind energy profiles of the study countries. Nine of the study countries have installed wind energy capacity in 2012, from only three countries in 2000.

China's leadership on wind energy installations – 155 GW total installed capacity in 2015 – is evident in terms of the share of wind energy in its TFEC (44 per cent in 2012). In 2014, about 45 per cent of global additions during that year, which was about 23.2 GW, were from China.[52] Deployment, however, has been much slower than what the Chinese government had anticipated. There are various reasons for this slump, but most important are fragmented permitting process and feed-in tariff rates that are insufficient to make projects economically viable.[53] It is also key to note that China's National Energy Agency had revealed that it would reduce deployment targets in its 13th Five-Year Plan: from 30 GW by 2020,

Table 3.9 Wind energy profiles

	Installed wind power capacity, MW, in 2015	Wind energy share of TFEC, in per cent			
		1990	2000	2010	2012
Bhutan	0.6				
Brazil	8,715			0.08	0.18
Chile	933			0.11	0.13
China	145,362		0.01	0.22	0.44
El Salvador	n.d.				
India	25,088		0.03	0.28	0.39
Indonesia	n.d.				
Morocco	787		0.07	0.45	0.46
Nepal	n.d.				
Philippines	216			0.02	0.02
South Africa	1,053			0.01	0.01
Thailand	223				0.02
Vietnam	n.d.			0.01	0.01
Zambia	n.d.				

Note: Dawa Zangmo provided data for Bhutan for the year 2016. Data for installed capacity for other countries are extracted from Global Wind Energy Council 2016, *Global Wind Report: Annual Market Update 2015*, p. 11. Data for wind shares of TFEC is extracted from Sustainable Energy for All Database 2017, available from the World Bank Database.

down to 10 GW.[54] Despite these reductions, a number of wind projects have already received approval from the government to proceed with construction. Onshore wind, in particular, which has become one of the most economical renewable energy generation technologies in the market, has become the de facto renewable energy technology of choice in China. Offshore wind capacity, nonetheless, is also being added. In March 2015, Ming Yang, for example, installed the first two-bladed 6.5-MW turbine in its Rudong project in Jiangsu Province. The project, thus far, is the largest Asian offshore wind farm. As of June 2015, China is fourth in the world in terms of operating offshore wind projects, about 310 MW, with 918 MW under construction that time.

New markets for wind energy are also developing elsewhere in the developing world. In Asia, for instance, a number of new wind energy installations were also deployed in Indonesia, the Philippines, Thailand, and Vietnam. In 2014, the Philippines completed Southeast Asia's largest individual wind project: the 150 MW project in the town of Burgos in the province of Ilocos Norte.[55]

The main hardware-related barrier that limits the penetration of wind energy is still the high generation and equipment costs. Regulatory and financing constraints are also key challenges. Nonetheless, the capital cost of wind power globally is in decline largely because of competition and technological advances especially as more players join the sector. Table 3.10 shows the capital costs for wind energy technology, as of 2015, which vary according to capacity and location. Declining costs, in the long term, are expected to boost the ability of wind energy to be rapidly deployed in developing countries.

It is also key to note that small wind systems are also increasingly being adopted in developing countries, especially in the context of energy access, albeit on a slow deployment rate. These turbines range from 0.1 to 3 kW with a rotor diameter ranging from 0.5 to 1.4 meters. They are often used in conjunction with other renewable energy systems such as a solar photovoltaic (PV) array.

The long-term trend progressively shows positive signs that the supply chain would also become more competitive. In many developing countries, such costs

Table 3.10 Capital costs for wind energy technology, per kW

Capacity	Capital cost	Location
Up to 100 kW onshore small-scale wind turbines	$1,900	China
1.5 MW to 3.5 MW onshore wind turbines	$925 to $1,470	India
1.5 MW to 3.5 MW onshore wind turbines	$660 to $1,290	China
1.5 MW to 7.5 MW offshore wind turbines	$4,500 to $5,500	Globally

Source: abridged from Renewable Energy Network 21 2015, *Renewables 2015: Global Status Report*, REN21 Secretariat: Paris, France.

would depend upon policy, markets, and other location-specific factors. Of particular interest in future cost declines is the entry of developing countries in the turbine-manufacturing sector, particularly China and India. China's Goldwind and India's Suzlon Group, for example, are among the world's top turbine manufacturers. In 2014, China even took 21.4 per cent of the global market shares for wind turbines.[56] Brazil has also become a turbine manufacturer. Andrade Gutierrez, for example, has joined with Alstrom of France to build a factory in Brazil.

Wind technology deployments not only respond to climate change mitigation and ensure reliable energy supply; they also help create local jobs and provide some monetary benefits, particularly in terms of payments to landowners who allow turbines on their property. Tapping wind energy potential, however, entails navigating potential trade-offs. The remoteness of potential sites entails higher upfront cost in the transport of the technical hardware and worker relocation. Remote locations also require additional cost in terms of connecting the new energy source with the grid. The land may have conflict in terms of its use. Urban areas, protected natural areas, and military exclusion areas, for example, could not be covered with wind turbines. Also, delicate ecosystems can be disturbed. Foundation work and interconnection cabling deployments in offshore installations, for example, can cause a degree of physical disturbance to the sea and surrounding seabed, with possible ecological ramifications. Related to that, wind installations have impacts on birds and other wildlife. These impacts can be direct, through fatalities or reduced reproduction, or indirect, through habitat loss and behavioral displacement. Noise pollution and landscape aesthetics, including shadow flicker caused by the turbine blades passing through the sun, are also potential trade-offs.

Solar energy

As with other renewable energy sources, the availability of solar energy – expressed in the popular statement on the amount of sunlight hitting the Earth – does not determine its role in the global energy mix. What matters are the availability and efficiency of conversion technologies and their market competitiveness. Two essential factors thus affect the practically harvestable potential of solar energy. First is the amount of solar energy available at a given location, which is subject to daily and seasonal variations. Second is irradiance intensity, which depends upon geographical and weather variations.

Equatorial countries receive more radiation than those at higher latitudes, making them countries with top potential for solar energy. By the end of 2014, REN21 estimates that a total of 181.4 GW solar energy capacity had been installed.[57] Table 3.11 shows the technical potential and installed capacity of solar energy in the study countries, as well as improvements in the share of solar energy in their TFEC over time.

Up from only three countries in 2000, seven of the study countries have installed solar capacity greater than 100 MW by 2014. All countries in the world, nevertheless, have some solar PV in operation. In 2015, China lead the study

Table 3.11 Solar energy profiles

	Installed capacity in 2015	Cumulative installed capacity, as of 2015	Solar energy share of TFEC, in per cent			
			1990	2000	2010	2012
Bhutan	12 MW					
Brazil				0.02	0.19	0.24
Chile	446 MW	848 MW				0.08
China	15.15 GW	43.53 GW	0.01	0.12	0.60	0.85
El Salvador						
India	2 GW	5.05 GW		0.01	0.07	0.13
Indonesia						
Morocco						
Nepal						
Philippines	122 MW	155 MW				
South Africa	200 MW	1.12 GW			0.10	0.12
Thailand	121 MW	1.42 GW				0.06
Vietnam						
Zambia						

Note: Dawa Zangmo provided data for Bhutan for the year 2016; data for installed capacity in 2015 for other countries are extracted from International Energy Agency – Photovoltaic Power Systems Program 2016, *2015 Snapshot of Global Photovoltaic Markets*, p. 18; data for solar energy share of TFEC is extracted from Sustainable Energy for All Database 2017, available from the World Bank Database.

countries in terms of installed capacity. China has also leapfrogged its consumption of solar energy, from a mere half of a per cent in 1990 to a whopping 85 per cent in 2012. Other countries that were able to substantially leap in solar energy installations include Brazil, India, and South Africa. Thailand's solar installations have also been increasing.

Currently, solar energy systems can be divided into two main categories. First are grid-connected systems, which can be building-integrated and building-adapted systems (distributed systems), and ground-based systems (utility-scale power plants). Second are off-grid and stand-alone systems, which can be solar cells integrated in consumer products, professional systems such as in telecommunication towers, and rural PV systems, such as solar home systems and mini-grid systems. These systems may be off-grid at the moment, but they can be designed as grid-ready for future use.

Although the market share of stand-alone systems is currently relatively small, their value for the user remains very high. Especially for access purposes, this value is affected by two key factors: the cost of storage and the efficiency of appliances. The latter is poised to increase rapidly with improved direct current appliances, including solar-powered refrigerators, agro-processing equipment, and irrigation pumps, among other hardware.[58] Stand-alone systems, thus, are set to see a market explosion in the very near future, particularly in developing countries, given friendly policy and funding support. This is because the systems are generally the user's only source of electricity, and the alternatives are either more expensive or less convenient. Stand-alone systems such as distributed solar photovoltaic, thus, remains a key technology in rural areas, where grid connection is simply expensive, if not impossible, to undertake. These small-scale systems are also fast becoming a key hardware for energy transition in many urban areas.

Utility-scale PV systems have also been entering the market on a commercial scale more rapidly. Among the study countries, solar energy capacity additions were at their highest in China, India, and South Africa.[59] In China, 84 per cent of its new solar capacity was in utility-scale power plants (10.6 GW). In 2014, most of these new Chinese large-scale installations were in Inner Mongolia (1.64 GW), Jiangsu (1.52 GW), and Qinghai (1.02 GW).[60] Utility-scale solar farms using concentrated solar power (CSPs) have also been demonstrated on the pilot scale. CSP technologies include parabolic troughs, linear Fresnel reflectors, power tower systems (usually based on molten-salt receivers integrated with thermal storage), and dish/engine systems. By end-2014, REN21 reports that 4.4 GW of installed capacity was delivered by CSP technologies – some of which were deployed in the global south.[61] The capital costs of solar energy technologies vary according to capacity and location. Table 3.12 shows these costs as of 2015.

Table 3.12 Capital costs for solar energy technology, per kW

Capacity	Capital cost	Location
3 kW to 5 kW residential rooftop solar PV	$2,150	China
100 kW commercial rooftop solar PV	$2,900	Globally
500 kW industrial rooftop solar PV	$3,800	Globally
Up to 250 MW ground-mounted utility-scale solar PV	$1,670	China
50 MW to 250 MW parabolic trough CSP, without storage	$3,100 to $7,000	Developed countries
50 MW to 250 MW parabolic trough CSP, with storage	$6,000 to $8,000	Globally
20 MW to 250 MW CSP tower, without storage	$6,000	Globally
20 MW to 250 MW CSP tower, with storage	$9,000	Globally

Source: abridged from Renewable Energy Network 21 2015, *Renewables 2015: Global Status Report*, REN21 Secretariat: Paris, France.

Although solar energy systems can be geographically suitable and can be installed in locations with favorable weather conditions, not all surfaces are suitable for solar energy conversion. Their installation is largely dependent upon the size of the system and their location. Siting decisions often carry with it some trade-offs. Amongst these are land-use conflicts especially in urban, agriculture, or forest areas. While small-scale, distributed solar energy use can be installed in almost all building structures, utility-scale solar farms require relatively large areas of land. Solar thermal power plants also need land of up to 8 square kilometers for a 250 MW plant with six hours of storage. Social issues could also arise, particularly when solar installations affect biodiversity, and landscape aesthetics. For concentrated solar power, there are concerns over impacts on fragile desert ecosystems, especially on sensitive habitats, where they are often sited. Thermal pollution to water resources is also possible, particularly in arid regions. A continuous supply of water for steam generation, cooling, and cleaning solar mirrors, which is required in CSP plants, also poses a future challenge. Some locations, especially in desert areas, may incur additional costs in terms of transporting and storing water to meet this need. In a grid-connected operation, particularly of large-scale, utility-size systems, the distance of the solar farm from demand centers also contributes to the cost. There are also challenges related to grid integration and associated grid stability of a VRE such as solar energy.

Geothermal

Electricity from geothermal energy is currently produced in 24 countries. Geothermal energy has also been in used for heating in 78 countries. REN21 reports that 12.8 GW installed capacity is from geothermal sources as of 2014.[62] Five of the study countries have installed geothermal energy capacity as of 2014: China, El Salvador, Indonesia, Philippines, and Thailand (Table 3.13). Of these five

Table 3.13 Geothermal energy profiles

	Installed capacity as of 2015, in MW	Geothermal energy share of TFEC, in per cent			
		1990	2000	2010	2012
China	27		0.21	0.26	0.27
El Salvador	204	1.50	2.39	4.36	4.58
Indonesia	1,340	0.12	0.32	0.50	0.49
Philippines	1,870	1.95	3.41	2.95	3.00
Thailand	0.30				

Note: only countries with potential are shown; data on installed capacity is from Ruggero Bertani 2015, Geothermal Power Generation in the World 2010–2014 Update Report in the *Proceedings of the World Geothermal Congress 2015*, Melbourne, Australia, 19–25 April; data for geothermal energy share of TFEC is extracted from Sustainable Energy for All Database 2017, available from the World Bank Database.

countries, Indonesia and the Philippines have tapped it more. The reason for this is straightforward: the potential for geothermal energy in these countries is among the world's highest. Although Indonesia has larger technical potential than the Philippines (about 40 per cent of the world's total),[63] it remains largely underexploited. The share of geothermal energy to TFEC in Indonesia, nevertheless, exceeds that of the Philippines in 2012. Being located on a volcanic belt, these two countries can expand their use of geothermal energy considerably.

The Philippines follows the USA as the second-highest geothermal power producer in the world, with 1.87 GW installed capacity as of 2014. Indonesia comes third at 1.34 GW. In 2014, about 650 MW of new geothermal power capacity was installed, which included new installations in Indonesia and the Philippines.[64] Geothermal resources in Indonesia are associated with volcanoes along Sumatra, Java, Bali, and the islands in the eastern part of the archipelago, and they are also mostly within forest areas. Table 3.14 shows current geothermal fields operated in the Philippines and Indonesia. In the Philippines, new contracts were issued in 2014, tapping additional capacities in Sta. Lourdes, Palawan; Biliran, Leyte; Mount Makiling; Kalinga, Apayao; Misamis Occidental; Negros Occidental; North Cotabato; Batangas; Mountain Province; and Ifugao.

China also exploits some of its geothermal energy potential. This includes the building of the Shaanxi Green Energy's district heating project at an installed capacity of 10 MW. Geothermal heat pumps are also being used in China; some of these were used to heat and cool some of the venues of the 2008 Beijing Olympics. In the future, China expects to install additional geothermal capacity in Tibet.

By cascading the temperature, the use of geothermal energy can be done more efficiently, thus improving the economics of the plant. One example has been described in Thailand, where a multipurpose geothermal combined heat and power (CHP) plant uses a well of 116°C to provide electricity (at a plant capacity of 300 kW) as well as hot water for refrigeration, crop drying, and a spa. In the Philippines, a geothermal CHP plant in Palinpinon uses a 160°C well to produce

Table 3.14 Operating geothermal fields in the Philippines and Indonesia

Philippines	Indonesia
20 MW in Maibarara, Leyte	2.5 MW in Mataloko
49.4 MW in Nasulo	5 MW in Ulumbu-Flores
108 MW in Mount Apo, Mindanao	11 MW in Sibayak
131 MW in Bacon-Manito, Sorsogon	60 MW in Dieng
192 MW in Palinpinon, Negros Oriental	87 MW in Lahendong
234 MW in Tiwi, Albay	110 MW in Ulu Belu-South Sumatra
458 MW in Mak-Ban, Laguna	200 MW in Kamojang
726 MW in Tongonan, Leyte	260 MW in Darajat
	227 MW in Wayang Windu

Source: author's compilation.

electricity and, at the same time, tap the remaining heat for *copra* (coconut meat) drying facility.

The cost structure of a geothermal project is determined by three activities: exploration, resource confirmation and characterization (drilling and well testing), and site development (facility construction). These costs vary considerably from project to project depending on well productivity and temperature and the depth to the geothermal reservoir. In addition, the rising cost of steel and competition from oil and gas activities for drilling-rig availability increases drilling costs for tapping geothermal energy. Typically, a reservoir takes 40 per cent of the total cost, while the power plant takes the remainder. The economic lifetime of the system is often assumed at 30 years. REN21 estimates that the capital cost for a 1-to-100 MW geothermal power plant ranges from $1,900 to $5,500 per kW.[65]

Compared to other energy resources, the exploitation of geothermal energy has a relatively low carbon footprint. Nonetheless, there are trade-offs that need to be considered. The potential gas pollution during drilling, field-tests, and installation of pipelines is a key limitation. The increased concentration of geothermal fluids, either steam or hot water, which usually contain gases as well as dissolved chemicals, during plant operation is another. Hydrogen sulfide, one of these gases, is heavier than air, very poisonous, corrosive, flammable, and explosive. Smaller proportions of ammonia, mercury, radon, and boron are also released in these facilities. Although their concentrations are usually benign, technologies for removing them can be installed nevertheless. The higher temperature of wastewater from geothermal plants compared to the surrounding environment is also a potential thermal pollutant. Another trade-off is regarding the subsidence phenomena or the gradual sinking of a land surface, which may occur as large quantities of fluids from geothermal reservoirs are extracted. The high-pitched noise of steam traveling through pipelines and the occasional vent discharge can also be an issue. There are also some issues with geothermal resources being below rainforests. Another set of issues is with regard to landscape aesthetics, especially with the sight of networks of pipelines and power-plant cooling towers.

Ocean energy

Ocean, since it covers almost 75 per cent of Earth's surface, is the largest collector of solar energy. In principle, oceans represent one of the largest renewable energy resources on Earth. Compared to VRE from sun and wind, the reliability and predictability of ocean resources give it an advantage. Ocean energy can be captured for practical use using five processes:

- Tidal head energy: among developing countries, the Gulf of Cambay in India has the largest tidal head and therefore has the most potential.
- Tidal current and ocean current energy: in developing countries, sites for tidal energy resource have been identified in South America and Asia. Potential locations for open ocean current flows have been identified in South Africa and East Asia.

- Wave energy: among developing country regions, South America has the greatest wave power densities.
- Ocean thermal energy: a few tropical regions with very deep water – a depth of 1 km or so – can deliver a feasible system, technically and economically, since they have large temperature difference.
- Salinity gradient energy.

The world, however, is only beginning to deploy ocean energy conversion systems. Currently, not many systems are operational. In 2014, ocean energy capacity remained at about 530 MW,[66] which are virtually pilot and demonstration projects. In addition to the existing 3.9 MW Jiangxa tidal power plant, which was completed in 1980 and upgraded in 2015, the Chinese ocean energy capacity comes from test sites in Weihai Shandong, Zhoushan Zhejiang, and Wanshan Guangdong. Three deployments are planned in China: a 300 kW wave energy device in Dawanshan Island, 300 kW wave energy converters in Shengshan Island, and floating turbines in Daishan.[67]

The technical potential for ocean energy has not yet been assessed in detail, but first indications are that at least China, the Philippines, and Indonesia, among the study countries, have huge technical potentials: in the range of 6 MW and 20 MW, respectively. However, these potential figures should be treated with caution, as they relate to non-mature technologies. Ocean energy is still progressing from the research stage and thus still needs to prove its technological worthiness before these technologies can be brought to the market. Given the current state of the technology, ocean energy entails a high cost of up to $5,870 for a plant less than 250 MW.[68]

Ocean energy technology, as with any energy resource, is not without its own trade-offs. In addition to its current cost and immaturity, these limitations are also technology and size-dependent. Tidal head energy systems, for example, when located in estuaries, will have an impact on currents and on sediment transport and deposits. Current subjects of investigation include the impacts of construction of the barrage on local biodiversity, of a large human-made seawater lake behind the barrage, and of offshore tidal lagoon systems on fishing, fish, bird breeding, and feeding.[69] Wave energy systems will also have a visual impact when large arrays of floating devices are installed near the shore. Underwater noise and vibrations can also be concerns, as well as impacts on fishing activities. To avoid an accident with surface vessels, these devices must be installed deep enough, resulting, however, in a lower energy yield. For ocean thermal energy devices that use closed-circuit hydraulics, spills of working fluids or leakage could be a concern. Large-scale wave energy systems have the potential to disturb ocean ecosystems and, therefore, harm marine life.

3.4.   Conclusion

The countries under study are on their different levels of transitions. Despite the availability of most of the required hardware, ramping up activities to close energy access gaps, heighten energy efficiency, and increase the share of renewable energy appears to be heterogeneously facilitated in the study countries. The hardware for achieving universal energy access, at least in the provision of modern energy for cooking and basic access to lighting in underserved areas, is ready for deployment. Improved cookstoves and solar home systems, the key hardware for closing this gap, need to be deployed and scaled rapidly. Access to productive energy for small-scale manufacturing and improved agriculture needs to be included in the portfolio of energy access hardware. The biggest opportunity for tapping energy efficiency as a key technology of the transition, which remains underexploited in many developing countries, needs to be harvested faster and wider. Bringing efficiency to the core of energy policy is an imperative as well as, most importantly, expanding its scope to other key energy-consuming sector in industry, transport, and agriculture. The availability and potential of renewable energy technologies and systems to provide new capacity and to replace dirty fossil fuel systems are also high in many developing countries – yet they are still regarded as niche industry.

In a number of countries under study, the role of biomass and hydropower as renewable forms of energy is substantial. Their inherent risks to human populations and the natural environment, however, entail the need for a new vision for the future of renewable energy in countries where they are exploited the most. In the longer term, the capacity that these sources provide needs to be replaced with less-risky technologies such as wind and solar.

The transformation of the level at which renewable energy is generated in the study countries and brought to their end users with higher efficiency represents the crux of achieving the sustainable energy transition ambition. All three key aspects of the transition hardware – for access, efficiency, and renewables – should be explicitly included in the longer-range energy transition ambition of developing countries. Integrating pockets of renewable energy as they are generated in sporadic spaces also has to pan out in future policy and investment directions. The next chapter describes how the deployment of the technical hardware can be brought to speed.

Notes

1 Sovacool, BK & Drupady, IM 2012, *Energy Access, Poverty, and Development: The Governance of Small-Scale Renewable Energy in Developing Asia*, Ashgate: New York.
2 Holdren, JP & Smith, KR 2000, 'Energy, the environment, and health,' in T Kjellstrom, D Streets & X Wang (Eds.), *World Energy Assessment: Energy and the Challenge of Sustainability*, United Nations Development Program: New York, pp. 61–110.
3 Sovacool, BK & Drupady, IM 2012, *Energy Access, Poverty, and Development: The Governance of Small-Scale Renewable Energy in Developing Asia*, Ashgate: New York, p. 7.
4 Ibid., pp. 12–16.
5 Ibid.
6 Pode, R 2010, 'Solution to enhance the acceptability of solar-powered LED lighting technology,' *Renewable and Sustainable Energy Reviews*, vol. 14, pp. 1096–1103.

7 Sovacool, BK & Drupady, IM 2012, *Energy Access, Poverty, and Development: The Governance of Small-Scale Renewable Energy in Developing Asia*, Ashgate: New York.
8 International Energy Agency 2015, *Energy Efficiency Market Report 2015: Market Trends and Medium-Term Prospects*, IEA: Paris, France, p. 22.
9 Yu, Y, et al. 2015, 'Ex-post assessment of China's industrial energy efficiency policies during the 11th Five-Year Plan,' *Energy Policy*, vol. 76, pp. 132–145.
10 International Energy Agency 2015, *Energy Efficiency Market Report 2015: Market Trends and Medium-Term Prospects*, IEA: Paris, France, p. 75.
11 Ibid., p. 76.
12 Ibid.
13 Akpinar-Ferrand, E & Singh, A 2010, 'Modeling increased demand of energy for air conditioners and consequent CO_2 emissions to minimize health risks due to climate change in India,' *Environmental Science & Policy*, vol. 13, pp. 702–712.
14 International Energy Agency 2015, *Energy Efficiency Market Report 2015: Market Trends and Medium-Term Prospects*, IEA: Paris, France, p. 113.
15 Li, T, Molodstov, S & Delina, L 2010, *Assessment Report on Institutional Arrangements for Energy Efficiency in Asia and the Pacific*, United Nations Economic and Social Commission for Asia and the Pacific: Bangkok, Thailand.
16 Moomaw, W, et al. 2011, 'Introduction,' in O Edenhofer, et al. (Eds.), *IPCC Special Report on Renewable Energy Sources and Climate Change Mitigation*, Cambridge University Press: Cambridge, UK & New York, USA, pp. 164, 178.
17 I thank Hartley Walimwipi for this point.
18 Roach, J 2015, 'For strong electricity, utilities are turning to pumped hydro,' *Yale Environment 360*, 24 November. See Section 4.5 for discussion on some roles for pumped-hydro in integration.
19 International Renewable Energy Agency 2015, *Renewables and Electricity Storage: A Technology Roadmap for Remap 2030*, IRENA, www.irena.org/DocumentDownloads/Publications/IRENA_REmap_Electricity_Storage_2015.pdf.
20 Roach, J 2015, 'For strong electricity, utilities are turning to pumped hydro,' *Yale Environment 360*, 24 November.
21 State Grid Corporation of China 2013, 'World's largest pumped storage power station with 3.6 GW installed capacity began construction in Fengning,' www.sgcc.com.cn/ywlm/mediacenter/corporatenews/06/293253.shtml.
22 Eskom 2016, 'Ingula pumped storage scheme,' www.eskom.co.za/Whatweredoing/NewBuild/IngulaPumpedStorage/Pages/Ingula_Pumped_Storage_Scheme.aspx.
23 International Renewable Energy Agency 2015, 'Hydropower technology brief,' www.irena.org/DocumentDownloads/Publications/IRENA-ETSAP_Tech_Brief_E06_Hydropower.pdf.
24 Ibid.
25 Renewable Energy Network 21 2015, *Renewables 2015: Global Status Report*, REN21 Secretariat: Paris, France.
26 Ibid.
27 Ziv, G, et al. 2012, 'Trading-off fish biodiversity, food security, and hydropower in the Mekong River Basin,' *PNAS*, vol. 109, pp. 5609–5614.
28 For a nuanced take on the contestations surrounding the Three Gorges project, see Bellette Lee, Y-C 2012, 'Global capital, national development and transnational environmental activism,' *Journal of Contemporary Asia*, vol. 43, pp. 102–126.
29 Zhou, Y 2010, 'Why is China going nuclear?,' *Energy Policy*, vol. 38, pp. 3755–3762.
30 Chen, H & Zhu, T 2016, 'The complexity of cooperative governance and optimization of institutional arrangements in the Greater Mekong Subregion,' *Land Use Policy*, vol. 50, pp. 363–370.
31 Ziv, G, et al. 2012, 'Trading-off fish biodiversity, food security, and hydropower in the Mekong River Basin,' *PNAS*, vol. 109, pp. 5609–5614.

32 International Energy Agency 2010, *Energy Technology Perspectives 2010: Scenarios and Strategies to 2050*, IEA: Paris, France.

33 Renewable Energy Network 21 2015, *Renewables 2015: Global Status Report*, REN21 Secretariat: Paris, France.

34 I thank Louise Tait for this point.

35 I thank Marcio Giannini Pereira for this information.

36 Rajendran, K, Aslanzadeh, S & Taherzadeh, MJ 2012, 'Household biogas digesters: A review,' *Energies*, vol. 5, pp. 2911–2942.

37 Weisman, W 2014, 'Biogas at home: A renewable no-brainer,' *Renewable Energy World*, 21 November.

38 Ministry of New and Renewable Energy, Government of India 2016, *Annual Report 2015–2016*, http://mnre.gov.in/file-manager/annual-report/2015-2016/EN/Chapter%201/chapter_1.htm.

39 Weisman, W 2014, 'Biogas at home: A renewable no-brainer,' *Renewable Energy World*, 21 November.

40 As observed for example in the *Pa Deng* community during the author's fieldwork in Thailand, November 2016 to January 2017.

41 Renewable Energy Network 21 2015, *Renewables 2015: Global Status Report*, REN21 Secretariat: Paris, France.

42 I thank Bharath Jairaj for this point.

43 German Advisory Council on Global Change 2008, *Welt im Wandel. Zukunftsfähige Bioenergie und nachhaltige Landnutzung*, WBGU: Berlin, Germany; also see Searchinger, T, et al. 2008, 'Use of U.S. croplands for biofuels increases greenhouse gases through emissions from land-use change,' *Science*, vol. 319, pp. 1238–1240.

44 Cherubini, F, et al. 2009, 'Energy- and greenhouse gas-based LCA of biofuel and bioenergy systems: Key issues, ranges and recommendations,' *Resources, Conservation and Recycling*, vol. 53, pp. 434–447.

45 Sagar, AD & Kartha, S 2007, 'Bioenergy and sustainable development?,' *Annual Review of Environment and Resources*, vol. 32, pp. 131–167; also see Foley, JA, et al. 2005, 'Global consequences of land use,' *Science*, vol. 309, pp. 570–574.

46 Lal, R 2004, 'Agricultural activities and the global carbon cycle,' *Nutrient Cycling in Agroecosystems*, vol. 70, pp. 103–116.

47 Haberl, H, et al. 2009, 'Towards an integrated model of socioeconomic biodiversity drivers, pressures and impacts: A feasibility study based on three European long-term socio-ecological research platforms,' *Ecological Economics*, vol. 68, pp. 1797–1812.

48 Berndes, G 2008, 'Future biomass energy supply: The consumptive water use perspective,' *International Journal of Water Resources Development*, vol. 24, pp. 235–245.

49 Lal, R 2004, 'Agricultural activities and the global carbon cycle,' *Nutrient Cycling in Agroecosystems*, vol. 70, pp. 103–116.

50 Renewable Energy Network 21 2015, *Renewables 2015: Global Status Report*, REN21 Secretariat: Paris, France.

51 Ibid., p. 20.

52 Ibid.

53 Smith, A, Stehly, T & Musial, W 2015, *2014–2015 Offshore Wind Technologies Market Report*, National Renewable Energy Laboratory, www.nrel.gov/docs/fy15osti/64283.pdf.

54 Jianxiang, Y 2015, 'Analysis: China to reevaluate offshore in new five-year plan,' *Windpower Offshore*, 16 June, www.windpoweroffshore.com/article/1351718/analysis-china-reevaluate-offshore-newfive-year-plan.

55 Gonzales, I 2014, 'SEA's biggest wind farm powers Luzon,' *Philippine Star*, 8 November.

56 Renewable Energy Network 21 2015, *Renewables 2015: Global Status Report*, REN21 Secretariat: Paris, France.

57 Ibid.

58 I thank Ryan Hogarth for this point.
59 Ibid.
60 Xinhua 2015, 'China adds 9.9 GW solar capacity in first nine months,' 20 October, http://news.xinhuanet.com/english/2015-10/20/c_134733002.htm.
61 Renewable Energy Network 21 2015, *Renewables 2015: Global Status Report*, REN21 Secretariat: Paris, France.
62 Ibid.
63 Holm, A, et al. 2010, 'Geothermal energy: International market update,' Geothermal Energy Association, www.geo-energy.org/pdf/reports/GEA_International_Market_Report_Final_May_2010.pdf, p. 53.
64 Bertani, R 2016, 'Geothermal power generation in the world 2010–2014 update report,' *Geothermics*, vol. 60, pp. 31–43.
65 Renewable Energy Network 21 2015, *Renewables 2015: Global Status Report*, REN21 Secretariat: Paris, France.
66 Ibid.
67 Ocean Energy Systems 2016, 'China,' https://report2015.ocean-energy-systems.org/country-reports/china/ocean-energy-policy/.
68 Renewable Energy Network 21 2015, *Renewables 2015: Global Status Report*, REN21 Secretariat: Paris, France.
69 Boehlert, GW & Gill, AB 2010, 'Environmental and ecological effects of ocean renewable energy development,' *Oceanography*, vol. 23, pp. 68–81.

4   Accelerating deployment

While the pathways to achieve the transition will vary across scales and levels of governance, the temporal dimension of the required change remains a constant: sustainable energy transition must occur as soon as possible. To achieve the ideal speed of the transition, the two options for scaling up – small-scale, distributed deployment (like a thousand flowers blooming) and large-scale, centralized deployment (as if we are mobilizing for a great emergency[1]) – need to be effectively integrated. Both options will be delivered using different schemes and supported by different policy settings and financial mechanisms. They will have their different potential trade-offs, yet there are also synergies. Finding a middle-way and linking the multiple approaches for deployments are necessary especially in the context of our increasingly networked and polycentric governance systems.

The traditional deployment approach to scaling energy generation and distribution involves a highly centralized mechanism where a large, monolith-like institutional arrangement directs, operates, and manages an equally large and concentrated system. This conventional understanding of electricity generation and distribution system, hence, involves central power plants fulfilling load demands and grids delivering generated electricity to customers. Sustainable energy transitions, however, tend to contest this monolithic, traditional system (4.1). To address energy access gaps (4.3), to harvest energy efficiency (4.2), and to contribute to the widespread use of renewable energy (4.3, 4.4) require multiple efforts that would involve small-, medium-, and large-scale interventions linked together to achieve acceleration and scale. All three aspects of transitions in the global south have to be deployed in concert. How could these multi-size, multi-level, and heterogeneously located and deployed efforts be supported, strengthened, and eventually linked together (4.5)? What are the ensuing tensions, and how could they be negotiated (4.6)?

4.1.   Future energy systems

Expansion till kingdom come – the tenet of the utility-scale business model in many developing countries – is no longer well suited to contemporary circumstances. In the same way, the traditional notion of electricity as a commodity to be produced in central power plants and delivered to consumers through long-distance transmission and distribution systems is also being challenged. Further disruptions can be expected in future arrangements.

The essential point of disruption is, indeed, already occurring at the point of distribution where customers interface with their electricity source. In the future, most energy will almost be locally generated in distributed systems located at roofs (such as arrays of solar home systems, solar utility photovoltaic [PV], and micro wind systems, or a combination) and, in some cases, below ground (such as a micro-scale geothermal heating and cooling system).

In many developing countries, these systems will most likely be generated communally (such as a micro-hydro or a micro-grid). In rural, agricultural areas, many productive ventures will be powered by renewable energy systems, either as a stand-alone or as a part of a micro-grid. These systems are used to efficiently pump irrigation water, dry crops and produce, mill grains, provide cleaner cooking fuel, light efficient lamps, power efficient fans, fridges and TV sets, provide power for cottage industries, and charge battery storage systems, among others.

These distributed systems are either off-grid solutions to meet energy access in rural areas or on-grid solutions attached to the grid. In the latter, this means getting electricity at times when its local supply is not enough and feeding excess energy.

Many existing and newly constructed buildings, including residential houses, will be energy efficient, with good insulation and efficient appliances and lighting, and they will be designed with passive efficiency built onto them. In many developing countries, efficient cookstoves, fans, and refrigerators will be regular home fixtures. Further into the future, these and other home appliances will be connected to an app or a computer program that monitors and manages energy use. While consumers make use of this monitoring and management software built onto their smartphones as a response to price signals, they will also use this to evaluate their own energy consumption behaviors.

In an event of a grid failure such as blackouts, these houses, communities, neighborhoods, or buildings will use energy from their local storage, or in any case from community-owned and community-managed solar PV arrays and/or micro-hydro systems, which future households, community organizations, or building owners participate as a co-owners or shareholders of these renewable energy businesses.

The future will also see power companies and utilities that do things far different from what traditional firms like they used to do. They will act as power aggregators, connecting and linking all those houses, buildings, community systems, and other distributed renewable energy generators, operating them as power plants, and selling electricity to a larger grid. These power plants will be considered micro-grids, another fundamental and common fixture of future energy systems.

A micro-grid, usually with generation capacity of 10 kilowatt (kW) or below, is a network of renewable energy-generating homes, neighborhoods, and buildings in a geographically contiguous area. It manages energy produced in this scale at the same time that, if excess energy allows, it also feeds into a larger grid. A micro-grid can also tap into energy generated from small to mid-sized renewable energy generators such as a small solar or wind farm or a micro-hydro facility – on top of their household rooftop PV systems, for example. A micro-grid can be operated by a group of households, a business park, a community, a local neighborhood association, or a cooperative. Micro-grids hold great promise for achieving energy access, especially in rural, off-grid areas. At the larger scale, say a city or a province or a state, autonomous micro-grids can be linked or networked. They can then be expanded further upward the scale: to nations and neighboring nations.

Other energy services will also be made very efficient, in addition to them being powered solely by renewable electricity. The mobility of choice for example will be geared towards an extensive use of public transport including trains and boats in cities where there are waterways.

This future arrangement of energy generation, distribution, and consumption is a complete antithesis of the traditionally centralized and utility-scaled energy systems. It emerges from the ground, extends and branches horizontally, and reaches out vertically – in contrast to the top-down, expansion-oriented nature of conventional utility models. This means that new players in the energy landscape are created and are to be provided with capacity. As households become energy generators and participate in the energy business, new regulations, financing schemes, management support, and institutional arrangements will be devised to fully support them and their transition activities.

The new integrated, multi-actor, and multi-scale arrangements that the transition brings comes with a number of co-benefits. It contributes to accelerating sustainable energy transition since this innovation occurs in pockets of small and medium-size systems that can be, as already demonstrated in practice, easily organized, maintained, and scaled up in a system and network-type processes. It addresses universal energy access since many people who have no access are located in geographic areas that could never be connected to the grid for technical and economic reasons. It saves money as the need for new and large power plants and power lines are greatly reduced. It also saves carbon emissions as sustainable choices are made over unsustainable, fossil fuel-fired systems. It harvests energy efficiency potentials, both at supply and at demand side, with the help of technology, nudges, and changes in consumption patterns. It is far more resilient than centralized energy generation-and-grid systems, which are vulnerable to accidents and natural calamities. It is democratizing as a result of distributing control and extending autonomy and ownership to common people.[2] It allows ordinary citizens to learn about their energy consumption practices, thus nudging them to be more reflective about their own choices.

Most of the hardware aspects of sustainable energy deployment are, as described in the previous chapter, already commercially available. In developing countries, as well as in developed ones, though, there are still important gaps, including, most particularly, 'smart' hardware that would make home and community renewable energy systems smarter, as well as integrated system arrangements that would link them together. These technologies, nonetheless, have already emerged and are demonstrated in pilot areas with high levels of success. What is more important now is for policy to innovate simultaneously with these technological innovations. To accelerate the diffusion of sustainable energy systems for universal energy access and for low-carbon development, markets and citizens also need to be nudged by strong policy[3] that would rapidly encourage innovation in improving the required hardware, bring down the cost of these technologies, and scale up their deployment.

4.2. Harvesting energy efficiency

Expanding the coverage of energy efficiency policies is necessary for meeting the coupled ambition of climate mitigation and sustainable development. Energy efficiency is a key component of many nationally determined contributions (NDCs) to the Paris Agreement. At the same time, doubling the rate of improvement in global energy intensity by 2030 compared with historical improvements is one of the goals in the Agenda 2030 (SDGs). Efficiency in lighting appears to be among the easiest to scale, especially given the significant price drops in the price of LED bulbs in recent years. More work, however, remains to be done to fully harvest efficiency potentials in important energy consuming sectors such as appliances, buildings, agriculture, transport, and industrial equipment.

Target setting remains a key policy mechanism to expand the opportunity for maximizing efficiency gains. China has long-standing efforts in this regard. As part of its 13th Five-Year Plan, China seeks to achieve energy intensity improvements of 15 per cent from 2015 to 2020. Retiring old and inefficient steel manufacturing plants within this period is among the strategies in the Plan. India also sets plans to improve building energy efficiency, such as through its National Energy Efficient Fan Program that distributes efficient ceiling fans. This was after a successful rollout of lighting efficiency programs. The Philippines also has an Energy Efficiency Plan for 2016–2020 aimed at reducing energy intensity by 40 per cent by 2030 from the level in 2005. Thailand also incorporates an energy efficiency plan in its consolidated and integrated energy plan, aiming to reduce energy intensity by 30 per cent in 2036 versus the 2020 level.

Energy efficiency needs to be at the heart of future energy strategies, particularly for accelerating sustainable energy transitions. A number of measures, policy strategies, and funding mechanisms can be tapped to achieve this. India, for instance, has completed an innovative trading scheme to improve energy efficiency in the industrial sector with targets exceeded during its first implementation cycle.[4] More types of innovation in policy and financing are necessary in the future, especially in terms of expanding the scope and scale, from sector to sector. Moving from voluntary to mandatory energy efficiency regulations is also a must, as well as including other instruments in the policy toolbox. These include, among others, the systematic and structured phasing out of consumer subsidies,[5] putting a price on carbon, and raising taxes for carbon-polluting systems. Pricing is key in nudging consumers to make environmentally aware consumption choices.

Influencing energy prices through subsidies and taxes is a staple in energy policy in many developing countries. Often, they are employed as a means of social safety nets aimed at protecting low-income households; however, this practice tends to backfire in terms of increased energy demand, failing its intended objective. This relationship, however, is complex, especially when one brings into the equation the role of structural differences, in terms of regulations for example. Nonetheless, it is essential that subsidies to dirty polluting fuels be systematically removed. This eases out budget constraints in many developing countries and therefore helps them to deliver the objectives of energy transitions.[6]

4.3.   Scaling distributed energy

A lot has already been written about the promise of decentralized, small-scale energy generation systems, especially for meeting the energy access component of sustainable energy transitions in developing countries. Several technologies are already technically proven, piloted, and demonstrated and are commercially available for distributed generation purposes. These include solar PV systems, micro-hydro, wind energy, biomass combined heat and power, and small-scale, household-size storage systems. These technologies are appropriate for meeting energy needs in residential, commercial, industrial, and government facilities. Installation, maintenance, and fuel costs typically vary according to size, geographic location, financial incentives, policy support, local market maturity, and competition. Small-scale distributed generation systems are, in general, not susceptible to lock-in, inertia, or path dependence. Since they are smaller installations, they can be easily replaced as improved or more efficient technologies become available. Compared with large-scale installations, which are often associated with coal or hydro power plants, small-scale renewable energy infrastructure offer rapid buy-in from local communities.

Benjamin Sovacool and Ira Martina Drupady devoted an entire book to this topic describing and analyzing the opportunities, challenges, and limitations of these systems in developing Asia.[7] These will not be rehashed here; rather, the focus is on the key aspects of small-scale generation and its contribution to meeting the aims of sustainable energy transitions, in particular for accelerating and scaling up their deployment.

Distributed generation opens up doors for new players, such as private citizens, homeowners, indigenous communities, small-scale enterprises, cooperatives, associations, and other groups to participate in sustainable energy transitions and, in a growing instance, in the energy market itself. This entails introducing new capacities, while strengthening existing ones, in both operations and management of new assets, including addressing system breakdowns and ensuring sustainability of operations and systems.

Distributed generation systems are key for meeting the goals of universal energy access particularly in underserved areas and communities that the grid cannot reach. Off-grid systems offer the most economical approach to meeting these energy needs. It also has an important role in increasing generation capacity to meet the objective of accelerating the transitions in areas that are connected to the grid. Indeed, on-grid distributed systems become the more important component of the transition as it helps in securing reliability and stability of supply. It also has economic implications in that it can generate new sources of income for households, at the same time that it makes energy affordable for everyone.

Off-grid, small-scale, distributed installations

Accelerating the deployment of off-grid distributed systems can significantly advance the ways we could meet the global ambition of universal energy access. Off-grid systems can directly respond to basic energy poverty such as lighting and inefficient heating and cooking. In developing countries, there are at least four common types of technology hardware to meet these ends. These technologies, as demonstrated in perhaps hundreds of installations worldwide, can easily be adopted to suit local needs. These technologies are improved cookstoves, solar home systems, biogas digesters, and micro-hydro dams. Depending on need, local resources, and capacity, these technologies can operate either as a stand-alone system or as a combination of two or more technologies. Each of these technologies brings with it a number of benefits depending on the type of energy poverty it seeks to address. At the same time, they also have some limitations and challenges.

Improved cookstoves for cooking and heating purposes efficiently use biomass as fuels. They address health issues in many households in developing countries, particularly in terms of reducing indoor air pollution. Cutting the fuel by half as a result of this innovation significantly reduced the stress to forests. They can also be installed quickly and maintained without requiring additional skills. They have some limitations, however, especially in terms of cultural practices as this basically changed people's appreciation of their food, for example.

Solar home systems, in the range of 10 to 150 Watt-peak (Wp), are fast becoming the new norm, especially in terms of basic lighting provision. Some large systems can even provide enough energy to power radios, television sets, and other electric appliances. The transition from using kerosene lamps or candles towards electric lighting has a number of social and economic benefits to households, especially to children and women.

Biogas digesters usually provide fuel for cooking, but some households use it for generating electricity too. Their size range from 1 to 8 cubic meters, with feedstock coming from a variety of sources: from animal manure to agricultural and domestic wastes. While these systems have a number of benefits such as reduced cost for cooking fuel, reduced reliance on traditional forms of biomass, and improved sanitary practices, they are not free from challenges. The sufficiency of feedstock remains a key challenge for many households, for example.

Micro-hydro dams are also almost a constant feature in community renewable energy in developing countries. These structures utilize low-voltage distribution systems ranging from 5 kW to 10 megawatt (MW). Their allure is due to their multi-use other than for electricity. For instance, they can be tapped to provide mechanical energy for processing agricultural products. Compared with the technologies mentioned above, however, micro-hydro dams require skillsets and capacity for operation and maintenance, which can be a key challenge when deployed. Nonetheless, experiences in Indonesia, for instance, where micro-hydro in the range of tens of kW and thriving in community-based organizations in the absence of regulatory regimes, suggest a very promising approach to sustainable energy transitions in many developing countries with potential for this technology.[8]

Opportunities for bringing stand-alone systems together and networking them into a micro-grid are also becoming more relevant, technically efficient, and economically effective, and they are, therefore, favorably accepted in a number of locations and communities in the developing world. Accelerating the deployment of these technologies and new systems requires a number of development interventions. Some of these are discussed below.

On-grid, small-scale, distributed installations

Distributed energy systems also contribute to meeting other aims of the transition agenda. They help in accelerating the deployment of renewables and the displacement of polluting systems. They add to energy supply diversity and enhanced system reliability. They reduce peak power requirements – at least during peak daytime use (and with proper management, even at night time), thus displacing or deferring capital investment for more expensive power plants. With generation close or even on the site of consumption, distributed energy generation systems help reduce transmission and distribution requirements, and, thus, avoid grid losses in conventional systems. This results in improved energy efficiency, which directly translates into economic and carbon savings. If interconnections are used to bring in variable renewable energy (VRE) from distant sites to points of consumption, the cost for transmission and distribution can be significantly increased. These challenges are further discussed below.

As generation becomes more widely distributed, the number of electricity sources reverses the traditional direction of flow of energy service: from utility-to-consumer to consumer-to-utility. This has implications in the current business orientation of many utilities in developing countries at the same time that it opens up a new technical challenge to distribution grids. As renewable energy produced in distributed systems is fed into the system, the grid needs to assume the function of transporting electricity bi-directionally, i.e. both from utility to point of consumption and vice versa.

The future arrangement will still see some role for centralized power stations, but they will have an additional role – that is, to cater a large number of smaller, distributed systems. Two changes can be envisaged when this occurs. First, additional high-voltage distribution lines will be required, especially when new supply comes from MW-size VRE power plants. Second, coordinating the operation of a large number of new VRE systems will be imperative in the electricity distribution and transport networks, which entail making grids smarter through information and communication technologies. These implications are further discussed in the section on integration below.

On-grid distributed systems can be either a small-scale solar PV array installed on rooftops, a micro-hydro system, a small-scale wind system, a small-scale biogas digester, or a portfolio of these systems connected in a micro-grid to serve the energy needs of household or community consumers. Such installations capture the imagination of many – mainly because of its allure to bring new opportunities to households and many businesses. The financial attractiveness of investing in these systems, such as rooftop solar PV, however, will be a moving target: as larger amounts of distributed renewable energy generation, mostly VRE sources, can add stress to the traditional energy retail businesses in developing countries. Tariff structures can easily be affected, especially as the underlying share of fixed costs in the power system are accounted for in the new generation-distribution dynamics. Centralized utility business models are also affected, bringing them to obsolescence as distributed energy systems crowd out the market. This, as a result, democratizes the power sector as consumers are provided with more control and, hence, responsibility.

Accelerating the deployment of on- and off-grid distributed energy systems

Since most renewable energy technologies can be rapidly deployed in a smaller scale, their contribution to accelerating the transitions is evident when distributed energy multiplies and scales up both on- and off-grid systems.[9] As communities, both in urban and in rural areas, gained access or transition into distributed energy systems, several co-benefits are incurred, including growth of local businesses; improved education and medical services; local job creation; and improved social cohesion and community wellbeing.

With increased deployment of distributed generation systems, however, challenges are poised to occur: the quality of supply, the stability of the grid,[10] safety, operation, maintenance, and standardization. Small-scale distributed systems are also introducing huge challenges for the distribution industry and requiring some fundamental changes in traditional business models.

It could be challenging to regulate and govern multiple, smaller projects because they entail duplicate regulatory costs and incur high costs for complying with measurement, reporting, and verification requirements. They are perceived to be less bankable, especially compared to large-scale projects, primarily because of their high transaction cost. Since packaging a small-scale energy project loan or investment proposal requires the same effort as a large-scale project, developers and financiers have less incentive to process them. Their low return on investment also makes them less attractive for investment.

Distributed generation systems, which are mostly small scale, generally require low-level financing. However, this is also a challenge since many development banks operating in developing countries do not have much experience in providing numerous microloans (and in case they do, they are often failing in terms of sustaining it). The transaction costs are higher, especially, when compared to a single, large-scale business. However, there are now examples of mechanisms to aggregate and even commoditize multiple, small-scale projects into large-scale investment vehicles. For instance, yieldcos are raising significant capital for small-scale distributed energy projects. These, however, also pose some difficulties.[11]

4.4. A room for monoliths?

The economic potential of centralized power generation systems is maximized if, and only if, they are located close to load centers, which, with few exceptions, are densely populated urban areas. As much as possible, therefore, large-scale renewable energy generators can maximize their profit potential by connecting generation systems directly to urban centers. This has direct implications, especially for outlying areas and remote communities, who, in turn, could remain underserved if off-grid solutions are marginalized. In many developing countries, these underserved areas are already not getting the same degree of reliable and affordable energy access as their urban counterparts. Hence, too much focus on centralized generation can only perpetuate inequality and injustice.

Large facilities and extensive infrastructure also require large-scale investments, which, in turn, need long periods of recouping. This long-term aspect ensures the longevity of path dependence in which players, including funders and project developers and eventually consumers, are locked into conditions that may no longer be valid in the future. For these and other reasons, a centralized approach to energy access provision may not be an excellent approach for achieving universal energy access. Rather, a focused on small-scale, and distributed approach to renewable energy generation offers the most optimistic option to meet this sustainable development objective.

Beyond the issues of energy access, however, utility-scale and centralized renewable energy generation offers some importance, especially in terms of accelerating the transitions. In one of the technical models showing how countries can transition their energy systems, most of the efforts rest upon having utility-scale systems, mostly from VRE sources, particularly wind and sun energy – both to meet new and expanding energy demand and for replacing polluting systems.[12] The continued role for large-scale systems in the future will be largely seen in terms of new installations such as utility-scale solar PV, concentrated solar thermal (CST), onshore and offshore wind farms, and geothermal.

In recent years, many in developing countries have started rolling out technological deployment of these systems. Five of the study countries have, for example, started tapping into the potential of large-scale solar power aside from utility-scale solar PV, CST in particular. Table 4.1 shows examples of some of these ongoing and completed installations.

Utility-scale solutions offer a number of advantages for accelerating the transitions. First, they produce economies of scale, making them highly attractive

Table 4.1 Examples of concentrated solar projects in some study countries

	Capacity, MW	Project name	Location	Notes
China	1	Dalhan Power Plant	Beijing	Operating since 2012
	50	Delingha Solar Thermal Power Project	Delingha, Qinghai	Operational in 2017
	50	Supcon Solar Project	Delingha, Qinghai	Under construction
	200	Golmud	Golmud, Qinghai	Operational in 2018
	270	Delingha Solar Thermal Generation Project	Delingha	Operational in 2017
India	1	National Solar Thermal Power Facility	Gurgain	Operating since 2012
	2.5	ACME Solar Tower	Bikaner, Rajasthan	Operating since 2011
	25	Gujarat Solar One	Kutch, Gujarat	Under construction
	50	Abhijeet Solar Project	Phalodi, Rajasthan	Under construction
	50	Godawari Solar Project	Nokh, Rajasthan	Operating since 2013
	50	Megha Solar Plant	Anantapur, Andra Pradesh	Operating since 2014
	100	Diwakar Solar Project	Askandra, Rajasthan	Under construction
	100	KVK Energy Solar Project	Askandra, Rajasthan	Under construction
	125	Dhursar concentrating solar power project	Dhursar, Rajasthan	Operating since 2014
Morocco	3	Airlight Energy Ait-Baha Pilot Plant	Ait-Baha, Agadir	Operating since 2014
	20	ISCC Ain Beni Mathar Project	Ain Beni Mathar	Operating since 2010
	160	NOOR I concentrating solar power project	Ouarzazate	Operating since 2015
	200	NOOR II	Ouarzazate	Operational in 2017
	150	NOOR II	Ouarzazate	Operational in 2017

	Capacity, MW	Project name	Location	Notes
South Africa	55	Bokpoort concentrating solar power project	Groblershoop, Northern Cape	Operating since 2016
	100	KaXu Solar One	Poffader, Northern Cape	Operating since 2015
	50	Khi Solar One	Upington, Northern Cape	Operating since 2016
	100	Xina Solar One	Poffader, Northern Cape	Under construction
Thailand	5	Thai Solar Energy 1	Huai Kachao	Operating since 2012

Source: author's compilation.

options for policymakers, project developers, and financiers who often seek grand infrastructure projects to support. (This is countered, however, with the large-scale financing risks attached to megaprojects.) Second, they create more labor efficiency in terms of more energy per working-hour spent on them. (While this may be true, this advantage has to be appreciated in terms of the number of jobs created, which, in this case, can be actually few compared to say, a portfolio of small-scale projects.) Third, they make regulations easy to implement because they are few in numbers. Fourth, they lead to standardization, making the production of component parts easier. (This advantage, however, can also be realized in small-scale systems.)

More often than not, large-scale installations, despite the appetite of funders to support them and the other mentioned advantages, have some key challenges (in addition to the bracketed issues above). Benjamin Sovacool and Christopher Cooper demonstrate how larger megaprojects can become highly challenged as they grow in their size and complexities.[13] They make five key propositions about the challenges of megaprojects and argue that:

- Megaprojects can lead into competing constituencies, instead of cooperation, and, at times, can even exclude involvement and participation leading to resentment or opposition.
- Megaprojects can fail with increasing complexities, couplings, and cost overruns.
- Megaprojects can fail economically in that they consolidate their benefits among a small group of elites at the same time that they spread their costs across a broader range of social actors within and across countries and across generations.

- Megaprojects can erode transparency, accountability, and hence democracy since it tends to reinforce centralized control.
- Megaprojects tend to have overestimated benefits while undervaluing its impacts.

In addition, challenges regarding land availability pose a hurdle for big installations. Competition for land use complements this barrier. The challenges attached to large-scale energy infrastructure, thus, require balancing it with small, distributed systems. For scale to be achieved, they need to be integrated and efficiently linked. These processes of integration, however, are processes that are also filled with tensions.

4.5.   Small meets big

Accelerating sustainable energy transitions requires that the energy system be improved by linking both distributed and centralized systems. In developing countries where population increases, urbanization intensifies, and consumption increases, the future of energy means increase in energy demand across households, industries, and service sectors. Stability, reliability, and affordability of supply, thus, become imperative but ensuring that supply is sustainably sourced, efficiently generated and consumed, and universally accessible is similarly important. A key challenge in the future, however, as more renewables get into the system, will be to match load demand and supply of energy properly. A key challenge is the need to understand, appreciate, and navigate the partly fluctuating nature of some renewable energy sources – or VRE sources, which range from minutes to annual seasons.

   Of all types of renewable energy, except from large hydropower, VRE from wind and solar PV sources currently provide a minor role in the energy mixes of many developing countries. Instead, hydropower and conventional fossil fuel-fired power plants continue to bring the lion's share of the needed energy demand in these countries. A future scenario envisaged in a low-carbon, decarbonized, and climate-safe world, however, entails that VRE overtakes these traditional fuels and becomes the leading source of energy supply. As everything is electrified – from lighting to cooking to transport to heating and cooling to productive energy, the challenge of providing energy that is reliable, affordable, modern, and sustainable also increases.

   Reliability and stability, i.e. ensuring that demand and supply are balanced, is key for ensuring that access is provided to all consumers. In traditional systems, flattening the 'valleys' and 'peaks' in energy-demand profile is already a key technical challenge. This becomes more important in sustainable energy futures where more valleys and peaks can be expected from VRE sources. For instance, as more solar energy comes online during the sunny daytime hours, demand for utility electricity is pushed down further and further (the valleys). Just as the sun is setting and solar energy declines, however, consumers are also getting home from their work and turn on their appliances. At this time, net load demand rises very rapidly to the early evening peaks (the peaks). In many developing countries, intense urbanization and increasing population are expected to contribute to more valleys and peaks.

The physical nature of electricity requires that demand and supply be in balance at all times. While the traditional, large-scale power plants maintain this balance simply by adjusting their outputs to power demand at a given time, the introduction of more VRE to the traditional system can easily lead to a more volatile supply profile. Ensuring flexibility is also important during the transition process where significant amounts of polluting power plants are retired and replaced with more VRE. In this regard, the future energy system needs to be flexible so that it can easily integrate high shares of VRE sources into the mix. The challenge of integration and flexibility is defined by at least three key aspects:[14]

- Variability: the fluctuating output of VRE power plants requires that dispatchable generators can quickly increase or decrease its production.
- Scarcity: at times when demand is high but supply from VRE is low, the system needs to import or take from other generators.
- Abundance: at times when supply is high but the demand is low, conventional generators need to be powered down. This can pose a significant challenge to the economic viability of solar and wind energy, which can affect revenue streams and the recovery of project investments.

Given the broad impacts of VRE to the system, successful integration in developing countries will likely depend upon the balanced use of the following technical and non-technical measures in the short and long term.

> *Strategy 1: targeting energy efficiency measures at peak demand hours.* In developing countries, especially in large load centers such as in urban areas, this means focusing on improvements in lighting and air conditioning. Technological hardware to substantially cut energy use in these services is already widely available and affordable. These technologies could cut demand at times when they are most needed.
>
> *Strategy 2: deploying peak-oriented renewable energy systems.* Dispatchable renewable energy from hydropower (which many developing countries count as a key energy supplier), biomass energy, geothermal energy, and CSPs can be used to smooth out energy demand during peak hours. Some wind farms can also be sited in areas where they can generate energy in the evening.
>
> *Strategy 3: adopting time-of-use pricing to nudge consumers to reduce consumption during peak hours.* The price of energy should reflect its use to certain hours, i.e. cheaper at times when demand is low and vice versa. Although seldom in use, even in developed countries, if not totally absent, time-based tariff solutions can be done either through time-of-use tariffs where energy is priced differently based on predefined blocks of hours, e.g. peak

versus off-peak, or real-time pricing where the price varies at every single hour of the day.

Strategy 4: siting VRE generators closer to the load. With solar and wind energy hardware advancing technically – for instance, wind energy generations even in lower wind speed locations are now possible with improved wind turbine technologies – VRE generation can be sited closer to where the demand is.

Strategy 5: using more sophisticated system operations such as improving production forecasts for VRE. Predictions in network operations must be integrated into the new system. Forecasts – especially about long periods of low VRE, which require the system to meet demand by importing electricity elsewhere – can be integrated in networks. This entails matching supply and demand with good-quality information on the availability of renewable energy sources in the space and time required.

Strategy 6: micro-grids. VRE generators can be pooled into a complementary portfolio such as wind plus solar plus run-of-river hydropower to create a virtual power plant or a micro-grid. Connecting micro-generators to this network of virtual power plants reduces expenses that could be incurred to construct new transmission and high-voltage distribution systems. Micro-grids are either low- or medium-voltage distribution systems with distributed generators, storage devices, and controllable loads. Although some micro-grids are isolated from the main grid, a number can be connected to the main power network where they trade electrical energy outputs in the larger system. In Nepal, for example, two community-owned micro-hydro projects – the 23 kW Leguwa Khola installation in Dhankuta district and the 40 kW Syaure Bhumi installation in the Niwakot district – have been connected to the Nepal power grid through an agreement with Nepal Electricity Authority.[15]

Strategy 7: interconnection. Flexibility can also be achieved through grid interconnection with neighboring power plants, storage, and demand-side response measures. The more grids can be connected with one another to form larger grids over larger areas, the more spread out the potential for VRE will be and the more spread out load will be, both of which will serve to smooth out the peaks and valleys in the demand and supply curve.

Strategy 8: improving transmission and distribution systems. In cases where the best VRE sources are located far away from load centers, which will be the case in many developing countries, adequate capacity must be available on the transmission lines. Reliability of supply would be heavily dependent upon the integrity of interconnections of critical nodes and links up to the point where electricity finally reaches consumers. This, however, represents a key challenge among developing countries where the age of the grid is often old. New transmission lines that will connect VRE generators to areas where demand is entail additional cost. Already, transmission and distribution costs often account for more than twice the cost of electricity generation on most electricity bills in many developing countries. This represents a huge burden to consumers, especially for poor people.

Strategy 9: demand-side management. Flexibility can be achieved with an actively managed distribution system especially in rapidly urbanizing centers in developing countries where energy demand in households, industry, and the service sectors are growing alongside new population.[16] This can be done through voltage control in rural systems and fault level control in urban systems through network switching. The rise of modern information and communication technologies (ICTs) opens up new opportunities for monitoring and managing demand at various scales. There are two types of strategies for reshaping demand loads in the future: by influencing the load through energy efficiency (which reduces demand) and by managing demand-side response through instantaneous measures. Demand-side response can be performed either through load shifting by transferring demand (e.g. shifting the use of washing machines to different time period) or through load shedding by interrupting demand for short intervals (e.g. stopping the functioning of air conditioning systems for a given amount of time) or by adjusting demand intensity (e.g. reducing industrial production at a particular time).

Strategy 10: smart grids. For more efficient use of network capacities, strong and smart grids are necessary to smooth VRE output and connect flexible resources together. A smart grid is an electricity network that can intelligently integrate the actions of all users connected to it – generators, consumers, and those that do both, the prosumers – to efficiently deliver sustainable, economic, and secure electricity supply. Among developing countries, China is leading in terms of investing in smart grids – about 70 per cent of households are already connected to it with full coverage expected in the short term.[17] India, in 2013, has also released its *Smart Grid Vision and Roadmap* aimed at transforming the entire Indian electricity system into a smart grid over the next decade. Deploying smart grids entails substantial cost, especially in developing countries, and requires new and additional forms of financing.

Strategy 11: electricity storage. Linking electricity to other sectors such as transport and heat can contribute to stronger flexibility, and it opens up the opportunity to accelerate the transitions beyond the electricity sector. For instance, electric vehicle fleets may provide a valuable new opportunity to expand energy storage. In addition, space and water heating and cooling can be augmented by thermal storage systems and co-generation. Pumped storage hydropower dominates current power storage capacity. While they were originally built as a cost-saving measure for managing peak demand and for allowing continuous operation of inflexible base-load power generation plants, they are also now seen as complementary technologies for helping mitigate the challenges of integrating VRE into power systems. Although pumped storage hydropower has high technical potential, their potential is limited by the restrictions in terms of site availability and obviously the social and environmental risks attached to large hydropower. In that case, small-scale storage systems, while not yet commercially competitive, can be more appealing in the future. Already, some applications in Africa and South Asia have been rolled out in off-grid facilities to address access issues in rural areas.[18] With high levels of VRE penetration expected in the future, technologies for storing excess and abundant generation will be imperative.

4.6.   Conclusion

The technological strategies for the deployment of the transition hardware discussed in Chapter 3, including approaches for their integration – as discussed in this chapter – need to be accompanied with upgrades in the operations and management of power systems as well as, more importantly, the re-design of institutions, policies, and markets that would support them. Every region and country and utility is different, and each will need to customize its portfolio of deployment and integration solutions. The suite of hardware measures described in the last two chapters extensively requires innovations in organization and management of these new technological systems. Existing institutional arrangements, policy mechanisms, and market designs need to be reviewed and subsequently revamped to meet these new challenges, including the multiplicity of support and delivery mechanisms for each of the three complementary aspects of the transition: access, efficiency, and renewable energy. Deployment and integration can reach their full potential only when the technological responses are coordinated and complemented by strong, responsive, adaptable, useful, and coherent policy measures and collaborations between government, development providers, funders, consumers, grid operators, and other key actors.

Failure to integrate the hardware requirement for linking small and big generation systems, improving storage hardware, and making grids smarter with innovative institutions, effective policy, and relevant markets could result to curtailment, hence ineffectiveness and inefficiency. In the renewable energy deployment and integration field, curtailment occurs when renewable energy generated by VRE are 'lost' and thus are not used to meet demand. It usually occurs when the available output from renewable energy exceeds the ability of the grid to take it.

While smart metering, demand-side management, and other approaches can make technological leapfrogging for sustainable energy transitions, a clear institutional framework is essential for leading deployment and integration measures, developing new markets, and ensuring the security and stability of the grid. Tariff structures also need to evolve to maximize the opportunities for deployment and integration. They are necessary in nudging consumers towards more awareness and responsiveness to their energy consumption profiles. When tariffs reflect the cost of energy more accurately, consumers learn more about when they need to reduce their energy consumption, prompting them to make more efficient choices.

The future of energy also needs innovation in market development, inasmuch as it needs innovation in regulations. Market frameworks in developing countries need to be adjusted, opening up a larger role for VRE. Very few power systems, if not zero, are currently attuned to this emerging reality. New business models need to be supported. For example, electricity consumers can be turned into active participants in the electricity market through the introduction of an aggregate service provision model. An aggregator – currently absent in traditional markets – can be introduced as a new actor gathering consumer demand and VRE suppliers. As this, and other new business models, emerges and develops, ongoing collaborative reflection and knowledge sharing across actors, including consumers, is imperative to bring these models into maturity.

Developing countries also need to find new and secure investment in a range of new assets needed for integration, including flexible power plants, especially large-scale renewables with storage, storage itself, demand-side management, transmission and distribution, and smart grids. Price signals also play a large role. With the development of small-scale distributed energy resources such as rooftop solar PV, household batteries, and more actively engaged consumers, the market can be actively tuned in to the needs of the transition through price signals. Introducing a sufficient carbon price can help in setting up these price signals. Acknowledging that this policy measure takes time, and given the urgency of the transition, appropriate price signals can be introduced through other means such as feed-in tariffs and renewable energy certificates, which help create additional revenue streams for VRE suppliers on top of the market price. These and other mechanisms are discussed in more details in the next three chapters on policy, financing, and institutions.

Notes

1 For example, see Delina, L 2016, *Strategies for Rapid Climate Mitigation: Wartime Mobilisation as a Model for Action?*, Routledge: Abingdon, Oxon, UK & New York, USA.
2 For discussion on ownership, see Palit, D & Malhotra, S 2015, 'Energizing rural India using micro grids: The case of solar DC micro-grids in Uttar Pradesh State, India,' www.teriin.org/index.php?option=com_publication&task=details&sid=1789&q=&It emid=151.
3 See some of these policy recommendations in Bhattacharyya, S & Palit, D 2016, 'Mini-grid based off-grid electrification to enhance electricity access in developing countries: What policies may be required?,' *Energy Policy*, vol. 94, pp. 166–178.
4 Chapter 6 explores this innovation, alongside other mechanisms and strategies, in more detail.
5 This is particularly important in developing countries where some subsidies are essential for ensuring that basic needs are duly met.
6 See the discussion on subsidies in section 6.2.
7 Sovacool, BK & Drupady, IM 2012, *Energy Access, Poverty, and Development: The Governance of Small-Scale Renewable Energy in Developing Asia*, Ashgate: New York.
8 International Renewable Energy Agency 2016, *Policies and Regulations for Private Sector Renewable Energy Mini-Grids*, IRENA: Abu Dhabi, United Arab Emirates, p. 86.
9 I thank Ryan Hogarth for this point.
10 I thank Hartley Walimwipi for pointing this out.

11 See section 6.4 for some examples.
12 Jacobson, M, et al. 2015, '100% wind-water-sunlight energy for all countries, excel spreadsheet,' http://web.stanford.edu/group/efmh/jacobson/Articles/I/AllCountries.xlsx.
13 Sovacool, BK & Cooper, CJ 2013, *The Governance of Energy Megaprojects: Politics, Hubris and Energy Security*, Edward Elgar: Cheltenham, UK.
14 International Energy Agency 2016, *World Energy Outlook*, IEA: Paris, France, p. 499.
15 I thank Tri Ratna Bajracharya for this information; see also International Renewable Energy Agency 2016, *Policies and Regulations for Private Sector Renewable Energy Mini-Grids*, IRENA: Abu Dhabi, United Arab Emirates, p. 62.
16 I thank Ryan Hogarth for this point.
17 Yang, C-J 2015, 'Opportunities and barriers to demand response in China,' *Resources Conservation and Recycling*, vol. 121, pp. 51–55.
18 International Renewable Energy Agency 2016, *Renewable Power Generation Costs 2014*, IRENA: Bonn, Germany.

5 Policy turn

Strong, effective, stable, and coherent policy support through predictable and stable government legislation, policy framework, and targets is imperative in accelerating sustainable energy transitions. Policy is key in facilitating and negotiating the processes that would drive and accelerate the sociotechnical transitions of energy systems. Policy is also required to address the growing demand for scant resources, and to mobilize them. These resources include the hardware described in Chapter 3, alongside the financial, human, and institutional capacity to support every aspect and every stage of the transition. Policy also sought to level the playing field where renewable energy can compete fairly with other forms of energy, especially given the inertia to change of the incumbent sociotechnical regime. A more ambitious policy mix, with strong long-term commitment from governments, will always provide a stronger signal to investors and the larger public to support and engage with it.

The process of providing a general framework for accelerating the transitions entails a leadership role for governments in terms of policymaking to realign, coordinate, drive, and sustain collaborative actions across state and non-state actors and institutions. Creating an enabling environment for accomplishing this task is also necessary, especially in developing countries, where there is perceived high risk towards a new energy system that aims at changing an intricately, socially, politically, and economically intertwined incumbent system. This chapter describes the policy measures that have been used to overcome this challenge and to assist scaled-up deployments of sustainable energy technologies.

Governments have a key role in the transition because markets and private actors, by themselves, are inadequate to address the technological, financing, and social challenges that impede the acceleration of energy transitions.[1] In many developing countries, the centrality of governments and strong policy in accelerating the transition processes can be seen as a response to the following challenges. First, since actors in current energy markets, particularly private firms, can simply free ride on the technology innovations produced by other actors, there is less investment in transition that benefits the wider society. Second, the current energy infrastructure shaped around incumbent fossil fuel-based technology, such as pipelines, may no longer be relevant in an end-state where renewable energy becomes the dominant fuel. Third, many private investors still perceive the transition as a risky investment, hence less attractive particularly for its cost. Fourth, current energy markets are distorting the prices of energy services, which fail to reflect the negative social and environmental problems associated with energy production and consumption. The role of innovative policy and strong implementation can be seen in responding not only to these distinct challenges but also to the crosscutting issues that transcend them. Governments, broadly, can lead the transitions in terms of stronger policy directions in at least the following ways: providing a clear direction and an end-goal for the transition; developing baskets of policy mechanisms to support the ambition of energy access, energy efficiency, and renewable energy deployment; sending appropriate price signals; and pushing renewables by giving it priority support. The sections of this chapter are organized following these strategies.

5.1.   Plans and targets

Nationally determined end-goal is needed to set a coherent direction for navigating the future. Accelerating the transitions requires innovative policy approaches that would clearly layout what the end-state after these processes are done could be like. While the processes of identifying that future state can be challenging, achieving an overarching picture of what a sustainable future would mean and look like is vital.

As will be shown below, a number of developing countries had already started recognizing this imperative. These are evidenced primarily in the presence of policy frameworks and some quantitative targets, which, although varying in scope and ambition, are showing that energy transitions have already been considered in development agendas. There will still be challenges ahead, especially in terms of accelerating the transitions, implying the need for updating and extending the ambitions set in policy frames and targets.

Policy framework

Policy is enshrined in either legislation or regulatory issuance, or both. Many developing countries, for years, have already started building up some key policy frameworks to encourage, facilitate, and manage transitions albeit not explicitly for this purpose. Many of these policy frameworks were produced against the backdrop of energy security, which in developing countries pertain to the reliability of supply by developing sufficient generation capacity to match demand. These policy documents, however, it can be understood, are also recognitions that renewable energy, energy efficiency, and energy access are key development agendas. Registered in the form of legislation, plans, or visions, these documents have contributed to defining and orienting many developing countries towards some level of support towards the transition.

Universal energy access policy framework

Explicit policy, programs, or plans directed at the achievement of full access to electricity are already present in many developing countries. Often, the goal of universal energy access is inscribed within general energy policy documents and is included in national targets and government pronouncements (see Table 5.1 for examples). The greater goal of the transition to fully transform energy systems requires some trade-offs in developing countries where energy poverty – the inverse of energy access – remains a key challenge.

In some applications, the transition from traditional to modern forms of fuel may require, in the short term, the use of fossil fuel technologies merely due to their higher efficiencies. An example is the replacement of traditional biomass with fossil-based fuels for cooking such as liquefied petroleum gas (LPG). In the long-term, however, it is critical that the transition towards modern energy sources using renewable energy is introduced as a key means for achieving universal energy access.

The long-term view that merges access with transition ends requires formulating, introducing and implementing renewable energy deployment programs to secure the energy future of households and communities in many developing countries. Indeed, the transition requires that renewable energy resources have to provide almost all energy requirements in developing countries. Policy and programs to achieve renewable energy access need to be cognizant of this imperative. This means that energy use in households and communities need to evolve towards modern use – with almost all energy needs being met by renewable electricity.

In addition, policy frameworks for energy access have to be also carefully designed so that they consider institutional arrangements and cultural norms of these communities – not just a focus on the economic and technical feasibilities of these new systems. The social acceptance and sustainability of the technology are always, as studies have shown, reflective of these non-technical considerations.

Table 5.1 Examples of policy framework documents supporting electricity access

	Policy documents
Brazil	Luz para Todos (Light for All), 2003
India	DeenDaval Upadhyaya Gram Jyoti Yojana rural electrification program, 2014 National Electricity Policy Integrated Energy Policy Rural Electrification Policy
South Africa	Integrated National Electrification Program Non-grid Electrification Policy Guidelines, 2012 Free Basic Electricity Policy Free Basic Alternative Energy Policy
Zambia	Rural Electrification Act, 2003

Source: author's compilation.

This entails a portfolio approach to accelerating the transitions within which strengthening end-user capacity remains at its core.

Energy efficiency policy framework

The role of energy efficiency and maximizing its potential has already been introduced in formal policy documents of some developing countries (see Table 5.2 for examples). Energy efficiency policy is formulated at both the energy supply-side and the demand-side. However, it is key that demand-side energy efficiency policy frameworks are clearly instituted in developing countries to maximize the opportunity for harvesting its potential contribution to accelerating the transitions.

For energy efficiency to contribute meaningfully to accelerating the transitions, energy efficiency policy has to be regularly evaluated finding new opportunities to

Table 5.2 Examples of policy framework documents supporting energy efficiency

	Policy documents
Brazil	National Policy on Energy Efficiency, 2007 National Electricity Conservation Program (PROCEL), 1991 *Demand side* Utility Energy Efficiency Obligation, 1998 *Supply side* PROCEL Build, 2003 Energy Efficiency Program in Public Buildings, 1997 PROCEL Education, 1995 PROCEL Seal (Appliances), 1993 PROCEL Label, 1993 PROCEL Public Lighting
China	Energy Conservation Law, 2008 Energy intensity reduction target, 2006 *Demand side* Demand side management (DSM) implementation measures, 2010 Retirement of inefficient plants, 2007 Expansion of local cogeneration, 2006 Efficiency upgrade for coal-burning industrial boilers and kilns, 2006 Efficiency upgrade for electric motors, 2006 Energy efficient products for government procurement, 2006 General work plan for energy conservation and pollutant discharge reduction, 2006 *Supply side* Government promotion of energy efficient products, 2009 National building energy standard, 2008 Efficient light bulb subsidy program, 2008 Top 1000 industrial energy conservation program, 2006 Energy labelling program, 2005 Medium and Long-term plan of energy conservation: ten energy conservation programs, 2004 Minimum energy performance standards (MEPS), 1989

	Policy documents
India	Perform, Achieve, Trade (PAT) Scheme, 2011 Energy Conservation Act 2001, amended 2010 National Mission for Enhanced Energy Efficiency, 2009 Demand Side Management, 2009 Bachat Lamp Yojana Lighting Program, 2009 UJALA Scheme (LED-based domestic efficient lighting program) Comprehensive energy labeling program for appliances 2006, amended 2009 Energy Conservation Awards, 1999
Indonesia	Energy Management Regulation No. 14, 2012 Presidential Instruction on water and energy savings (20/2005; 2/2008; 13/2011) Ministry of Energy Regulation No.31, 2009 Energy efficiency labeling program for appliances, 2009 Energy Law No. 30, 2007 Ministry of Energy Decree No. 2, 2006 Mandatory energy conservation of government office buildings No. 10, 2005 Development of National Electricity Industry 2003–2020, 2003 Buildings Law No. 28, 2002
Nepal	Energy Strategy, 2010 Nepal Electricity Crisis Mitigation Plan, 2009 Nepal Standard Act, 1981 Industrial Policy, 1974
South Africa	National Energy Efficiency Strategy, 2005 (reviewed 2008) Integrated Resource Plan, 2010 Income Tax Act – Regulations on tax allowances for Energy Efficiency Savings Municipal Energy Efficiency and Demand Side Management grant program Standard Offer Incentive Scheme
Thailand	Energy Efficiency Plan 2015–2036, 2015 Energy Conservation Program, 1992
Vietnam	Law on Economical and Efficient Use of Energy, 2010 National Target Program on Energy Efficiency, 2006

Source: author's compilation.

improve existing targets. Moving from lighting and appliance efficiency – which are almost already achieved in many developing countries – to buildings and industrial equipment efficiency offers new opportunities for improved policy design. It remains imperative in designing efficiency policy frameworks to be cognizant of its inherent challenges including behavioral failures as shown explicitly in the rebound and backfire phenomena. Backfire occurs when energy consumers who save on energy cost through energy efficiency spend their savings on other energy-intensive activities or increased their demand for new energy service. Addressing rebound is a complex process, but it most likely entails and needs institutionalizing policy that seeks to address consumer behavior such as through improved nudges and pricing energy pollution.

Renewable energy policy framework

Policy frameworks for supporting sustainable energy through legislation are also becoming more common (see Table 5.3). While a number of these documents already show clear state support towards renewable energy, that level of support needs to be ramped up. Some examples of these proposed improvements include unhindered, preferential, and priority access for renewable energy to the grid.

Table 5.3 Some examples of policy framework documents supporting renewable energy

	Policy documents
Bhutan	Renewable Energy Policy 2011
Brazil	2010–2019 Plan for Energy Expansion, 2010
Chile	Law 20.698
China	Notice of further improvement of new energy demonstration implementation, 2013 Notice on integrating and accommodating wind power, 2013 Notice on the development of construction of distributed solar photovoltaic (PV) power grid demonstration park, 2013 Notice on the establishment of demonstration areas for large-scale solar PV power generation, 2012 Interim measure of distributed solar power generation on-grid service agreement, 2012 Notice on new energy demonstration city and industrial park, 2012 Wind power technology development, 12th Five Year Special Plan, 2012 Solar power technology development, 12th Five Year Special Plan, 2012 12th Five Year Plan for National Strategic Emerging Industries, 2012 Solar industry 12th Five Year Development Planning, 2012 The 12th Five Year Plan for Renewable Energy, 2012 Interim measures on the management of offshore wind farm, 2010 Building integrated solar PV program, 2010 Renewable Energy Law 2006, amended 2009 Offshore wind development plan, 2009 International science and technology cooperation program for new and renewable energy, 2008 Support for biogas projects, 2006 Provincial frameworks The 12th Five Year Plan for Renewable Energy of Beijing Shandong Province village renewable energy regulations, 2008 Shandong Province one million rooftops sunshine plan, 2008 Hainan Province plan for the construction of wind farms, 2007
India	Solar cities development program, 2011 National Solar Mission (Phase I and II), 2010 Integrated Energy Policy, 2006 National Electricity Policy, 2005 Electricity Act, 2003 National Policy on Biofuels National Offshore Wind Energy Policy

	Policy documents
Indonesia	National Energy Policy (Government Regulation No. 79), 2014 Ceiling price for geothermal (Ministerial Regulation No. 17), 2014 New Geothermal Law No. 21, 2014 Electricity Law No. 30, 2009 Energy Law No. 30 2007 Blueprint of National Energy Management 2005–2025, 2005 Green Energy Policy (Ministerial Decree No. 2), 2004 Small distributed power generation using renewable energy (Ministerial Regulation No. 1122, 2002
Morocco	Renewable Power Tenders 2010, updated 2016 Net-metering Law 58, 2016 Law No. 13-09, 2015 National Integrated Project for solar electricity production and National Agency for Solar Energy, 2010 Renewable Energy Development Law 13, 2009 Law of self-generation 16, 2008
Nepal	Energy Strategy, 2010 National Rural Renewable Energy Program
Philippines	Ensuring the adequacy and readiness of the National Transmission System to accommodate new generating capacities from RE technologies, 2011 Guidelines for issuing renewable energy service and operating contracts, 2009 Renewable Energy Act, 2008 Electric Power Industry Reforms Act, 2001 New and renewable energy program (Executive Order 462) 1997, modified 2000 Mini-hydro Law, 1991 Act to promote the exploration and development of geothermal resources, 1978
South Africa	Renewable Energy Independent Power Producer Program, 2011 Integrated Resource Electricity Plan 2010–2030, 2011 National Energy Act No. 34, 2008 Integrated Energy Plan for South Africa, 2003 White Paper on Renewable Energy, 2003 Non-grid Electrification Policy Guidelines, 2012 Solar Water Heater Rebate program
Thailand	Alternative Energy Development Plan 2015–2036, 2015 Renewable Energy Development Plan 2008–2022, 2009
Vietnam	National Power Development Plan 2011–2030, 2011 Electricity Law, 2005 Decree No. 45/2001/ND-CP on electric power operation and use, 2001 Green Growth Strategy, 2012 Strategy for the development of renewable energy up to 2030 (with outlook to 2050), 2015 Revised National Electric Development Master Plan, 2016
Zambia	Zambia Vision 2030 The National Policy on the Environment, 2007 National Energy Policy, 2008 National Climate Change Policy, 2016 Statutory Instrument No. 79 Grid Code Regulations Statutory Instrument No. 15, 2011 Renewable Energy Feed-in Tariff Regulatory Framework for Zambia

Source: author's compilation.

Priority dispatch needs to be explicitly embedded in these documents to ensure that renewable energy is first integrated into energy system before supplies from other sources. Planning frameworks supporting renewable energy also need to mention a planning regime that balances renewable energy support and deployment with public engagement and environmental protection. This provision is necessary to address possible tensions that could be created in terms of surface area ownership, conservation, traditional use, and commercial interests as accelerated deployment occurs. These frameworks also need to respond to entry barriers common among many developing countries such as lengthy permitting processes, high application costs, and lack of local or regional capacity to deal with renewable energy development applications. In the near future, countries should also address the fragmentation of their renewable energy policy frameworks. Making them coherent, complementary, and up-to-date requires reflexivity and close cooperation among policy designers.

Targets

Targets provide a marker for all transition actors so that they can assess the situation and act in their own best interests. Although targets do not set legal obligation, the establishment of a goal or a target may increase public support, spur confidence of investors and developers, and provide a basis for possible future policy or regulation direction. In many developing countries, targets remain the most prevalent indication of support to renewable energy deployment, to increase energy efficiency gains, and to close energy access gaps. The Nationally Determined Contributions (NDCs) that make the core of the Paris Agreement provide some of these target indicators (see Table 5.4).

Access targets can be voluntary or mandated objectives to address underserved and un-electrified populations. Renewable energy targets are voluntary or mandated amount of renewable energy, usually a percentage of total energy supply. The approach taken for renewable energy targets varies by country and can include a percent share of electricity production, a share of total primary and/or final energy supply, an installed capacity target, or total amounts of energy extracted from renewable sources. In addition, the timeframes for these targets also vary. Some countries have also technology-specific goals.

Brazil has produced a National Energy Efficiency Plan 2011 (Plano Nacional de Eficiencia Energética), which provides an overarching national energy efficiency policy framework. The plan directs the necessary actions to reach an electricity consumption reduction target of 10 per cent or about 107 terawatt-hour by 2030 as indicated in the National Energy Plan for 2030 (Plano Nacional de Energia 2030). Brazil's 45 per cent renewable energy target by 2030 incorporates a previously announced target made when then US President Barack Obama visited Brazil in June 2015, where, together with then Brazil President Dilma Rousseff, they jointly announced an increase of non-hydro sources to 33 per cent by 2030.[2] Prior to the announcement, Brazil has already established its renewable energy target through the country's 2010–2019 Plan for Energy Expansion. The Plan calls

Table 5.4 Energy access, energy efficiency, and renewable energy targets in the study countries' NDCs

	Access target	Energy efficiency target	Renewable energy target
Bhutan	Mentions almost 100 per cent access to electricity in urban areas, and 94 per cent in rural areas	No numerical target, but mentions promotion of energy efficiency in transport, appliances, buildings, and industrial processes	No numerical target, but mentions: diversifying energy supply mix through promotion of renewable energy (solar, wind, small hydro, biomass) other than large hydro and creating investment opportunities. (Renewable Energy Policy 2011 suggests a target of 20 megawatts [MW] renewable energy by 2020 to be generated equally from solar, wind, and biomass systems.)
Brazil	Mentions 'energy access' but provides no further details	Achieving 10 per cent efficiency gains in the electricity sector by 2030	Reaching a share of 45 per cent renewable energy in the energy mix by 2030
Chile	No mention	No mention	Law 20.698 requires that 20 per cent of energy supply be generated from renewables by 2025
China	No mention	Lowering the carbon intensity of gross domestic product (GDP) by 60 to 65 per cent below 2005 levels by 2030	Increasing the share of non-fossil energy carriers of total primary energy supply to around 20 per cent by 2030
El Salvador	No mention	No mention	Increasing the share of renewable energy at no less than 12 per cent of the total electricity generated in 2014 by 2025
India	Mentions the 304 million Indians without access to electricity, and the National Electricity Policy and the Integrated Energy Policy, which underscore the focus on universalizing access to electricity	Reducing the emissions intensity of GDP by 20 to 25 per cent by 2020 below 2005 levels; lowering the emissions intensity of GDP by 33 to 35 per cent by 2030 below 2005 levels; achieving total avoided capacity addition of 19,598 MW and fuel savings of around 23 million tons per year	Increasing the share of non-fossil based power generation capacity to 40 per cent of installed electric power capacity by 2030 (equivalent to 26 to 30 per cent of generation in 2030)
Indonesia	No mention	No mention	At least 23 per cent of energy use coming from new and renewable energy by 2025

(Continued)

Table 5.4 (Continued)

	Access target	Energy efficiency target	Renewable energy target
Morocco	No mention	Achieving 12 per cent energy savings by 2020 and 15 per cent by 2030	No mention
Nepal	Mentions that 56 per cent of the population has regular access to electricity for lighting. Mentions access to energy program through the National Rural Renewable Energy Program	No numerical target but broadly mentions energy efficiency as a key policy target	By 2020, expand energy mix focusing on renewables by 20 per cent; by 2050, achieve 80 per cent electrification through renewables
Philippines	No mention	No numerical target in its NDC but mentions grid efficiency improvement and high-efficiency technology for conventional power generation	Broadly mentioned renewable energy laws in its NDC, but no mention of a numerical target
South Africa	Mentions 'access to energy' but provides no further details	No numerical target, but mentions high-efficiency coal-fired power plants	No numerical target, but mentions investments in renewable energy projects
Thailand	No mention	Refers to existing target: reducing energy intensity by 30 per cent below the 2010 level in 2036 (Energy Efficiency Plan 2015–2036)	Refers to existing targets: achieving a 20 per cent share of power generation from renewable sources in 2036 (Power Development Plan); achieving a 30 per cent share of renewable energy in the total final energy consumption in 2036 (Alternative Energy Development Plan)
Vietnam	No mention	Mentions reducing emission intensity per unit of GDP by 20 per cent compared to the 2010 levels (cites National Target Program on Energy Efficiency 2006, and Law on Economical and Efficient Use of Energy 2010)	No mention; however, key policy approved following their NDC submission includes targets for renewable energy; this includes the National Strategy on renewable energy development (Decision 2068/Qd-Ttg/11-2015), which requires renewable energy share in total primary energy consumption to be 31 per cent in 2020,

	Access target	*Energy efficiency target*	*Renewable energy target*
			32.3 per cent in 2030, and 44 per cent in 2050; the plan also requires renewable energy-based electricity in national total electric production to rise to 38 per cent in 2020, 32 per cent in 2030, and 43 per cent in 2050
Zambia	No numerical target, but mentions off-grid renewables and grid extension to non-electrified rural areas	No numerical target, but broadly mentions energy efficiency	No numerical target, but mentions programs in fuel switching, and off-grid renewables

Source: author's summary from United Nations Framework Convention on Climate Change 2016, *NDCs as communicated by Parties*, www4.unfccc.int/submissions/indc/Submission%20Pages/submissions.aspx, and from other sources.

for the production of 116.7 gigawatt (GW) hydropower from large-scale dams by 2019 up from 83.1 GW in 2010, 7 GW from small hydro from 4 GW in 2010, 8.5 GW from biomass from 5.4 GW in 2010, and 6 GW from wind from 1.4 GW in 2010.

China's renewable energy targets are first strongly committed in the 2007 Medium and Long Term Development Plan for Renewable Energy, specifying China's commitment to increasing renewable energy share to 15 per cent of its 2020 primary energy consumption. In the country's latest update to its 12th Five Year Plan, China decided to aim for a target of 350 GW of hydro, 200 GW of wind, and 100 GW of solar installed capacity by 2020, while limiting coal burning to a maximum of 4.8 billion tonnes of the standard coal equivalent also by 2020.[3]

On the federal level, India has implemented two major renewable energy-related policies: the Strategic Plan for New and Renewable Energy, which provides a broader framework outlining the mission, objectives, goals, implementation, and evaluation plan for the country's renewable energy sector; and the National Solar Mission 2010–2022, containing capacity targets for solar energy. In August 2015, the government officially adopted plans to increase its solar capacity to 100 GW installed capacity by 2022, up from the original 2010 target of 20 GW. Installed capacity targets in other renewable energy technologies are also increased: 60 GW for wind, 10 GW for biomass, and 5 GW for small-scale hydro.[4] Complementing India's renewable energy plan is its National Mission for Enhanced Energy Efficiency.

The Nepal NDC, among few others in the study countries, has clearly and specifically stipulated how it intends to meet its renewable energy targets. This includes scaling up deployments of the following: 4 GW of hydroelectricity by

2020 and 12 GW by 2030; 2.1 GW of solar energy by 2030 with arrangements to distribute it through the grid; additional 220 MW of electricity from bio-energy by 2030; additional 50 MW of electricity from small and micro hydro-power plants; and biogas up to 10 per cent as energy for cooking in rural areas.[5] The Nepal NDC also mentions the following targets in terms of technologies: 600,000 institutional solar power systems; 4,000 improved water mills; 130,000 household biogas systems; 1,000 institutional biogas systems; and 200 community biogas plants.

Although the Philippine NDC is silent with regard to its renewable energy targets, other sources show its plans on tripling its renewable energy capacity up to 15 GW by 2030 and increasing the share of electricity production from renewables up to 40 per cent. The country has also set its energy efficiency targets through an Energy Efficiency and Conservation Roadmap, which mandate energy savings equivalent to 10 per cent across energy demand sectors by 2030.

Just like the Philippine submission, the NDC by South Africa is also silent about its renewable energy targets. However, its Integrated Resource Electricity Plan 2010–2030 has set new installed renewable energy capacity target of 17.8 GW for 2030.[6] Just like other study countries, South Africa also continues to place premium on the role of coal in domestic energy generation. Its Integrated Resource Electricity Plan has indicated that 16.4 MW of additional coal capacity are either planned or already committed for construction. By 2030, the plan aims at achieving an energy mix with energy from coal combustion contributing 48 per cent of the capacity, while renewable energy will account for only 21 per cent.

Of the study countries, Thailand has explicitly mentioned its ongoing transition initiatives, highlighting how three key documents are shoring up the country's sustainable energy targets. Thailand's NDC was formulated based on already approved national energy plans. These plans laid out the numerical targets by which Thailand aims to achieve energy security and competitiveness. Three 20-year plans (2015–2036) related to the electricity sector are being implemented: Power Development Plan, Alternative Energy Development Plan, and Energy Efficiency Plan. These plans seek to achieve 20 to 30 per cent renewable energy in Thailand's energy mix, while reducing energy intensity by 30 per cent relative to 2010 by 2036. The Power Development Plan seeks to increase contributions from renewable energy, including hydro sources, from 8 per cent in 2014 to 20 per cent in 2036.[7] In this envisaged future, fossil fuels remain significant contributors: natural gas provides up to 40 per cent, while coal contributes up to 25 per cent. There is also a place for nuclear capacity in the Plan: 5 per cent at most. The Alternative Energy Development Plan targets to increase installed capacity of energy from waste, biomass, biogas, wind, solar, and energy crops from 7,279 MW in 2014 to 19,635 MW in 2036.[8] The Plan puts priority on power generation from waste, biomass, and biogas, while looking at the promotion of solar and wind power deployment at a later stage when cost becomes competitive with liquefied natural gas. The Energy Efficiency Plan sets up sub-targets for energy savings in the industrial, commercial, residential, and transport sectors, through compulsory and voluntary measures.[9] In 2016, the Thai Government decided to integrate these three key Plans into what has become the Thailand Integrated Energy Blueprint 2017–2036.

It is important to mention that these targets are also complemented by new fossil fuel-based development. Notably, among the study countries, China has been the world's top coal producer.[10] Indonesia's domestic coal resources, one of the world's largest, also factor in the decision to expand coal-fired power. The country is the world's third-biggest coal producer.[11] Indonesia also continues to consider expanding the role of coal-fired power plants to meet increasing domestic demand. The Indian government also supports the coal industry in its aim to double domestic coal production to 1.5 billion tons by 2020.[12] India's Five Year Plan reflects this intention with a 60 per cent target for new coal plants.[13] On April 2015, nonetheless, the Indian Ministry of Power had announced that every new coal-fired power plant should be accompanied by a renewable power plant of at least 10 per cent of the generating capacity.[14] The Philippine government has also announced the construction of more than 10 GW of coal-fired power plant capacity by 2025 to meet domestic demand.

Echoing the discussion on the normative ambition of a full transition to renewable energy systems as a key component of the sustainable energy transition agenda, policy frameworks and targets need to be continually and regularly improved. Of key importance is how renewable energy can be supported as they quickly displace and replace fossil fuel-fired power plants. This requires ensuring that the dynamics of policy design and target setting would allow an occasion for reflection. This is essential as markets, technologies, institutions, and social behaviors evolve. Cohesion among fragmented policy frameworks and targets also needs to be a key objective in the future development of energy transition policy. This is particularly the case in many developing countries where transition-related policies are mentioned explicitly as stand-alone documents, with no clear linkages to other policy documents. While fragmentation allows for creativity and innovation in policymaking, national governments have to ensure the presence of an overarching framework and targets that would bind fragmented policy, targets, and regulations together.

One emergent example of this policy turn is Thailand's agenda to build competitiveness and ensure energy security in the area of sustainability transitions. Called 'Thailand 4.0,' this 20-year program aims at integrating the efficient use of renewable energy with smarter grids, improving storage technologies, small-scale renewable energy generation, hybrid systems, and the deployment of electric vehicles. Another emergent direction is the adoption of a new goal of 100 per cent renewable electricity generation, which is being promoted as official policy in many developing countries in the Pacific. Fiji and Vanuatu, for example, have plans to increase the share of renewables in their respective energy mixes towards full renewable electricity by 2030. These emerging approaches to bundle all possible opportunities for accelerating the transitions respond to the call for a portfolio approach necessary in the policy turn.

5.2.   A portfolio approach

Policy basket for achieving universal energy access

Sustainable energy transitions require that access to modern forms of energy is provided for all. Where universal energy access has yet to be achieved, many developing countries need to revisit this policy and ensure that it occupies a priority place in policymaking. This can be accomplished with strong policy direction as demonstrated in China, for example. At the end of 2015, the Government of China reported that it has achieved universal energy access, concluding the largest national electrification program in history. Some aspects of the energy access challenge, however, persist: reliability, affordability, and sustainability – and China remains one of the countries with serious issues regarding access to clean cookstoves. Many developing countries still need to address these vital access concerns. Decentralized solutions, particularly in terms of deploying renewable energy technologies, remain critical.

Small-scale solar-powered systems, such as solar lamps and solar rooftop photovoltaic (PV), need to be scaled up, alongside options for mini-grids, in communities without access to basic lighting services. The mini-grid option is already being considered as a key part of some key access initiatives; but its large-scale deployment needs to be considered and included in the strategies of many developing countries. India's Deen Dayal Upadhyaya Gram Jyoti Yojana initiative, which is aimed at electrifying every Indian home by 2022, is one recent example of the use of mini-grid strategy for achieving universal energy access. The design of effective policies to increase energy access through off-grid and mini-grid systems need to take into account several key criteria. These include the energy needs of communities the system will serve; the quality of the hardware; the capacity of the community to operate and maintain these systems; and, most importantly, the affordability of the system, including the capacity of end-users to repay it in time.

Universal full access to clean cooking, which remains a prevalent development challenge in many countries in the global south, needs to be achieved in parallel to universal lighting. In India, for instance, 63 per cent of the population still lacks this access. China, despite reporting universal energy access, has close to 450 million people still relying on traditional use of biomass for cooking. India is another country with huge challenge regarding access to clean cooking. Addressing this challenge requires a new set of policy, including mechanisms by which households can replace their inefficient and polluting stoves affordably. The Government of India, for example, has pledged to distribute free LPG tanks and fuel to about 50 million Indian households by 2019.

In addition to lighting and cooking services, many people in developing countries also need universal access to productive use of energy. Examples of these services include fuel-efficient farm machineries for tilling, harvesting and drying; irrigation facilities such as efficient and renewable energy-powered water pumps; and small-scale machineries for supporting cottage industries.

Addressing the challenge of energy poverty requires a dedicated suite of policies to promote the objectives of universal, modern, reliable, affordable, and sustainable energy access – one that goes beyond addressing the challenges and gaps regarding lighting and cooking services. This is a challenge that goes beyond energy policy since it entails addressing key complementary areas, particularly household income and investments. Ensuring that end-users can afford these systems, can repay it in time, and can operate and maintain them without much external intervention is necessary. While the technological hardware already exists to address these needs, the absence of effective policy that provides and strengthens the capacity of poor people in developing countries to own, manage, operate, and sustain these technologies in the long term remains a vital challenge to be addressed.

Policy basket for maximizing energy efficiency

The traditional understanding that governments can only pursue development through approaches that strongly linked economic productivity with increased, yet inefficient, energy consumption is no longer true. Many developing countries have the biggest opportunity for harvesting the low-lying fruits provided by energy efficiency using a portfolio of policy options on efficient lighting, appliances, building, mobility, and industry.[15] The benefits of energy efficiency improvements are manifold. For one, energy efficiency measures result in financial resources savings, which represent additional opportunities for investing in the transition. Since energy saved from these measures means reduced need for energy generation, energy efficiency is creating virtual power plants. For energy efficiency potentials to be effectively harvested, a strategic direction in the form of high-level policy standards that not only encourage but also mandate energy efficiency is imperative.[16]

Some examples of energy efficiency policy options for residential and commercial buildings include labeling; building codes; energy audits; financial incentives and mechanisms to support the purchase of efficient appliance or equipment, and/or construction of energy efficient buildings; and awareness campaigns on best practices. For industrial energy efficiency, the following options have been available: mandatory efficiency standards for industrial equipment; energy audits; demand side management programs; financial incentives and/or mechanisms to support the purchase of replacement or new efficient industrial equipment; and awareness campaigns on best practices.

Of the abovementioned approaches, labeling, codes, and standards are fast evolving in support of sustainable energy transitions. These include standardizing practices and equipment, as well as codifying energy efficiency improvements in appliances, equipment, and buildings. Table 5.5 shows some examples of sustainable energy-related codes and standards in the study countries.

Appliance and equipment standards are either voluntary or mandatory. In the last ten years, however, there has been a considerable move towards making standards mandatory. These include labeling and informing consumers about the

Table 5.5 Examples of sustainable energy-related codes and standards in the study countries

	Renewable energy technology standards	Energy efficiency standards
Brazil		PROCEL Build, 2003 Energy Efficiency Program in Public Buildings, 1997 PROCEL Education, 1995 PROCEL Seal, 1993 (Appliances) PROCEL Label, 1993 PROCEL Public Lighting
China	National certification and Implementation Supervision Commission, Energy Bureau on strengthening the PV products testing and certification work 2014 Interim measures for new power access network supervision 2014 Interim distributed PV power generation service guide of China Southern Power Grid Company Ltd. 2013 Code of practice of the PV manufacturing industry 2013 Market entry standards for wind equipment manufacturing industry 2010	Government promotion of energy efficient products, 2009 MEPS, 1989
India		Indian industry program for energy conservation, 2001
South Africa		SANS 941: Energy efficiency of electrical and electronic apparatus Building Regulations & Building Code (SANS 10400-XA:2011) with SANS 204

Source: author's compilation.

efficiency or specific energy consumption of appliances and equipment aimed at nudging them to make more intelligent choices. Mandatory labeling and standards programs, which are increasingly becoming the norm in many developing countries, set penalties for noncompliance, such as prohibition of manufacture, sale, purchase, or import of appliance or equipment that do not conform with the standards. By contrast, manufacturers adhering to set standards are provided with incentives.

Another key energy efficiency strategy is building codes. These codes regulate the overall energy use per unit of residential or office floor space, and are either mandatory or voluntary. Most building codes, nonetheless, specify some forms of incentives and penalties. A number of building codes in developing countries, often mandating maximum energy consumption per unit of area for new construction, have been developed in the last ten years, and continue to evolve (see Table 5.6). Retrofitting existing buildings – a strategy that can be easily scaled in developing countries – is also fast becoming a common specification in new building codes. Their implementation is also evolving: from voluntary to mandatory, for example.

The Energy Conservation Code of India, launched in 2007, for instance, is intended for new commercial buildings having a connected load of more than 500 kilowatts (kW). The Code, which seeks to define the norms of energy performance for buildings in India, made mandatory compliance for those obtaining environmental clearances for new building construction.

Energy efficiency remains the most economical strategy for achieving the transition in developing countries. It should, therefore, be widely considered in policy and continually improved (e.g. by moving from voluntary to mandatory obligations). Some examples of a staged approach to efficiency are from China and India. Both countries have moved towards mandatory energy efficiency targets for

Table 5.6 Examples of building energy codes in the study countries and their status, as of 2013

	Building energy codes	Code implementation for new residential buildings	Code implementation for existing residential buildings	Code implementation for new non-residential buildings	Code implementation for existing non-residential buildings
China	National building energy standard, 2008	Mandatory	Mandatory	Mandatory	Mandatory
India	Energy Conservation Building Code, 2007	Voluntary		Voluntary	
South Africa	National Building Regulations and Building Standards Act 103, 1977, last amended in 2008 Building Regulations & Building Code (SANS 10400-XA:2011) with SANS 204	Voluntary		Voluntary	

Source: author's compilation; status of implementation is extracted from International Energy Agency 2013, *Modernising Building Energy Codes*, IEA: Paris, France, pp. 22–23.

designated industries with obligations for yearly energy use reductions. India is combining it with a trading scheme for efficiency certificates. In addition to its improved building code mentioned above, it is also increasing its energy efficiency targets in the sector through its National Energy Efficient Fan Program that distributes efficient ceiling fans. India also plans to harvest more energy efficiency gains from its transport sector once its 'green tax' plan is implemented.[17] Between 2015 and 2016, the Government of China announced the closure of 100–150 Mt of inefficient steel capacity within five years as one of the key aspects of China's Circular Economy Promotion Plan. This strategy is expected to produce new gains in industrial energy efficiency and could easily yield energy savings and emissions reduction. The Philippines is also expanding its energy efficiency program. It has released its new Energy Efficiency and Conservation Action Plan 2016–2020 aimed at reducing energy intensity by 40 per cent by 2030 from its 2005 level. A key component of this Plan is energy labeling and efficiency standards for air conditioners and refrigerators.

Widening the scope of energy efficiency programs is a key strategy for accelerating the transitions. This means pursuing several strategies, approaches, projects, and programs in parallel. Industry-wide efficiency schemes, which are fast becoming the norm, need to be included in the energy efficiency strategies of developing countries – in addition to efficient lighting and appliances. The experiences in China and India show that targets become effective when they are taken at the sectoral level, as well as through strict implementation. A legal framework and strong institutional arrangement to enforce these mechanisms are critical elements if energy efficiently has to meaningfully contribute to accelerating the transitions.

Policy basket for renewable energy deployment and retirement of fossil-based energy systems

Accelerating the transition requires providing enabling policy mechanisms that will, in parallel, speed up the deployment of renewable energy technologies while accelerating the retirement of polluting energy systems. The next two sections deal with these complementary policies, highlighting the need for multiple strategies for dismantling polluting energy systems and for accelerating the diffusion of multi-scale and multi-size sustainable energy systems.

5.3.   Sending signals

Governments need to send price signals that are reflective of the goal of the transition. Price is important, especially in market economies where price provides a key signal for investment. It is key that the risks of energy resource and its impacts on the natural and social environments in terms of emissions and climate change have to be fairly and transparently reflected on the price of energy. To do this, governments need to establish policies or reform existing ones. Reform seeks to correct the inefficiency of current pricing systems and to contribute to the internalizing of external costs associated with the extraction, processing, combustion, and distribution of polluting fossil-based energy.

Price reform policies include the introduction or removal of regulation fees and charges, taxes, and subsidies. Fees or charges, for example, can be levied on the extraction and use of a fossil fuel such as coal and oil. Taxes can be used to raise revenues as compulsory payments to governments. Increasing taxes encourages efficiency to the consumer-taxpayer since they discourage consumption habits that lead to higher tax payments. Subsidies are either fiscal benefits such as tax exemptions or rebates, or financial assistance such as grants or low-interest loans that governments provide to encourage or boost the productivity of a particular industry. Subsidy reform is imperative for a fossil fuel industry that has, for a long time, generously been at the receiving end of public subsidies.[18]

While pursuing energy price reforms in developing countries is imperative for driving the transition, they have to be designed and implemented well alongside social protection for poor people. While necessary, facilitating these reforms will take the strongest political will for two key reasons. First, it entails losing substantial revenues in key industries – which, in developing countries, may substantially affect the standing of public coffers, hence affecting the quality of public service. Second, any reform can be an unpopular political move, which has direct implications to the political careers of politicians in government service.[19] Despite these trade-offs, about 40 national jurisdictions and over 20 cities, states, and regions have already decided to introduce price reform, particularly by putting a price on carbon pollution.[20]

Pricing energy-based emissions

Properly charging those who emit carbon with a fee, a tax, or a reduction of their subsidies for their use of the atmospheric, terrestrial, and marine carbon sinks – and for the costs of the climate disruption these emissions have and will cause – will help to accelerate the transitions. A price on carbon must achieve two basic and interrelated goals. The first is divesting from or discouraging the use of fossil fuels, ideally with increasingly painful economic consequences; and the second is investing in or encouraging the development of their replacement: more energy efficiency and renewable energy technologies.

Existing carbon prices range from about $1 per ton of emissions in Poland and Mexico to $137 per ton in Sweden.[21] Carbon pollution is also priced (and traded) in parts of China – the only country with a price on carbon among those studied here as of this writing. China has regional emission trading schemes (ETS) in the cities of Beijing, Chongqing, Guangdong, Hubei, Shanghai, Shenzhen, and Tianjin as early as December 2013. A nationwide ETS is expected in China in the second half of 2017.[22] ETS is also being considered in Indonesia, Thailand, and Vietnam. South Africa will introduced its own scheme. India has, since 2012, experimented on a trading scheme to promote efficiency through a Perform, Achieve, and Trade Scheme. A majority of the study countries have mentioned setting a carbon price as a strategy to meet their NDCs (see Table 5.7). While

Table 5.7 Carbon pricing in NDCs

	Mention of carbon price
Bhutan	International
Brazil	International
Chile	International
China	Domestic
El Salvador	None
India	International
Indonesia	International
Morocco	International
Nepal	International
Philippines	None
South Africa	Domestic
Thailand	International
Vietnam	International
Zambia	International

Source: extracted from United Nations Framework Convention on Climate Change 2016, *NDCs as communicated by Parties*, www4.unfccc.int/submissions/indc/Submission%20Pages/submissions.aspx.

bringing this key strategy into reality is an important next step, expanding their scope to include not only key emission sectors such as energy but also other consuming sectors such as industry, manufacturing, transport, and agriculture and, at the same time, regularly reviewing these prices – ensuring that they are periodically increased – are vital for achieving its intended purpose quickly.

Pricing energy-based emissions can take either the form of a tax which puts a price on each ton of carbon emission produced, or an ETS, which uses market mechanisms to price carbon.

ETS

An ETS places progressively stricter limits on fossil fuel use by requiring carbon polluters to purchase allowances or permits to discharge carbon dioxide to the atmosphere. An ETS then functions as a market for those permits. The Chinese experience on city-based markets is the only example we have at the moment among the countries studied here. Supporters of cap-and-trade argue for two key strengths of ETS in accelerating the transitions. First, it sets a steadily declining ceiling on carbon emissions. This means that as time goes by, it will be very expensive for polluters to dump their carbon pollution. Second, the system creates a market that rewards companies for slashing their emissions while punishing those who could not. In summary, an ETS sends key signals regarding the long-term profitability of private firms and the efficient use of private capital. The basic idea for an ETS is for private firms to reduce their emissions below their allotment so that they can sell their permits in the open market. Those needing new permits to pollute will then need to buy these at a price. As the permits increase in their price, polluting the atmosphere will become an inefficient activity, hence discouraging future investment on these systems and, by contrast, encouraging investment in the transition. The key for an ETS to be effective in delivering sustainable energy transitions, thus, is for it to be guided by a law that strictly places an impermeable lid on the amount of carbon that enters the atmosphere. In other words, for an ETS to function in its intended purpose, these permits must be very limited in number, and the price should be very high enough to actually divest investor appetite for supporting dirty energy systems and to encourage them to invest instead on replacement technologies.

While a cap-and-trade system promises, in theory, that it could provide more certainty in emissions reductions, it has, in practice, shown to be subject to easy manipulation that allows additional emissions. The Chinese experiment with the ETS has, in a number of ways, shown these challenges.[23] If the permits become too expensive, regulators would likely sell or distribute more permits to keep the price 'reasonable' to polluters. Once this happens, an ineffectively designed ETS, in the long run, could not lead to real changes required to accelerate the transitions.

Carbon tax

The second mechanism to price emissions is an outright tax on fossil fuels. A carbon tax vis-à-vis an ETS is simpler to design – especially for governments whose main revenues come from taxes. Many developing countries have substantial experience with taxation; hence, this option is relatively more promising, compared to a cap-and-trade market. A carbon tax can also cover the entire economy, including automobiles, household use, and other units, which are complicated to reach in a cap-and-trade system. For sustainable energy transition to be driven fast, however, such tax should steadily increase. In contrast to an ETS, which gives a highly fluctuating spot price, a carbon tax can clearly put a price on energy sector-based emissions for many years ahead. This predictability means that a carbon tax could raise a clear amount of revenue that can then be used for targeted purposes to support accelerated transition, or as rebates to the public, or both.

Regardless of mechanism (a tax or an ETS), pricing carbon can easily impact the poor if these schemes are not properly designed. Electricity prices, as a result of pricing changes in electricity generation, for instance, can easily impact all consumers, with poor people absorbing most of these impacts. The absence of strategies to counter the economic hardship created by higher energy prices could easily result to the inability of the poor to even purchase their basic needs. To address this, a carbon tax can be designed as revenue neutral, meaning that the revenues it generated are used to reduce existing taxes or are returned to the public as rebates or as support for them to participate with transition-related activities such as investing in renewable energy businesses or by putting up solar home systems, etc. Examples of these strategies can be found in the tax on emissions in British Columbia in Canada[24] and in the defunct carbon price in Australia.[25] In both instances, the price on emissions led to actual emissions reduction without incurring substantial economic losses and social impacts to citizens, particularly the economically poor.

Suspending subsidies to polluting energy systems

Price reforms also involve revisiting other key support that carbon polluters enjoy and cutting them. Public subsidies that the fossil fuel industry, for instance, has generously benefited from are not only hampering fair competition for their replacement but are also incentivizing and perpetuating high-carbon development pathways in many developing countries. Keeping fossil fuel prices artificially low – under the rationale of making it affordable especially for poor people – posits difficulty for sustainable energy to compete and discourages energy efficiency and conservation.

Removing fossil fuel subsidies sends the right signal for accelerating the transitions.[26] The elimination of perverse energy sector subsidies surely has negative effects in terms of business competitiveness of traditional energy players. The long-term benefits of staged, structured, and systematic elimination of fossil fuel subsidies far outweigh these short-term impacts. If subsidies can be totally phased out, governments in many developing countries can end up as the ultimate winners. These implications are profound since it creates new fiscal spaces for public budgets that can easily lead to the reduction of national budget deficits. Consumers are also provided with the signal and incentive to carefully consider their consumption choices since energy is now priced appropriately compared to their previous artificial low cost. Properly priced energy consumption increases the opportunity for harvesting energy efficiency gains. The major benefit, however, is in the form of accelerating sustainable energy transitions. Since energy subsidies are distorting price signals, which, in turn, increase the barriers to entry for sustainable energy technologies, their removal could lead to the flattening of the competition landscape. In many developing countries, the benefits of subsidy removal can primarily accrue in terms of addressing energy poverty since subsidies are beneficial mostly only to the wealthier sectors of society such as energy corporations, not the poor that this unfair policy purports to support.[27]

Phasing out subsidies, just like carbon pricing, needs the strongest possible policy push. Some strategies to achieve this include: adoption of strict timelines for their phase out with specific and measurable outcomes; transparency in public disclosure of all subsidies for fossil fuels; and shifting subsidies from fossil fuel to support the acceleration of the transitions, including energy access and the rapid deployment of renewables. Some of the countries under study have already successfully accomplished part of these strategies (see Table 5.8 for some examples).

Table 5.8 Examples of successful subsidy reforms

	Year	Energy source	Description
Brazil	1993–2003	Electricity	Lowered subsidies equivalent to 0.7 per cent of GDP.
Chile	1995	Coal	Subsidies were removed after coal production prices became apparently high compared to other countries. Removal resulted to increase in income by more than 1 per cent among Chilean households.
Indonesia	2005–2009, 2013	Oil and gas	Subsidies declined from 3.5 per cent of GDP in 2005 to 0.8 per cent in 2009. However, this share had increased in 2013 due to public protests.
Philippines	2001–2006	Electricity	Subsidies were totally reduced from 1.5 per cent of national GDP to zero.

Source: abridged from Sovacool, BK 2017, 'Reviewing, reforming, and rethinking global energy subsidies: towards a political economy research agenda,' *Ecological Economics*, vol. 135, p. 161, Table 6.

The subsidy landscape continues to be raptured, albeit in different scale and intensity. The plunge in oil prices since 2014 has provided, in many ways, an impetus for subsidy reform, which could now be achieved without having a major upward impact on energy prices or inflation. In 2015, China issued plans to phase out selected fossil fuel subsidies to help in their emissions reduction program. Morocco, also in 2015, has begun reforming their subsidy policy at the same time that it expands investment into renewable energy. Also that year, Indonesia cut subsidies for both gasoline and diesel, with the complete removal of diesel subsidies under consideration. In 2016, the Government of India introduced direct cash transfer program for household kerosene consumers and launched a program to progressively raise kerosene prices. Thailand, also in 2016, announced to deregulate compressed natural gas prices. Expanding subsidy reforms and carbon pricing initiatives is key for accelerating the policy turn to support accelerated energy transitions; however, placing priority support towards access, efficiency, and renewables equally needs to be reflected in this policy push.

5.4. Prioritizing renewables

Sequence matters. The transitions require heavy and priority investments on the cheapest, quickest, and cleanest options – at the same time that investments toward polluting energy systems are substantially discouraged. In developing countries, these can be done through large-scale harvesting of energy efficiency[28] and staged and structured transitions in renewable energy generation, in parallel. A decision to prioritize spending billions on expensive, too-long-to-complete, carbon-polluting power plants could lock developing countries into a less advantageous economic position in the future. Hence, policy has to be designed and introduced to deliver a focused, long-term commitment to sustainable energy transitions – and not on perpetuating carbon-based development pathways. Key to this is a clear policy that guarantees markets for renewable energy generators.[29]

Policy on guaranteed markets can be broadly categorized either as price-based or quota-based. Price-based policy and its instruments aim to provide a more predictable revenue stream to alleviate risk-return profiles of renewable energy investments, especially in less mature technologies such as large-scale solar and ocean energy. Examples of these instruments are net metering and feed-in tariff (FiT) schemes. Quota-based policy and its instruments aim to induce private finance for more mature technologies such as wind and hydro energy. Renewable energy credits traded in over-the-counter transactions, such as renewable energy quotas or obligations, are examples of quota-based instruments. Tenders also fall into this policy basket.

Key in the success of these policy options is the stability and predictability of the policy itself or a portfolio of these policies while being adaptive to changing environments, i.e. policies are continually improved as technologies and markets mature. The capacity for reflexivity and flexibility is vital. Upcoming market developments, improvements in institutional capacity, and the availability of funding support, among other dynamic factors of the transitions, should always be accommodated in the design of these schemes to avoid unnecessary public spending. Ensuring that these qualities are achieved requires that policymakers are provided with the capacity to effectively design and efficiently implement these schemes.

Price-based instruments

Net metering

Net metering schemes are mostly applicable to small-scale generators such as households with installed rooftop solar PV. Net metering allows grid-connected generators to sell their excess power into the grid and obliges utilities to purchase this excess. Excess power forwarded to the grid is often paid either through a reimbursement or a rebate and may be based on retail or wholesale prices. The pricing may also consider the time-of-day value of the power. Credit may be forwarded to the customer either at the level of the retail electricity price (under net metering) or lower than the retail price (under net billing). Table 5.9 shows some of existing net metering schemes in some study countries. (Vietnam is also considering a net metering scheme.)[30]

FiTs

FiTs, which have almost become the de facto economic support policy for attracting investments in the renewable energy sector, have been demonstrated to have high impact in the deployment of wind energy, solar PV, biomass, and small hydro

Table 5.9 Examples of existing net metering schemes

	Net metering schemes
Brazil	The scheme allows renewable energy generators with capacity of up to 1 MW to sell their surplus electricity back to the national grid in return for the electricity billing credit to be recuperated within three years.
India	The scheme runs in the state of Uttar Pradesh for rooftop solar PV at INR7.06 per kilowatt-hour (kWh) for 25 years.
Morocco	The scheme covers solar PV and onshore wind plants connected to high-voltage grid to sell not more than 20 per cent of their electricity.
Philippines	The scheme is limited up to 100-kW systems.

Source: author's compilation.

in a number of countries. A FiT guarantees a price for the sale of renewable electricity over a specified period and allows the supply of investment to determine the resulting volume or capacity. FiT policies were conceived to create more price certainty at levels that would guarantee risk-adjusted returns. FiT rules, however, differ by country, and even within states or provinces. The level of incentive also varies, either as a guaranteed minimum price or on top of wholesale electricity price (which is called the feed-in premium).

A 'standard' FiT includes an obligation to connect renewable energy projects to the grid, their priority dispatch, and the purchase of any electricity generated at a fixed minimum price, which is generally above the market level for a set time period. To take into account technological maturity, FiT payment usually declines over time according to a rate known at the time of initial contracting. This approach minimizes the risk of investment and, if designed appropriately, should provide attractive risk-adjusted return on investment. One example is provided by the Philippine FiT scheme, where a digression rate of 0.5 per cent is applicable after two years for run-of-river hydropower, wind, and biomass energy, and 0.6 per cent after a year for solar energy.[31] As shown in Table 5.10, the trends and developments related to sample FiT policies vary from country-to-country.

Although the transaction costs involved with FiTs tend to be lower – which makes it attractive to investors, concerns over the design and best practices regarding its payment and cost structure have been raised. For this reason, and others, there has been generally little investment in renewable energy systems despite the presence of FiTs in many developing countries.[32] The two-year experiment with FiT in South Africa and its subsequent termination in the absence of signed contracts is one example.

Approved in 2009, the South African renewable energy FiT program was designed to cover generation costs, plus a real after tax return on equity of 17 per cent, and would be fully indexed for inflation. Project developers have generally regarded the initially published FiTs as generous: $0.156 for wind, $0.26 for concentrated solar troughs with six-hour storage, and $0.49 for solar PV per kWh

Table 5.10 Examples of some FiT policies in some study countries, per kWh, grid-connected

	Small hydro	Solar	Wind	Geothermal	Biomass	Biogas
China		2016, Zone-dependent: RMB0.8, RMB0.88, RMB0.98	2009, region-dependent: EUR0.052, EUR0.055, EUR0.059, EUR 0.062		2010, From biomass: CNY0.75	Municipal solid waste: INR6.91
India, State of Uttar Pradesh, 2016	INR6.47 (<5 MW); INR5.32 (5 MW-25 MW)	INR7.06 only for <5MW			Based on rice husk: INR6.88 Based on bagasse: INR6.14	
Indonesia	2006, for multiple sources up to 10 MW capacity: 60 per cent of utility's generation costs for low voltage 80 per cent of utility's generations costs for medium voltage			2016, region dependent: $0.122, $0.176, $0.254		
Philippines, 2015	PHP5.90	PHP8.69	PHP8.53		PHP6.63	
Thailand	2014: THB4.90 (<200 kW)	2015, rooftop solar PV: THB6.85 (<10 kW), THB6.4 (10–250 kW), THB6.01 (250 kW-1 MW) 2015, community ground-mounted solar: THB5.66	2014: THB6.06		2014: THB5.34 (<1 MW), THB5.34 (1 MW-3 MW), THB4.24 (>3 MW)	2014, Landfill gas: THB5.60 From waste products: THB4.82 From energy crops: THB5.34
Vietnam			2011:VND1,614		2014: VND1,220	2014: solid waste: VND2,114

Source: author's compilation

produced. Despite suggesting certainty in pricing, considerable uncertainty about the nature of the procurement and licensing process remained. Further uncertainty was introduced when in March 2011 a surprise release of a consultation paper calling for lower FiTs than the original was released. The paper suggested FiTs that are 25 per cent lower for wind, 13 per cent lower for concentrated solar, and 41 per cent lower for solar PV. The paper argues that parameters such as exchange rates and the cost of debt had changed and that the capital component of the tariffs would no longer be fully indexed for inflation. More policy and regulatory uncertainties complicated the matter further. A legal opinion, for example, concluded that the FiTs could amount into non-competitive procurement and were therefore prohibited in public procurement regulations. Following these uncertainties, the Government of South Africa decided to terminate the original FiT program in favor of a competitive bidding process.[33]

Quota-based instruments

Tendering

Tenders, also called auctions or reverse auctions, are procurement mechanisms by which sustainable energy supply or capacity is competitively solicited from sellers who offer bids at the lowest price they would be willing to accept. Compared to FiTs, tenders can be more complicated to administer and often require stronger institutional arrangements, especially in terms of ensuring transparency.

Public authorities organize tenders for a given quota of renewable energy supplies, and ensure their payments through public auctions. Auctions or obligations set both the total share of electricity and a maximum price per unit of electricity. Developers then submit prices for contracts in a one-off bidding round to compete for funds and contracts. The government then evaluates the tenders based on price and other criteria, such as environmental requirements, technological specifications, and local manufacturing. Based on these criteria, the winning bidder signs a contract for a certain number of years and a guaranteed purchase for its generated electricity. Table 5.11 presents some examples in the study countries with renewable energy tender schemes.

Brazil has the oldest auction-based energy market, which is also considered as among the most sophisticated and efficient in the world. The Brazilian experience demonstrates the significance of auctions in facilitating new, large-scale investments in renewable energy generation. In 1998, Brazil started reforming its energy sector in response to a deep financial and operational energy crisis. These reforms included the creation of a competitive wholesale market, a spot market, and independent public institutions to regulate, monitor, and administer an energy market. Despite opening up the market and advances in institutional arrangements, project developers and investors, in the beginning, were not able to see long-term opportunities for meeting increasing demand through generation capacity expansion – hence the low level investment and low rates of new installations.

Table 5.11 Examples of renewable energy auction schemes in the study countries

	Renewable energy auction schemes
Brazil	Brazil Renewable Energy Auctions, 2007 Electric power auctions – wind, 2009 Brazil Inova Energia Program Electric power auctions – biomass, 2008
China	Support for biogas projects, 2006 Special funds for the industrialization of wind power equipment, 2007 Interim measures on renewable energy development fund imposition and management, 2012 Renewable electricity surcharge, 2009, amended 2011 and 2013 Renewable electricity generation bonus, 2013 The State Development and Reform Commission's notice on promotion of PV industry by exerting the price leverage effect, 2013 Notice on the related issues of the application of subsidies based on electric quantity of distributed PV power grid, 2013
India	Solar power generation based incentive, 2008 Generation based incentives for wind power, 2008 Renewable energy certificate system, 2011
Indonesia	Electricity purchase from small and medium scale renewable energy and excess power, 2012 Power purchase from solar PV plants, 2013 Purchase of electricity from geothermal plants, 2011, 2012 Geothermal business activities, 2007, 2010
South Africa	Renewable Energy Independent Power Procurement Program
Zambia	Zambia solar PV tender, 2016 Zambia scaling solar program, 2015

Source: author's compilation.

During the dry periods of 2001 to 2002, Brazil experienced reduced hydropower capacity, its primary source of energy. As a result, energy supply was rationed. This triggered the second wave of reforms, which began in 2003. This time, the government focused more on ensuring adequate and reliable power supply. A series of new energy policy were instituted, including: emphasis on centralized planning of power expansion; competitive tenders to build and operate new generation and transmission facilities; and mandatory long-term bilateral contracts between new independent power producers or transmission companies and financially viable distribution companies. In concert, these policies aimed to provide more revenue certainty and to attract long-term financing for new generation capacity.

Public auctions for renewable energy generation through small hydro, wind, and biomass energy were structured so that these sources would compete among themselves. In all cases, the auctions are fully competitive and are generally technology neutral. Annually run, auctions are designed according to project durations and technology types. There are also sporadic auctions, which are project specific or for reserve energy. Winning bidders sign direct contracts with distribution companies in proportion to their forecast demand. They then make financing agreements with banks, often with the Brazilian Development Bank (BNDES), which offers concessionary finance for auction winners. As a result of these auctions, cost-intensive generation projects were disincentivized, and wind power generation became more decentralized. Each year, during the last ten years, multiple auctions have been held, with impressive capacity and price outcomes.

The Brazilian experience with renewable energy auctions points out to four key principles for effective tenders: transparency and predictability of competitive procurement arrangements, and robust government oversight and regulation. Also key is the need for improving the operational and financial sustainability of electricity distributors, which would take the responsibility for securing adequate and reliable power transmission. Strengthening the financial system, in particular national development banks, which would provide means of financing, is also evidently vital in this case.

Although other study countries still have little experience with renewable energy auctions, this instrument offers one way to improve deployment rates, especially of large-scale installations. The level of sophistication reached in Brazil, however, may not fit the reality of other developing countries. For example, structural issues such as weak public sector capacity – including regulation and development financing, vulnerable economies, and weak investment climates – can limit the full potential of auctions. Issues of corruption related to bidding processes could also easily pose a limitation.[34]

Quotas

Quota systems can be based on obligation or certificate mechanisms in which investors, generators, or utilities have to achieve specific target and are penalized if they do not. They are also called Renewable Performance Standards in some countries. Green certificates, green labels, or renewable energy credits are credited through the generation of renewable electricity. To meet the obligation, it is possible to generate renewable energy, enter into a contract with others to do so, or buy a valid tradable credit in the marketplace. Of the study countries, the following have set up quota systems: Bhutan (not tradable), China (not tradable), India (tradable), Philippines (not tradable), Vietnam (tradable), and Nepal (tradable). There is, as of this writing and to the best of the knowledge of the author, no documented experience suggesting how quota systems fared in these countries.

Fiscal incentives

Other direct financial incentives used to support renewable energy technologies include: tax credits and rebates, grants, and direct subsidies. These incentives make it easier for renewable energy technologies to compete in the energy market by lowering the cost of renewable energy technologies or by increasing the value of renewable energy sold.

Production tax credits and incentives, including tax reduction and exemption schemes, are becoming more common in many developing countries. An investment tax credit, for example, allows investments in sustainable energy to be partially or fully credited against an investor's tax obligations. Production tax credits provide investors with a tax credit based on the amount of renewable energy generated by their facility. They are also called renewable energy conversion payments aimed at helping reduce the payback period and, therefore, increase the rate of return, making investment in renewables more attractive. Table 5.12 shows some examples of these schemes.

Many governments – and, in some instances, energy utilities – also provide investment grants, subsidies, and rebates, which are one-time direct payments to help defray the cost of investment. Credit enhancements and guarantees also help mitigate underlying credit risk of renewable energy projects. Private investors, for example, have commonly requested sovereign guarantees. These are guarantees made by governments stating that they will cover financial liabilities in the event of default. One example is the South African Renewable Energy Independent Power Procurement Program where the Government's Department of Energy provides guarantees. Some governments have also started imposing levies and fees on imported renewable energy components to protect domestic manufacturers. China, for example, has been imposing 42 per cent anti-dumping duties on German, Italian, and Spanish solar-grade polysilicon.[35]

Table 5.12 Examples of some tax incentive schemes to support sustainable energy transition

	Tax-related schemes example
Bhutan	10-year corporate income tax exemption for sustainable energy projects Additional 5-year tax holiday for remote projects (until 2025) 10-year corporate income tax exemption for manufacturers (until 2019) Sales tax and customs duty exemption for spare parts
Brazil	Wind turbine component tax exemption
China	Preferential tax policies for renewable energy, 2003 Reduced VAT for renewable energy, 2001 Notice of VAT policy of large-scale hydropower enterprise, 2014 Notice on the policy of PV electricity VAT, 2013
India	Accelerated tax depreciation benefit
Indonesia	Income tax reduction
Nepal	Subsidy of 40 to 75 per cent on different renewable energy technologies, mostly for rural population
Philippines	7-year tax holiday and exemptions Reduced corporate income tax of 10 per cent instead of 30 per cent at the expiration of the tax holiday
Vietnam	Accelerated depreciation tax relief for renewable energy projects, 2013

Source: author's compilation.

5.5. Conclusion

Strong, credible, predictable, and coherent policy is required to accelerate energy transitions in developing countries. The choice of policy instrument is key in transmitting signal of support to investors, aid providers, funders, and the public at-large since it shows the degree of commitment on the part of government. The greater the commitment means the louder the signal, implying reduced risks and uncertainties. The strength of the policy lies on its credibility, institutionalization, and predictability. Policy instruments that clearly provide avenues for more predictable revenue streams, therefore, might be more suitable than instruments whose support levels are more difficult to ascertain ex ante. Policy coherence is also important. The fragmentation of state policies in many countries in the global south reduces coherence, making monitoring and reporting a challenge. In the longer-range future, more integration across access, efficiency, and renewables solutions and their policy is necessary to allow cohesive, credible, and predictable transition. While ensuring that these policies are eventually in concert with each other should be a long-term objective, mainstreaming current policy, especially targets and existing price-related instruments, is also essential in the short-term. This policy turn is necessary in scaling up the opportunities for the transition.

Notes

1 Anadon, LD, Bunn, M & Narayamurti, V (Eds.) 2014, *Transforming US Energy Innovation*, Cambridge University Press: Cambridge, UK.
2 The White House 2015, *U.S.-Brazil Joint Statement on Climate Change*, www.whitehouse. gov/the-press-office/2015/06/30/us-brazil-joint-statement-climate-change.
3 China Energy Development Strategy Action Plan (2014–2020), www.lse.ac.uk/ GranthamInstitute/law/energy-development-strategy-action-plan-2014-2020/.
4 India Ministry of New and Renewable Energy 2015, 'Schemes for installing large solar power plants,' http://pib.nic.in/newsite/pmreleases.aspx?mincode=28.
5 Government of Nepal 2015, *Intended Nationally Determined Contributions to the Paris Agreement*, communicated in February 2016, p. 8.
6 Government of South Africa 2013, *Integrated Resource Plan for Electricity (IRP) 2010–2030: Update Report 2013*, www.doe-irp.co.za/content/IRP2010_updatea.pdf.
7 Government of Thailand 2015, *Thailand Power Development Plan 2015–2036*, www. eppo.go.th/power/PDP2015/PDP2015_Eng.pdf.
8 GIZ 2015, 'Thailand: Renewable energy policy update,' http://thai-german-cooperation. info/download/20150520_pdp_re_%20policy%20factsheet.pdf.
9 Pichalai, C 2015, 'Thailand Energy Efficiency Development Plan 2015–2036,' 4 June, www.renewableenergy-asia.com/Portals/0/seminar/Presentation/03-Overview%20 of%20Energy%20Efficiency%20Development%20Plan%20(EEDP%202015). pdf.
10 British Petroleum 2015, *BP Statistical Review of World Energy June 2015*, BP: London, UK.
11 Ibid.
12 Institute for Energy Economics and Financial Analysis 2014, 'India's electricity-sector transformation,' http://ieefa.org/wp-content/uploads/2015/08/IEEFA-Indian-Electricity-Sector-Transformation-11-August-2015.pdf.
13 International Energy Agency 2015, *World Energy Outlook 2015*, IEA: Paris, France.

14 Kenning, T 2015, 'New India renewable targets put country on path to 69GW of PV by 2019,' *PV Tech*, 29 April, www.pv-tech.org/news/india_ramps_up_renewable_purchase_obligations_target.

15 Li, T, Molodtsov, S & Delina, L 2010, *Assessment Report on Energy Efficiency Institutional Arrangements in Asia*, United Nations Economic and Social Commission for Asia and the Pacific: Bangkok, Thailand.

16 Delina, L 2012, 'Coherence in energy efficiency governance,' *Energy for Sustainable Development*, vol. 16, pp. 493–499.

17 The Plan includes taxes of one per cent on small petrol, LPG and compressed natural gas cars, 2.5 per cent on certain diesel cars, and 4 per cent on larger cars and sport utility vehicles.

18 International Institute for Sustainable Development 2013, *A Guidebook to Fossil-Fuel Subsidy Reform for Policymakers in Southeast Asia*, IISD: Global Subsidies Initiative, Geneva.

19 The Australian carbon price is case in point where it led to a change in government.

20 The World Bank October 2016, *State and Trends of Carbon Pricing 2016*, World Bank, Ecofys & Vivid Economics: Washington, DC.

21 Ibid.

22 The Straits Times 2017, 'Singapore to impose carbon pricing in a move to cut greenhouse gas emissions,' 17 February, www.straitstimes.com/business/economy/singapore-to-impose-carbon-pricing-in-move-to-cut-greenhouse-emissions?xtor=CS3–17.

23 See discussion on the limitations of the Chinese ETS experiment in Section 6.2, Carbon-related revenues.

24 Murray, B & Rivers, N 2015, 'British Columbia's revenue-neutral carbon tax: A review of the latest "Grand Experiment" in environmental policy,' *Energy Policy*, vol. 86, pp. 674–683.

25 Jotzo, F 2011, 'Australia's carbon price,' *Nature Climate Change*, vol. 2, pp. 475–476.

26 International Monetary Fund 2013, *Energy Subsidy Reform: Lessons and Implications*, IMF: Washington, DC.

27 See Sovacool, BK & Dworkin, M 2014, 'Chapter 8: Energy subsidies and freedom,' in *Global Energy Justice: Problems, Principles, and Practices*, Cambridge University Press: Cambridge, UK, pp. 256–273; also see Sovacool, BK 2017, 'Reviewing, reforming, and rethinking global energy subsidies: Towards a political economy research agenda,' *Ecological Economics*, vol. 135, pp. 150–163.

28 Li, T, Molodtsov, S & Delina, L 2010, *Assessment Report on Energy Efficiency Institutional Arrangements in Asia*, United Nations Economic and Social Commission for Asia and the Pacific: Bangkok, Thailand.

29 Protecting these niche industries is common in history. Computer chips, for instance, went from being high-priced luxuries to cheap commodities only because the United States Air Force and NASA bought them in bulk until their prices fell to a level where the private market took over. Also see Zuzhang, X 2014, 'Unlocking financial resources,' in A Halff, BK Sovacool & J Rozhon (Eds.), *Energy Poverty: Global Challenges and Local Solutions*, Oxford University Press: Oxford, UK, pp. 411–440.

30 I thank Thanh Nguyen Quang for providing this data; see Government of Vietnam 2015, *National Strategy on Renewable Energy Development 11/2015*, Government of Vietnam: Hanoi, Vietnam.

31 Philippine Energy Regulatory Commission 2015, *Resolution Adopting the Feed-In Tariff Rates for Wind*, 12 May, www.erc.gov.ph/Files/Render/media/Order,%20ERC%20Case%20No.%202015-002%20RM.pdf.

32 Frankfurt School-UNEP Collaborating Centre for Climate and Sustainability Energy Finance 2016, *Global Trends in Renewable Energy Investment 2016*, UNEP & Bloomberg New Energy Finance: Frankfurt, Germany, p. 58.

33 Eberhard, A, Kolker, J & Leigland, J 2014, *South Africa's Renewable Energy IPP Procurement Program: Success Factors and Lessons*, Public-Private Infrastructure Advisory Facility: Washington, DC.

34 See for example Liu, T, Wang, Y & Wilkinson, S 2016, 'Identifying critical factors affecting the effectiveness and efficiency of tendering processes in Public-Private Partnerships (PPPs): A comparative analysis of Australia and China,' *International Journal of Project Management*, vol. 34, pp. 701–716; Auriol, E, Straub, S & Flochel, T 2016, 'Public procurement and rent-seeking: The case of Paraguay,' *World Development*, vol. 77, pp. 395–407.
35 Parnell, J 2016, 'China to extend anti-dumping duties on EU polysilicon,' *PV Tech*, 29 April.

6 Financing turn

Accelerating the transitions requires major shifts to increase public and private investment in and financing of the transitions to fill the necessary investment needs. This chapter surveys multi-level funding sources and mechanisms for supporting the transitions. Funding mechanisms developed endogenously, using state apparatuses, are discussed (6.2) alongside funding support brought about by external actors, such as from bilateral and multilateral arrangements (6.3), as well as from non-state sources (6.2 and 6.3). These varieties of exogenous support, both flowing from north-to-south and from south-to-south, are important since public finance policy alone cannot improve the economics, scalability, and diffusion of sustainable energy systems.

The chapter first scopes the challenges and costs for facilitating sustainable energy transitions in developing countries (6.1). It then describes the current approaches by which some developing countries are filling these funding gaps by discussing various sources of funds, how they are presently utilized, and how these mechanisms can be innovated to address the need of accelerated transitions. The chapter closes by describing the broad implications of the multiple sources of finance, and the need for a financing turn to support the longer-range futures of sustainable energy in developing countries.

6.1. Funding challenges

Financing is a key challenge for many developing countries especially when the need for accelerating the pace of change is factored in. An influential determinant of whether sustainable energy infrastructure would attract financing will be the cost of capital. Even though the levelized costs of energy are now often lower for several renewable energy sources than for fossil fuel generation, their deployments are still more capital intensive. This is a key barrier to energy transition in many developing countries.

In energy system deployment, the costs of electricity generation are often a fundamental aspect in decision-making, although they vary according to sources. Some renewable energy technologies, solar PV and wind in particular, are already gradually reaching various levels of competitiveness. Table 6.1 shows the costs of electricity generation according to sources.

Table 6.1 Costs for electric generating technologies, $/kW

Technology Type	Mean installed cost	Installed cost standard deviation (SD) (+/-)	Fixed Operations and Maintenance (O&M) ($/kW-yr)	Fixed O&M SD (+/-)	Lifetime (yr)	Lifetime SD (yr)
PV <10 kilowatts (kW)	$3,897	$889	$21	$20	33	11
PV 10–100 kW	$3,463	$947	$19	$18	33	11
PV 100–1,000 kW	$2,493	$774	$19	$15	33	11
PV 1–10 megawatt (MW)	$2,025	$694	$16	$9	33	9
Wind <10 kW	$7,645	$2,431	$40	$34	14	9
Wind 10–100 kW	$6,118	$2,101	$35	$12	19	5
Wind 100–1000 kW	$3,751	$1,376	$31	$10	16	0
Wind 1–10 MW	$2,346	$770	$33	$16	20	7

Source: National Renewable Energy Laboratory, 2016. 'Distributed generation renewable energy estimate, updated February 2016,' www.nrel.gov/analysis/tech_lcoe_re_cost_est.html. Note: these values are only meant to provide rule-of-thumb information, accurate enough for a first pass screen of economic viability.

For renewable energy grid-connected systems, such as utility-scale installations, which aim to compete with electricity from the grid, the levels of competitiveness are usually referred to as 'grid parity.' The concept of grid parity is based on a comparison of the levelised cost of electricity (LCOE) and electricity prices in a specific year. LCOE is the average total cost to build, operate, and maintain a power generation plant over its lifetime divided by its total energy output also over its lifetime. LCOE, hence, can be used to determine the minimum cost at which the generated electricity may be sold to break-even. Nevertheless, the use of LCOE in decision-making has to be approached with caution, particularly given the assumptions made on the following:[1]

- The existing resource mix, which can directly affect the economic viability of a new investment because of the economics surrounding the displacement of existing energy systems. For instance, a wind resource displacing coal generation has different economic value than a wind resource displacing natural gas generation.
- Capacity factor values – the ratio of the plant's actual output over a period of time to its potential output when operating at full capacity continuously

over the same period of time – depend on existing capacity mix and load characteristics of specific region. Thus, systems with output that can be varied depending on demand (dispatchable technologies) have more economic value than less flexible systems (non-dispatchable or variable technologies), such as intermittent resource-dependent systems.

- Utilization rates, which entail less or additional capacity due to varying demand.
- The ease of access to capitalization varies with the technology, location, market, institutional capacity, and other factors, as reflected in the terms and conditions of financial support.

Given these limitations, direct comparison of LCOE across locations and technologies can be problematic and misleading. Because of this, another measurement of economic competitiveness, the levelised avoided cost of electricity (LACE) has been proposed.[2] LACE considers avoided cost – a measure of what it would cost the grid to generate the electricity that is otherwise displaced by a new generation project – in its computation. Avoided costs are summed over the project's lifetime and then converted to a stream of annual payments. To determine LACE, this sum is then divided by the average annual output of the project. LACE can then be compared with LCOE to provide a measure of whether or not the project's value exceeds its cost. For illustration, Table 6.2 presents a summary

Table 6.2 Average LCOE and LACE of select energy generation technologies in the United States, in 2022, $\$_{2016}$/MWh

	Average LCOE	Average LACE	Average difference
Dispatchable technologies			
Coal 30 per cent with carbon sequestration	140.0	58.7	–81.3
Advanced nuclear	99.1	57.3	–41.7
Geothermal	43.3	65.3	21.9
Biomass	102.4	58.3	–44.1
Variable technologies			
Wind – onshore	52.2	53.2	1.0
Wind – offshore	145.9	57.8	–88.1
Solar PV	66.8	64.7	–2.0
Solar thermal	184.4	69.9	–114.5
Hydroelectric	66.2	57.4	–8.8

Source: United States Energy Information Administration 2017, 'Levelised cost and levelised avoided cost of new generation resources in the Annual Energy Outlook 2017,' April, www.eia.gov/forecasts/aeo/pdf/electricity_generation.pdf, accessed 13 May 2017, Table 4b. Note: for illustration purposes only, LCOE and LACE are location-specific and vary widely.

of LCOE and LACE, computed by the United States Energy Information Agency (US EIA) for select generation technologies in 2020, based on a 30-year cost recovery period.[3] Note that this is a US case and is used here only to illustrate the divergences between LCOE and LACE.

When the LACE of a particular technology exceeds its LCOE at a given time and place, that technology would generally be economically attractive to build. A negative difference indicates that the cost of the project exceeds its value to the system, as measured by LACE; a positive difference indicates that the project brings in value in excess of its cost by displacing more expensive generation options. By 2020, the US EIA projects negative net differences for all technologies except for geothermal.[4] Thus far, onshore wind and hydroelectric, among other renewable energy technologies, appear to be the most competitive generation technology – even more competitive than conventional coal and nuclear. The growing solar energy market, demonstrated in many developing countries by utility-scale solar photovoltaic (PV), however, is also evident of the dynamics towards cost reduction in these settings.

Estimates of the total cost of the transition, particularly the deployment of its hardware components, vary according to scale, location, market, capacity, policy environment, and other factors. At the global level, the German Advisory Council on Global Change estimates this cost to range from $200 billion to $1 trillion per annum by 2030.[5] Stanford's Mark Jacobson and Mark Delucchi project this cost to be $100 trillion spread over 20 years, or approximately $5 trillion yearly, but decreasing to 80 per cent by 2030.[6] In their most recent working paper, dated 7 April 2017, the Stanford study placed the cost to move the entire global energy system to 100 per cent wind, water and sunlight-based systems in 2050 at about $124.7 trillion.[7] In developing countries, estimates range from $156 billion per year[8] to $565 billion.[9]

The huge cost of the transition is expected to be traded-off by avoided costs in new fossil-fuel based power plant construction; in prospecting, mining, and distribution of fossil fuels; maintenance of existing fossil-based power plants; in immense pollution and its public health implications; and in the impacts of unmitigated climate change to social, economic, and natural systems. Of these many avoided costs, that of climate takes the lion's share. Estimates of the cost of climate change vary from as low as $4 billion per year[10] to as high as $109 billion per year,[11] with larger cost to be expected for runaway climate change. Also needed to be included are other non-monetary costs from social, ecological, and political changes accruing from climate impacts. The expected cost of climate change today and the future represents huge budgetary expenditures, especially in developing countries where national budgets are already constrained and are already committed to other expense items. These costs can be minimized only if the transition occurs in earnest.

To be able to compete with electricity generation rates in utility markets, the costs for deploying offshore wind and solar technologies – two key technologies for accelerating the transitions – need to be further and quickly brought down. In parallel, current fossil fuel-based electricity generation costs also need to be brought up to take account of the externalities of its production, through a carbon tax, air pollution and water regulations, etc. This is where financing policy becomes very important; yet it is also the most contentious.

In many developing countries, the large-scale, high-capital cost of the replacement system is exacerbated by other risks related to currency exchange rate and country politics. Financing energy access, particularly to support small-scale installations, also faces high transaction cost. The same can be said with energy efficiency, especially with strategies involving equipment replacements. These risks conspire together to place transition financing at a disadvantage creating high-barriers to entry and limiting private sector investment interest in the transitions.[12] While these hurdles apply to fossil fuel infrastructure as well, they are more nuanced in energy transitions since they are still largely considered niche industries in many developing countries.

Investments towards energy solutions are also often not particularly appealing to institutional investors given the perceived lack of liquidity of energy-related investments. Most of institutional investors' capital is invested in stocks and bonds, some of which are held by companies that invest in infrastructure. Unlocking this cache of institutional investment for large-scale sustainable electricity infrastructure is key to the transition and must be supported with policy nudges.

The hurdles to achieve a financing turn are many and go beyond issues related to costs. Many investors, financiers, and project developers still perceive greater policy risks with efficiency and renewable energy investments. Since the primary role of private companies is to seek profits, investors would only invest in the transitions if there were clear incentives in making these investments in the first place. More often, private firms also tend to prefer enhancing their existing competencies, which means maintaining and sustaining status quos rather than supporting alternatives that require change.

Addressing the financial hurdles to achieve and accelerate the transition requires closing both costs and perception gaps via a strong policy push and institutional support. However, in many developing countries, policy and institutions themselves are also challenges that pose key risks. Among these policy risks are their relative uncertainties, fragmentation, and structural weaknesses. Administrative difficulties include the lack of skilled personnel to coordinate transition efforts. In addition, other hurdles in bringing access, energy efficiency, or renewable energy projects online include aspects such as the lengthy, often convoluted, siting and permitting processes, embedded corruption, and red tape.

Addressing these challenges require a turn in ways that policy for financing energy solutions is done. Policy needs to be cognizant of the need to increase the commercial viability of transition-related activities. New business models that address the key challenges on how the market perceived transition activities are imperative both as means to provide new revenue streams and spread, to reduce, risks. The stability and coherence of regulations and policy mechanisms, as well as the many actors and institutions involved, are equally important as investors and the public at-large engage with transition-related activities. Also vital is to sharpen and strengthen coordination and linkages efforts between development partners, particularly among end-users and solutions providers in development cooperation type of solutions.[13]

Given the scale of investments needed – from manufacturing to project construction to operations and maintenance – and the complementary requirement of acceleration, understanding where the funding could come and efficiently allocating it is key in the transition finance turn. Public policy to level economic playing field is a vital component, but providing appropriate amount of funds is equally important. Having strong and capable institutional and regulatory architecture to facilitate the mobilization of transition finance is also vital. To achieve this turn, at least three financing streams need to be mobilized, i.e. domestic, international, and emerging alternative schemes. Both public and private actors are present in each of these streams.

6.2. Mobilizing domestic finance

Both national and local governments have to enable a policy environment that would shift current financing modalities and unlock new mechanisms towards smart and innovative approaches for financing the transitions. Broadly, public finance mechanisms have a twofold objective: direct mobilization or leverage of commercial investment in sustainable energy projects, and indirect creation of scaled-up and commercially sustainable markets for sustainable energy technologies. The most common types of public finance mechanisms used to achieve these objectives include:

- credit lines provided by national development banks, other state financial institutions, rural banks, and co-operatives to other national and local actors for providing debt financing or loans to projects
- loans and equity participation from local and national public financial entities provided by investors into publicly listed companies or channeled directly onto private companies
- government guarantees to share with commercial financial institutions and to sponsor the risks of providing financing to projects and companies
- debt financing provided directly to projects and using existing assets as collateral
- loan softening programs to mobilize domestic sources of capital
- financing of private equity funds that invest risk capital in companies and projects
- equity financing provided directly to companies and projects
- grants to share project development, transaction, or capital costs
- grants or loans provided by national, state, provincial, or local governments to both state-owned energy suppliers and non-state players
- consumer loans, microfinance, and leasing to help small and medium-size enterprises set up small-scale infrastructure
- bonds for projects, which are debt obligations issued directly to capital markets to raise funds.

Domestic financing for the transition can be secured through mobilization of the following: public funds in government budgets, revenues generated from carbon pricing, freed-up funds from subsidies removal, banking assets, private capital, and debt and equity from domestic capital markets. Maximizing the opportunities for capital mobilization from across these sources is necessary for facilitating a transition finance turn.

Government budgets

Government budgets provide transition finance flows through taxation revenues it accumulates and supplemented by levies and other charges. Funds for the transitions can then be channeled from this source through grants, direct spending, and loans channeled through national development banks, rural banks, and, in some cases, public agencies. Often, grid improvement is funded by these budgets. But these funds can also be used to provide direct investments to non-state actors through equity holdings in private sustainable energy firms or co-funding, grants, or loans to entities such as energy cooperatives and small- and medium-sized energy enterprises.

Not all sustainable energy transition activities, however, can be financed directly from government budgets. Often, national budgets in developing countries are limited in volume, with many agencies even competing for funding. In addition to scarcity, revenue sources also face additional challenges regarding their reliability and sustainability. The political economy of public funds – it being subject to politics and power play – is another challenge. For these reasons, governments have to secure additional funding from other sources. Some of these can be generated directly from carbon emitting sectors.

Carbon-related revenues

Carbon pricing instruments are economic mechanisms to mobilize domestic, sometimes international, public and private climate finance while providing incentives for transition-related actions. A price on carbon can support all aspects of sustainable energy transitions and, at the same time, reflects the impact of emissions to human health, local environment, and climate – which are considered market externalities. In countries where carbon pollution is priced, they are currently too low – hence, inadequate to send the right signal to pursue, lest to accelerate, the transitions.

Carbon pricing holds promise in transition finance. With a carbon price of $25 per ton, for instance, one analysis has shown that $30 billion can be collected by 2020.[14] Another analysis estimates this potential to be up to $50 billion globally.[15] Revenues can be collected from carbon pricing instruments such as an expanded tax base by introducing a carbon tax, such as energy taxation, or through auctions of emission allowances in a cap-and-trade system or an emissions trading scheme (ETS). For carbon price to meaningfully contribute to transition finance turn, the design and coverage of the instrument and the level of the carbon price matters. A significant amount of political will – first in putting up relevant policies into effect, and then to enforce and enhance them over time – is also imperative for success. China's experiment with a small-scale ETS provides an illustration.

In 2013, China introduced pilot cap-and-trade systems in seven of its major provinces and cities: Shanghai, Beijing, Chongqing, Tianjin, Shenzhen, Hubei, and Guangdong. The price of carbon, however, varies across these markets. Following the joint U.S.-China climate statement in September 2015, the central government announced that it would initiate a national ETS. It is expected to be online in 2017. The Chinese experiment with the ETS, however, is not free of challenges. Amongst these include: less developed capacity for market regulation and infrastructure; less participation from Chinese firms in the domestic carbon market; low trading volume; the small scale of the market; and weak management and institutional capacity. As a consequence, these limitations had sent wrong signals to financial institutions and other private actors who participated less in the trading. Given the low level of funds derived from the Chinese carbon trading platforms, it is unlikely that the carbon market would be able to provide adequate support for the country's sustainable energy transitions.[16]

Other than China, South Africa is also expected to introduce its own carbon-pricing instrument – a hybrid carbon tax with an offsetting system.[17] The carbon tax bill has set a carbon tax rate of ZAR120 ($11) per ton of carbon dioxide equivalent for emissions above the thresholds. The bill also provides an increasing rate of 10 per cent per year. To lessen the impact of the carbon price, 60 per cent of emissions will be tax-exempt up to 2020. When this relief is taken into account, the effective tax rate will range between ZAR12 ($1) and ZAR48 ($4) per ton, which is very low – hence raising the question as to its potential to make a dent in South African emissions.

Often, policymakers are presented with a dilemma about which instrument to use in pricing carbon pollution. Between a carbon tax and an ETS, taxation, it seems, has a number of attractive features, especially in developing country contexts. Some of these features are:

- lower complexity and administration costs, since the information needed to tax emissions can be easily obtainable compared to firm-level data on individual emissions required in an ETS. For this reason, a carbon tax could be implemented more quickly and easier to administer, thus reducing the likelihood of failure.
- institutional readiness, since almost every country has already institutionalized a tax revenue collection system.
- harder to evade, because of better availability of relevant information.

Regardless of instrument, however, structural adjustments need to be processed in an equitable and orderly way for a carbon price to be effective. This means that its distributive consequences need to be ameliorated in some ways. The case of the South African proposal illustrates this by starting at a relatively low level and with a promise of scaling up over time. Some of the revenues could also be used to assist people on low incomes who are adversely affected by price changes. To elicit local information and compliance, as well as support for it, revenues can also be shared with local governments for their local transition activities.

Obviously, there are significant political challenges associated with introducing a pricing mechanism. Introducing a new tax, for example, can be an uphill battle for its proponents and, therefore, may take longer time to process. Carbon pricing may also have some less impact in countries where renewable energy, such as large hydropower, already represents substantial share in the energy mix.

Fossil fuel subsidies removal

Fossil fuel subsidies represent expenses in public budgets, and thus cost the tax-payers. In 2015 alone, after-tax energy subsidies were estimated at $4.9 trillion globally, or about 7 per cent of global gross domestic product (GDP). The volume of after-tax subsidies in the study countries is huge – a total of $2.4 trillion, or about half of total global subsidies. The subsidies in China are the highest, most of which are support for coal at about $1.8 trillion, or 38 per cent of the world total.[18] Table 6.3 presents the per capita energy subsidies in the study countries in 2015.

Since subsidies often take huge portions of national budgets in many developing countries, the amount and quality of public service such as healthcare, education, and public infrastructure such as roads and electrification are seriously

Table 6.3 Post-tax subsidies, in 2015 $ per capita (nominal)

	Petroleum	Coal	Natural Gas	Electricity	Total
Brazil	247.47	21.42	13.40	49.81	332.10
Chile	354.94	82.46	22.55		459.94
China	122.95	1,198.21	15.73	18.28	1,355.16
El Salvador	108.80	0.03		89.84	198.67
India	76.19	124.80	7.55	7.60	216.13
Indonesia	294.15	36.77	14.86	44.87	390.65
Morocco	118.95	18.50	3.81		141.26
Philippines	27.21	30.24	3.63		61.08
South Africa	305.39	405.44	7.16	80.63	798.62
Thailand	151.65	131.98	60.49	13.22	357.34
Vietnam			14.49	46.32	60.81

Source: extracted by the author from International Monetary Fund 2015, *How Large Are Global Energy Subsidies?* 29 June, www.imf.org/external/np/fad/subsidies/data/codata.xlsx.

affected. Subsidies also create an uneven-level playing field for sustainable energy options since they are intended to keep energy prices low. With artificially lower cost, incentives for improving energy efficiency are also lowered since consumers are encouraged to excessively consume more energy. The removal of fossil fuel subsidies, therefore, can result to a number of co-benefits.

Subsidy removal results to substantial gains for public budgets, the environment, and social welfare. It improves economic framework for supporting sustainable energy transitions, especially if the subsidies are redirected towards transition finance. The current low energy prices offer a window of opportunity for governments in developing countries to phase out fossil fuel subsidies.

Reforming or phasing-out harmful or costly subsidies, however, is not simple given the complex interests surrounding this policy. Understanding its key actors and their interests, therefore, is key in the design of fossil fuel subsidy removal. Efforts to raise awareness on the actual cost of fossil fuel-based development, especially in issues related to pollution and community health cost, are also necessary. Despite the political difficulty in phasing-out fossil fuel subsidies, some developing countries have experimented with it, with some level of success. The conversion of cooking fuel from kerosene to liquefied petroleum gas (LPG) in Indonesia provides one illustration.

For decades, the Indonesian Government has been subsidizing kerosene, the principal fuel for households and transport. As the Indonesian population and price of oil increased, kerosene subsidy has become a huge burden on government budget. To illustrate, kerosene subsidy between 2001 and 2009 had ranged from 1.9 to 3.7 per cent of the GDP.[19] To reduce the pressure on public budget brought about by kerosene subsidy, the government initiated a three-year program that would transition kerosene use to LPG. Beginning in 2006, subsidized kerosene was withdrawn in favor of support to LPG cylinders. Consumers were provided with start-up LPG cooking system: a cooking stove and an LPG cylinder. The transition, however, resulted to increased kerosene and LPG prices, which also led to soaring inflation. As the price of basic cooking fuel rose, the Indonesian public protested. The government quickly addressed it by creating more distribution nodes for LPG supply and supporting former kerosene suppliers and distributors as they transitioned into LPG distribution. In the end, the kerosene conversion program stabilized the new demand for LPG. The program, in general, incurred government savings, generated new jobs, and reduced greenhouse gas emissions. There are also positive effects on consumers including safety, relative costs, and ease of use of their new fuel.[20]

The Indonesian case shows how to navigate the many trade-offs of a subsidy phase-out program. It also shows how strong political will takes a centerpiece in transition processes, especially in messy and complex systems dominated by multiple interests. The case, however, has to be appreciated in its context: a much larger subsidy phase-out necessary to make impact in the transition would be most likely navigated in a much more complex environment than the Indonesian kerosene subsidy phase out.

Domestic banking

Domestic banks at the local (such as rural banks) and national (such as development banks) levels are crucial to financing multilevel transitions. In China, state development banks assume critical roles in facilitating green financial flows towards the sustainable energy sector. As these banks amplify their financing support towards renewables, they also send positive signals to other financing institutions. Indeed, these state banks are key in reducing perceived risks,[21] sharing and pooling risks, and building specialized skills in many transition-related infrastructure projects.[22] This example of supportive national development banks illustrates the need for developing or strengthening the institutional context of the financing turn. In many developing countries, national banks are important in transition finance since they can provide preferential, low and stable interest rates for the deployment of transition hardware. Governments need to provide support by creating conducive financing environment. This entails the design of new strategies and plans to turn the portfolio of domestic banks into as 'green' and 'transition friendly' as possible.

Governments can support domestic banks in at least two ways: loan refinancing and loan guarantees. These strategies can be designed to help in alleviating the risks of investment away from banks by sharing it with governments. Governments can then use these approaches as an incentive or as leverage for requiring banks to treat the sustainable energy transition sector as a priority sector. The Reserve Bank of India, for example, had, in 2015, used this opportunity when it asked bank creditors to treat loans to renewable energy projects as a priority sector lending area in exchange for some concessions such as refinancing and guarantees.[23] Central Banks can also set up subordinated debt facilities at low interest rates and with long tenures, which they can then pass on to local commercial and development banks with institutional capacity and experience for management. The experience with the Clean Energy Development Bank Ltd. and the Himalayan Bank Ltd. in Nepal provides some examples.[24] Governments can also nudge the banking sector towards supporting the transition sector by initiating regulations. For instance, banks could be mandated to internalize environmental sustainability in their operations by establishing and institutionalizing green credit information and risk management systems.[25]

Public debt and equity from domestic capital markets

Revenues for the transition can also be raised using debt from domestic capital markets. While this may not be applicable to all developing countries, some fast-developing economies in the global south may, given their prior experience with this mechanism, exploit the potential of public debt and equity to finance the transitions and scale them quickly. Green bonds, the de facto term for public borrowing instrument in financing environmentally related projects, are already increasing in terms of saliency and volume. In 2015, the Climate Bonds Initiative reported that $41.8 billion labeled green bonds were issued globally.[26] About 46

Table 6.4 China's green bond issues, as of March 2016

Market	Issuer	Volume, in billion
Domestic	Shanghai Pudong Development Bank	$5.3
	Industrial Bank of China	$1.9
	Bank of Qingdao	$0.6
	Concord New Energy	$30.9
Hong Kong	Xinjiang Goldwind Science and Technology	$0.3
International	Agricultural Bank of China	$1

Source: Dai, W, Kidney, S & Sonerud, B 2016, *Roadmap for China: Scaling Up Green Bond Market Issuance*, Climate Bonds Initiative, www.climatebonds.net/files/files/CBI-IISD-Paper2-Final-01B_A4.pdf.

per cent of this volume went to support renewable energy projects, and about 20 per cent was for energy efficiency activities.

China, India, and Brazil have, to some extent, already developed policy frameworks to support green bonds. Green bond markets in these countries have registered some successes. In 2015, China issued $1 billion of green bonds; India issued $1.1 billion; and Brazil issued $600 million.[27] China has also exploited the bond market for expanding its international transition-related activities, while making domestic impact (see Table 6.4).

The potential of public debt in transition finance is illustrated by security of returns, which to some key investors is important than the volume of profit. Investors in bonds usually receive a fixed rate of return, normally as an annual coupon, plus the principal of the bond upon maturity. Compared with other forms of investment, bonds typically offer a lower rate of return to investors but the investment return tends to be more secure, and are therefore often attractive especially to very large institutional investors.

The scale of finance that can be raised through bonds is significant and will be principally determined by the issuer's commitment to meet bond repayments. Estimated at $100 trillion in mid-2013,[28] bonds represent the largest pool of capital in the world,[29] even overshadowing the equities market.[30] Investments required by the transition can take advantage of this large cache of capital. Already, a cohort of investors representing approximately $24 trillion of assets under management, at the September 2014 United Nations Climate Summit, has called for climate action saying they stood ready for providing investment of more than $5 billion in bonds.[31]

In developing countries, bond issuance for transition-related objectives and activities can be used for revenue sourcing or scaled up to increase revenue volume. To maximize the potential of green bonds in many developing countries, however, several challenges need to be hurdled, including:[32]

- limited knowledge of bond issuance process, which entails improving capacity building programs through market education activities and strengthening public institutions

- lack of a concrete long-term pipeline of sustainable energy projects, which entails identifying a priority list of specific projects, ensuring their financial viability, and ensuring transparency for investors
- weak or lack institutional arrangements to support activities involved in the bond market.

In some developing countries, some capacities to address these limitations are already in place where some national governments, development banks, and municipalities have the experience in demonstrating successful bond issuance processes. Their established status could provide investors with an introduction to the green bond market without being exposed to significant risks.

In China, for example, its three main development banks (called policy banks): China Development Bank, the Export-Import Bank of China (known as the China Exim Bank),[33] and the Agricultural Bank of China are of sufficient size to issue larger benchmark sized bonds. In 2014, the Chinese development banks have already accounted for 27 per cent of the total outstanding bonds in China's domestic market.[34] Municipal bond issuances, which are common in developed countries, have also started to permeate some local governments in developing countries. The first of these was a green city bond issued by the City of Johannesburg in South Africa in June 2014. The proceeds of the municipal bond were allocated to renewable energy, waste-to-energy, and low-carbon transport projects.

For green bonds to scale and be aligned with the transitions, governments need to develop standards on what could constitute 'green' and 'transition friendly.' In many developing countries, this can be a hit or a miss, opening up opportunities for learning what works and what does not. Governments also have to recognize that investors, particularly institutions, demand large-scale investment opportunities. The benefit is tremendous if this is successfully tapped as it represents a huge leap forward in the financing turn. To achieve this, bond designers in developing countries need to create investment grade bonds of half a billion dollars upwards to make them easily secured.[35] Some large-scale access, efficiency, and renewable energy projects can easily fit this volume, but, for small-scale technologies and systems to access this investment, governments may need to lead an effort to bundle 'small' projects. Financial houses solely for the purpose of aggregating small-to-medium-scale sustainable energy projects can be created. Some examples include sustainable energy project 'warehouses' in the U.S. states of Pennsylvania and Kentucky[36] and Australia's Clean Energy Finance Corporation.[37] Since this would require new institutional arrangements and human skills to operate and manage, many developing countries need support in terms of capacity building in setting these 'warehouses' up.

Domestic private finance

Many pioneers in the private sector have developed low-cost energy systems at the household or village scale, from solar lanterns to biogas digesters to micro-hydro systems, using new business models for rolling out these products and systems, their processes, and distribution. Rural microcredit has been successful in providing the needed funding for rural electrification. The Grameen Shakti projects in Bangladesh, for example, have been instrumental in the provision of solar home systems in many Bangladeshi households. Scaling up innovations such as these require some form of policy nudges and political support. In many developing countries, where securing capital remains a huge issue, tapping in the capacity of these small-scale innovative approaches offer a tremendous opportunity for accelerating the transitions, especially its access component.

Privately owned and managed utility-scale renewable energy generation also needs policy support. In many developing countries, numerous efforts have been made to introduce private sector participation into the electricity generation sector to increase and improve supply and its reliability. Private sector finance is often channeled through independent power production projects, which are then supported by long-term power purchase agreements (PPAs) from either the state or the utilities. Thailand's success in the rapid deployment of solar PV farms can be attributed to this policy. Some regulatory changes, however, have lead to the reduction of renewable energy PPAs, particularly solar-related. Some experiences also showed that some of those who have awarded PPAs were not able to timely commission renewable energy power plants. This experience shows the complexity of the policy highlighting the imperative of complementary strategies. In the case of Thailand, capacity in terms of evaluating PPA proposals needs to be strengthened.[38]

6.3.   Mobilizing international finance

Many developing countries expect that their sustainable energy transitions will be partly supported by international sources. In their Nationally Determined Contributions to the Paris Agreement, many governments in developing countries have clearly indicated their willingness to increase their decarbonization targets with foreign assistance (see Table 2.10). While there is no precise definition as to what constitutes foreign assistance, it can be interpreted generally as the voluntary transfer of public or private resources, from a government or a non-government entity to another independent government, to a non-government organization, or to an international organization. In some cases, the private sector can also become a recipient of international funding. Foreign assistance, however, is not only limited to funding; other international sources also convey expertise, technology consultancy, and proposal development capacity building.[39]

Official development assistance

The international flows of funds for development purposes have its antecedent in post-war reconstruction efforts, and are often represented by official development assistance (ODA). Given the historical experience with ODA, the most common form of foreign assistance that can be used for funding the transitions, therefore, is ODA. ODA, in its vague definition, is centrally sourced from government

budgets to promote the economic development and welfare of developing countries. Some, however, opines that ODA is actually a mechanism by which some
countries illustrate their hegemony over others.[40] Officially, ODA is provided as
grants, concessional loans, or equity to countries and territories on the Development Assistance Committee's list of ODA recipients.[41] If ODA is provided as a
loan or equity, rules state that it must convey a grant element of at least 25 per
cent.[42] ODA is channeled through bilateral agencies and finance institutions or
multilateral development finance institutions and funds.

Recently, the volume of climate-related ODA has surged. In 2011–2013,
bilateral ODA for this purpose reached more than $16 billion per year, tripling
the 2005–2007 level of $5 billion per year. In 2013, $5 billion of the ODA
funding was spent on energy generation and supply.[43] The volume of multilateral climate-related ODA that year reached $3.4 billion,[44] and was channeled
through:

- African Development Fund (channel: African Development Bank)
- Asian Development Fund (channel: Asian Development Bank (ADB))
- Inter-American Development Bank Special Fund (channel: Inter-American
  Development Bank)
- Global Environment Facility (channel: World Bank)
- Climate Investment Funds (channel: World Bank).

Loans involve a transfer of finance for which repayment by the recipient is
required, while grant is a one-way finance. For a loan, repayment is required for
both the initial loan or principal and any interest accrued, usually over a fixed
period of installments. Since international climate finance is viewed by some as
a form of compensation or restitution owed by developed countries to developing countries, the use of loans to deliver support has been heavily criticized as it
places the burden of repayment on developing countries. Public finance loans for
energy transitions are, therefore, likely to include a high degree of concessional-
ity, which means that the loan will be delivered at the most favorable rates unlike
private sector debt. This kind of financial flow is often referred to as a concessional or soft loan. Examples of these are ADB loans to the energy sector shown
in Table 6.5.

Often, concessional loans for development are suitable for investments that
have some level of financial return, while still being below a threshold that would
attract commercial investment. Concessional loans, thus, make them suitable in
financing transition activities that have commercially uncompetitive returns on
investment and for interventions that require capital-intensive investments, such
as large-scale renewable energy systems.

Nonetheless, concessional loans are not free of conditions. To be granted
access, developing country borrowers are still assessed as to their capacity and
ability to meet future financial commitments. In many instances, many less developed countries still have little capacity to repay even soft loans. Loan defaults,
therefore, are not uncommon.

Table 6.5 Examples of ODA supporting sustainable energy transitions in developing Asia

Type	Year approved	Recipient country	ODA	Purpose	Amount, in $ million
Loan	2013	India	Hydro and Wind Power Development Project	To support NSL Renewable Power Private Ltd.	1,500
Loan	2013	Indonesia	Sarulla geothermal energy generation project	To support Sarulla Operations Ltd.	954
Loan	2010	Bhutan	On-grids and off-grid electrification projects	To support hydro, solar, wind, and biogas projects	21.59
Grant	2012	Indonesia	Scaling up renewable energy access in Eastern Indonesia	To improve institutional capacity to design and manage rural energy access programs	2

Source: extracted by the author from Asian Development Bank 2016, 'ADB Project Database,' www.adb.org/projects.

Multilateral development banks (MDBs) are significant actors in channeling transition finance. Some studies, however, have shown that some MDBs are not necessarily taking the transition agenda seriously. The ADB, for instance, has, despite its support towards the transitions in the Asia and the Pacific region, continued to ramp up its investments on carbon-polluting energy systems.[45]

In spite of rising ODA volume for transition-related projects in recent years, ODA remains variable and unpredictable primarily because of its voluntary nature. Since it comes directly from national budgets of donor countries, which are also subject to many pressures, predictability and variability of ODA are also affected.

Other emergent mechanisms involving ODA such as debt-for-climate swaps open up new vehicles for supporting energy transitions. Swaps free up some of the unpaid development loans in developing countries as contributing countries agree to cancel a portion of non-performing debt obligations of a developing country in exchange for an investment in transition-related projects in that country.[46] Debt swaps are attractive for developing countries' debtors because it allows them the possibility to relieve a portion of their debts that they are unlikely to ever repay in full. These, too, allow them to free up some amounts in their national budgets and use them to support the transitions. The historical experience on debt swaps to finance environmental conservation and health projects in developing countries[47] provides a rationale and examples for increasing the future volume of debt-for-transition swaps.

Although debt swaps are likely to be able to provide short-term finance – since they do not necessarily require new institutional arrangements – the mechanism, nonetheless, is an unstable source of public finance, especially over the longer term. As developing countries progress economically, for instance, there will be less incentive for developed countries to relieve their debt.[48] Debt-for-climate swaps may also be politically difficult, given the limited successes of similar campaigns as illustrated in the Jubilee 2000 debt relief experience.[49]

In the context of the Paris Agreement, the challenge related to availability and predictability of ODA is further exacerbated when separate accounting is eventually employed between development assistance and assistance towards transition-related interventions.[50] This could result in an unbalanced volume of funds with more money flowing in for climate interventions than for development. This has tremendous implications to many developing countries where issues related to health, education, and other social services remain key development challenges.

International climate finance

The United Nations Framework Convention on Climate Change (UNFCCC) has set the stage for international financial flows for both climate adaptation and mitigation. For mitigation purposes, Parties to the UNFCCC have underscored the requirement for developed countries to 'provide new and additional financial resources to meet the agreed full costs incurred by developing country parties with their obligations . . . including for the transfer of technology.'[51] As international climate agreements evolved, major outcomes of the Conferences of the Parties (COP) to the UNFCCC have continued to underline the importance of 'new and additional' climate mitigation finance for developing countries, meaning that climate finance has to be separately delivered and accounted from traditional ODA.

The first international climate finance mechanisms are the two instruments of the Kyoto Protocol: the Clean Development Mechanism (CDM) and Joint Implementation. Both are project-based development interventions designed to achieve emissions reductions at a cheaper cost for Annex 1 countries. However, these mechanisms, especially the CDM, has been criticized as an expensive way to reduce emissions in developing countries, mainly since the price paid appears to be far higher than the average marginal abatement cost.[52] The role of CDM in the transitions, given this critique and its performance, remains unclear.

As of 13 May 2017, there are 8,464 CDM projects, of which 7,770 are registered. Of the registered projects, only 3,049 (or 39.2 per cent) have been issued certificates of emissions reduction (CER).[53] Table 6.6 shows the number of CDM sustainable energy projects in the study countries.

Between 2004 and 2013, the CDM Executive Board reported that more than 1,500 metric tons of carbon dioxide equivalent was reduced through CDM

Table 6.6 Number of CDM sustainable energy-related projects in the study countries, as of 1 April 2017

	Bhutan	Brazil	Chile	China	El Salvador	India	Indonesia	Morocco	Philippines	South Africa	Thailand	Vietnam
Biomass energy		52	13	154	2	318	17	3	6	5	29	19
Energy distribution	1	2		12		4						1
EE households				6		62				3		
EE industry		1	1	12		88	5			6		
EE own generation		4	1	227		104	2		2	8	5	3
EE service				1		27				1		
EE supply side			1	20		31	5				1	
Fossil fuel switch		6	2	37		45	5			5		
Geothermal			1	2	2		14		4			
Hydro	5	115	34	1,346	2	212	21		10	3	7	210
Landfill gas		59	18	107	2	32	19	3	5	7	6	7
Mixed renewables				4		18						
Solar		1		162		182	1	2	1	6	26	
Wind		70	20	1,519		919	7	7	4	16	3	5

Source: extracted by the author from UNEP DTU Partnership 2017, 'CDM spreadsheet,' www.cdmpipeline.org/publications/CDMStatesAndProvinces.xlsx.

projects. At least $138 billion of finance for mitigation activities was also raised in developing countries.[54]

CDM projects, however, is quickly reducing in number. In terms of submissions, CDM projects started peaking in 2005, at an average of 100 submissions per month. By mid-2011, monthly submissions averaged 200 projects. By March 2012, the number of submitted CDM projects reached its zenith at 325 projects a month. This level of monthly submissions, however, was not sustained. Beginning in April 2012, submissions started slowing down, such that by December 2012, there were less than 25 submissions. Since then, submissions have been below 25 per month. In April 2016, only four CDM projects were added to the pipeline.[55]

The declining number of submissions is linked to the lack of demand for CERs, which reflect their low prices as well as the level of use of the CDM by Annex 1 Parties to meet their mitigation commitments. Many existing CDM projects are therefore expected to face difficulties as many CERs are being cancelled.[56] Beyond the lack of demand, one political economy analysis about the relative decline of CDM point out to at least two causes.[57] First is the weak embedding of the governance of CDM within the wider policy processes and structures of decision-making. Second is about CDM being seen as a business opportunity, where the private sector can claim credit for projects that would have happened anyway. As shown in Table 6.6, some examples of these are the proliferations of landfill gas projects, where all study countries, but Bhutan, have claimed additionality.

As the CDM decreases in relevance, other mechanisms to support transition initiatives in developing countries have been pursued. During the 15th COP in Copenhagen, Parties have established the Green Climate Fund. In the following year during the COP in Cancun, the Parties formally established the Fund. The Fund, which aims to raise $100 billion per year by 2020, became the centerpiece of long-term financing for international climate change response. The design of the Fund, nonetheless, is far from perfect, with persistent issues including where to source it, what the role of the private sector is, and how transparent its Board is.[58]

To address the issue regarding sources of fund, the United Nations Secretary General created the High Level Advisory Group on Climate Change Financing (AGF) in 2010 to study some potential sources. In its report, the AGF identified the following:[59]

- Auctions of emission allowances and domestic carbon taxes in developed countries based on a carbon price in the range of $20 to $25 per ton of carbon dioxide equivalent in 2020. Up to 10 per cent of total revenues could be allocated to the Fund from these mechanisms, or, by AGF estimates, about $30 billion.
- Carbon price on international transport. Between 25 and 50 per cent can be earmarked to the Fund, or about $10 billion.
- Redeployment of fossil fuel subsidies in developed country, or some form of financial transaction tax. Can contribute up to $10 billion.
- Multilateral development banks can contribute up to $11 billion.

- Direct budget contributions based on existing public finance sources.
- Private capital.

The AGF recommendations, however, are yet to be considered. Revenue sources for the Green Climate Fund remains unclear as of this writing. By March 2017, the Fund has raised only $10.13 billion equivalent in pledges. The top five pledges have come from the USA ($3 billion), Japan ($1.5 billion), UK ($1.2 billion), France ($1 billion), and Germany ($1 billion).[60] The highly unstable political landscape in some of these key pledgers further threatens the stability and predictability of the Green Climate Fund. While the Fund promises a new vital channel for financing the transitions, developing countries need to extensively locate and tap other sources of international finance. These could be done through bilateral or multilateral arrangements.

Foreign direct investments

In addition to the usual foreign assistance made as either a loan or a grant, international private investors may, depending upon national rules and investment climate among other considerations, invest directly in sustainable energy in developing countries. Foreign direct investments (FDI) are forms of equity transfer by multinational corporations seeking to establish or expand their operations overseas. FDI offers an opportunity for voluntary private sector engagement in the transition and is expected to play a crucial role in the transitions.[61] The potential for FDI contributions, however, is heavily constrained since only countries with favorable investment climate tend to enjoy this privilege.

Currently, around 10 per cent of global investment in developing countries, equivalent to $170 billion per year, is FDI. Only $2 billion of this total, however, have flowed in less developed countries.[62] The reason for this is straightforward and already mentioned: many least developed countries often fail to meet stringent criteria, which places developing countries as riskier locations to do business.

The reasons for higher risk perception towards investing in developing countries are complex, but it is mainly because of the scarcity of information and lack of sound data. Altogether, investment risks, market imperfections, policy uncertainties, and institutional limitations act in concert to hamper FDI flows to developing countries. Two indices that reflect, in some ways, the magnitude of these risks, imperfections, and uncertainties are depth of credit information index and the ease of doing business index (see Table 6.7). The depth of credit information index measures the rules affecting the scope, accessibility, and quality of credit information available through public registry or private bureau to facilitate lending decisions. The index ranges from 0 to 8, with higher values indicating availability of more credit information in a given country. Higher levels of credit information will generally attract investment.[63] The ease of doing business' index, which ranks economies from 1 to 189 with first place being the best, averages the country's percentile rankings on ten topics covered in the World Bank's Doing

Table 6.7 Indices of imperfections in the capital markets of the study
countries

	Depth of credit information index		Ease of doing business index	
	2013	2016	2015	2016
Bhutan	6	6	71	73
Brazil	7	7	121	123
Chile	6	6	55	57
China	6	8	80	78
El Salvador	7	4	86	95
India	7	7	131	130
Indonesia	6	6	106	91
Morocco	6	7	68	68
Philippines	5	5	99	99
South Africa	8	7	72	74
Thailand	6	7	46	46
Vietnam	6	7	91	82

Source: extracted by the author from The World Bank 2016, 'Depth of credit information,' http://data.worldbank.org/indicator/IC.CRD.INFO.XQ, and 'Ease of doing business,' http://data.worldbank.org/indicator/IC.BUS.EASE.XQ.

Business project. The ranking on each topic is the simple average of the percentile ranking on its component indicators. A high ranking (a low numerical rank) means that the regulatory environment is conducive to business operations.[64]

Given that most FDI will only flow to countries with favorable investment climate, the task for policymakers in developing countries would be to design attractive policy mechanisms, strengthen institutions, and aggressively open up markets for entrants in the sustainable energy sector.

South-South cooperation

International support, either private (FDI) or public (ODA), however, is no longer an exclusive province of developed countries. Over time, some developing countries have also started providing key assistance. Many times, these contributors have more appetite for risky investments than traditional north-south providers. South-South cooperation, or cooperation between and among developing countries, is already becoming a source of energy development finance. However, it remains unclear whether support for sustainable energy technologies will increase from this source. The fastest growing energy investment of this type has been support from China.

In Sub-Saharan Africa, for example, Chinese funding towards investments in electric power generation totaled $10.41 trillion between 2001 and 2013.[65] Many of these deals have been concluded for hydroelectric power plants, which, on average, have sizes between 9.6 and 600 MW. In all of Africa, approximately 63 per cent of all China-funded projects are hydroelectric-related. Between 1990 and 2014, a World Bank study finds that China has funded 23 projects of this kind in Africa[66] (see Table 6.8 for examples).

China's development lending funds for energy purposes are already of high volume. Between 2007 and 2014, in a matter of seven years, Chinese funds already

Table 6.8 Examples of China-funded hydroelectricity projects in Sub-Saharan Africa, 1990–2014

Country	Project	Capacity, MW	China funding, $ millions
Angola	CIF Cement	35	73.4
Cameroon	Memve'ele	201.2	637
Central African Republic	Boali III	9.6	25
Democratic Republic of Congo	Zongo II	150	367.5
Democratic Republic of Congo	Imboulou	120	341
Democratic Republic of Congo	Liouesso	19.2	40.3
Cote d'Ivoire	Soubre	270	571
Equatorial Guinea	Djiploho	120	257
Ethiopia	Fan	97	186
Ethiopia	Genale	245	451
Ethiopia	Gigel Gibe III	400	500
Gabon	Poubara	160	398
Ghana	Bui	400	621
Guinea	Kaleta	240	446.2
Mali	Gouina	147	467
Nigeria	Zungeru	700	1,293
Sudan	Merowe	12.5	87
Togo/Benin	Adjarala	147	308
Uganda	Isimba	183	556
Uganda	Karuma	600	1,688.4
Zambia	Kariba	360	279
Zambia	Lunzua	14.8	31.5
Zimbabwe	Kariba	300	389

Source: extracted from Eberhard, A, Gratwick, K, Morella, E & Antmann, P 2016, *Independent Power Projects in Sub-Saharan Africa: Lessons from Five Key Countries*, The World Bank Group: Washington D.C., Table D.1, p. 280–281.

represent half of the total available funds for global energy development finance.[67] During this period, China's contribution to the energy sector in developing countries reached a volume of $117.6 billion – almost equal to the combined finance provided by all MDBs.[68] In one estimate about $43 billion of the 2005–2014 funds were channeled to Europe and Central Asia, including Russia, $33 billion to Latin America and the Caribbean, $18 billion to Africa, $17.5 billion to South Asia, and $16 billion to East Asia and the Pacific.[69] Majority of these loans, about 66 per cent, however, are for fossil fuel projects, mostly coal. Hydropower projects constitute 27 per cent. Only 1 per cent is for wind projects. These statistics sit in contrast with the proportion of support provided by MDBs: mostly on hydro, growing in renewables, and reducing in fossil fuels.[70]

Chinese energy development funds were coursed through Chinese 'policy' banks, which include the Chinese Export-Import Bank, Industrial and Commerce Bank of China, China Development Bank, China Construction Bank, and Bank of China. In addition to these lending channels, China also supports other multilateral South-South initiatives to further institutionalize its development finance arm. China is leading, for example, the creation of two new MDBs: the BRICS' countries' New Development Bank, and the 23-Asian countries' Asian Infrastructure Investment Bank.

Given these developments, China is poised to be a major actor in finance provision for energy sector development. Whether it will assume a key role in sustainable energy transitions finance in developing countries, however, remains to be seen. Nonetheless, China has already demonstrated that it can support projects of this kind. In Ethiopia, for instance, two wind farm projects have already benefited from Chinese funding: the 50 MW Adama project ($123 million), the 51 MW Messabo Harrena project ($127 million), and the 100 MW Adama II project ($293.3 million).[71] Bringing this kind of project to scale while reducing support for fossil fuel and large-hydroelectric projects is now the new imperative for Chinese energy development interventions.

Regional transition finance

One key aspect of the financing turn for supporting the transition is to expand investment flows through regional trade and economic integration. This process is aimed at attracting and aggregating 'greener' economic activities and practices from one country, alongside that of others. One example of regional funding is the Energy and Environment Partnership (EEP) Mekong aimed at improving energy access and energy services in the Mekong region through the deployment of sustainable energy hardware. EEP Mekong facilitates inter-country cooperation, dialogue, and experience sharing. It also provides funding for pilot and demonstration projects, (pre)feasibility and strategic studies, capacity building and information sharing.[72]

New trade agreements at the regional level can also be used as new platforms for driving the turn in transition finance. Transition-responsive governments may look at how financial transactions, particularly those that cross borders, for instance, can enhance their environmental quality. Governments play a key role in meeting this end by instituting arrangements in the financial sector beyond their usual role on prudential oversight. This can be done through information and risk management, and by internalizing environmental stress testing for all financial institutions as key component of new trade deals.

6.4. Mobilizing innovative finance

New business models to support the transitions have recently emerged in many developing countries. Their emergence is essential in the financing turn and needs to be strongly supported. Some of these approaches include philanthropy, crowdfunding, small-scale public-private partnerships, microfinance, energy service companies (ESCOs), 'negawatts' sales, pay-as-you-go schemes, and one-stop-shops. When effectively deployed, these mechanisms have been proven to be able to provide some essential funds to support the transition.

Philanthropy can be used for activities that offer zero or low returns on investment. Large philanthropic organizations, which generate their revenues through an initial endowment that is managed in perpetuity, represent new, but limited, private sources of capital for some of the activities of the transitions. These include capacity building and some limited amounts for technology demonstration projects.

Crowdfunding platforms supporting renewable energy projects have recently attracted new retail investors and are fast becoming more mainstream means for raising money for development. Crowdfunding enables small and medium enterprises to raise capital from many small investors in exchange for equity, payments, or products, or a combination.[73] Crowdfunding was used, for instance, to raise funds for various Sustainable Energy for All efforts.[74]

Small-scale public-private partnerships for supporting micro and small-scale transition projects have also shown promise.[75] India's experience on leveraging public and private investments in its rural electrification efforts have successfully helped in providing electricity to more than 32 million households over the last decade.[76] In India's Uttar Pradesh, about 23 solar mini-grids were deployed in 2011 and 2012 under a build, operate, and maintain model where local operators run a system built by private firms.[77] In Nepal, some community-owned micro-hydro projects have been linked to the grid through a partnership between community owners and the Nepal Electricity Authority.[78] In Indonesia, a public-private partnership was used to develop Cinta Mekar, a 120 kW micro-hydro system, with cost born equally by a private company, a multilateral agency, and IBEKA, a not-for profit social enterprise.[79]

One emerging model of public-private partnership is the United Nations Economic and Social Commission for Asia and the Pacific's (ESCAP) pro-poor public-private partnership approach (5Ps). The model, a special purpose vehicle for operating and maintaining small-scale renewable energy systems, had been piloted in Laos and Nepal. The Nepal pilot project comprises solar PV and micro-hydro plants in Makwanpur and Tanahun districts; 5Ps is established with a 60 per cent private sector stake and a 40 per cent community stake. Here, the public sector owns no asset.[80]

ESCOs have been used to maximize energy efficiency improvements in developing countries. In Thailand, for example, ESCOs have become more common.[81] Zambia's PV-ESCO project is another example. Starting in 1996 as a cooperation project between the Stockholm Environment Institute, the Swedish International Development Agency, and Zambia's Ministry of Energy, the project first benefited communities in Nyimba, Chipata, and Lundazi with 50-Wp solar panels. Customers from these towns pay a monthly service fee for operation and maintenance, and funds towards a savings account for purchases of new batteries.[82]

In some developing countries, utilities and other organizations are allowed to sell 'negawatts.' Amory Lovins coined the term to refer to the energy saved because of efficient actions. For example, utilities could invest in energy efficient heating, ventilation, and air conditioning systems in clients' buildings and recoup the cost plus a profit by charging that client the same amount as prior to the installation for a fixed period, even though consumption has declined.

Microfinance or microcredit schemes allow purchasers such as small businesses, co-operatives, or households to take out a small loan from a credit institution to cover the cost of renewable energy technology purchase. The experience in Bangladesh with Grameen Shakti illustrates that microcredit can become a vehicle for the transitions, especially in achieving universal energy access.[83] In Thailand, a community network in Deng forest developed a microfinance scheme to distribute solar home systems and floating dome biogas digesters.[84]

Pay-as-you-go schemes provide financing through a metering system that allows consumers to pay in advance for energy access in small and regular installments. While most recent examples are used to provide access in underserved urban areas, these schemes can also be used in rural areas where customers can be charged a small upfront fee for a solar charger kit, for example. Consumers can then pay, either in advance or on a regular basis, depending on their consumption.[85] India's Solar Lantern Project, which used a 'fee-for-service' model, alongside a microfinance approach, was successful in distributing solar lantern kits in the rural areas of Andhra Pradesh, Himachal Pradesh, Maharasthra, Punjab, Rajasthan, and West Bengal without access to lighting services.[86] In the Thai-Myanmar border, an NGO called SunSawang are distributing solar home systems for a fee.[87] Other one-stop-shop schemes go beyond supplying renewable energy home systems to providing credit to pay for the systems.

6.5.   Conclusion

Accelerating the transitions requires a financing turn. The substantial transition cost entails that mechanisms and approaches for mobilizing transition finance are designed and executed strategically. This chapter described a portfolio approach to mobilizing transition finance in developing countries, which has to simultaneously occur across scales – from local to national to international – using public, private, and hybrid financing streams. Some key aspects of the financing turn include the following.

Access to affordable financing and flexible lending is essential. Scaling sustainable energy technologies, regardless of whether it is for distributed or utility scale deployment, are capital intensive – both for manufacturers of key components and for consumers who purchase this hardware. Funding and financing vehicles that reach target consumers, therefore, remain essential. Accessible, affordable, flexible, stable, and reliable finance is necessary for supporting transition-related activities: from achieving universal energy access to harvesting energy efficiency gains to rapid deployment of sustainable energy hardware. In many developing countries, this requires ready access to capital, which further entails the need for flexibility in lending terms. Examples of such approaches include zero to minimal collateral requirement, staged repayment terms, reduced interest rates, and preferential treatment. Ensuring the financial sustainability of transition-related hardware and systems, especially post-deployment, is also essential.

Sound planning, effective management practices, and adequate institutional capacity to facilitate transition finance are necessary. Although the availability of finance is important, efforts to remove policy barriers are equally necessary and need to be simultaneously accomplished. Many developing countries will need additional support to strengthen the capacity of their financial institutions: public, private, non-state, and financial intermediaries, as well as those of end-users. The goal is to develop sound planning mechanisms to facilitate capital-intensive investments, backed by appropriate risk mitigation instruments, in terms that capital providers and end-users can clearly understand.

All possible sources of funds need to be explored, including new channels provided by international climate finance mechanism, South-South capital, and emerging innovative business models. Access to new sources of funding becomes more important, especially in the absence of strong environment for private investment in many developing countries. Thus far, China-funded investments have been largely instrumental in funding hydropower projects in developing countries, but, at the same time, attract controversy.[88] UNFCCC mechanisms, such as the Green Climate Fund, can be tapped to fund the transitions; however, the Fund would first require stabilizing its funding sources. In addition, a number of emerging innovative systems, particularly for addressing energy access gaps in households and communities, have to be supported.

The fragmented sources of finance entail further challenge for developing countries, especially for those with weak institutional capacity. There are multiple actors involved in financing sustainable energy systems often with incoherent purposes and delivery strategies.[89] This needs addressing. Strong institutional capacity within developing countries is essential so that sustainable energy finance is efficiently tapped, channeled to its intended recipients, and monitored for their effectiveness and efficiency. Such institutions would also be necessary for tracking down the volume of finance that is flowing in, as well as for accounting them, whether they are 'new and additional finance' – a key aspect of the UNFCCC.

Notes

1 US Energy Information Administration 2017, 'Levelized cost and levelized avoided cost of new generation resources in the Annual Energy Outlook 2017,' April, www.eia.gov/forecasts/aeo/pdf/electricity_generation.pdf.
2 Ibid.
3 Ibid.
4 Ibid.
5 German Advisory Council on Global Change 2011, *World in Transition: A Social Contract for Sustainability*, WBGU: Berlin, Germany.
6 Jacobson, M & Delucchi, M 2011, 'Providing all global energy with wind, water, and solar power, Part II: Reliability, system and transmission costs, and policies,' *Energy Policy*, vol. 39, pp. 1170–1190; also through personal communication with Mark Jacobson in 2015.
7 Jacobson, M, et al. 2017, '100% clean and renewable wind, water, and sunlight (WWS) all-sector energy roadmaps for 139 countries in the world,' 7 April, https://web.stanford.edu/group/efmh/jacobson//Articles/I/CountriesWWS.pdf.
8 United Nations Framework Convention on Climate Change 2008, *Investment and Financial Flows to Address Climate Change: An Update*, FCCC/TP/2008/7, http://unfccc.int/resource/docs/2008/tp/07.pdf.
9 World Bank 2010, 'Generating the funding needed for mitigation and adaptation,' *World Development Report 2010*, World Bank: Washington, DC.
10 Stern, N 2006, *The Stern Review on the Economics of Climate Change*, Government of the United Kingdom: London, UK.
11 United Nations Development Program 2008, *Human Development Report 2007/8: Fighting Climate Change*, UNDP: New York.
12 Granoff, I, Hogarth, JR & Miller, A 2016, 'Nested barriers to low-carbon infrastructure investment,' *Nature Climate Change*, vol. 6, pp. 1065–1071.
13 Marquardt, J, Steinbacher, K & Schreurs, M 2016, 'Driving force or forced transition? The role of development cooperation in promoting energy transitions in the Philippines and Morocco,' *Journal of Cleaner Production*, vol. 128, pp. 22–33.
14 UN Secretary General High-Level Advisory Group on Climate Change Financing 2010, *Report of the SecretaryGeneral's HighLevel Advisory Group on Climate Change Financing*, 5 November, www.un.org/wcm/webdav/site/climatechange/shared/Documents/AGF_reports/AGF_Final_Report.pdf.
15 The World Bank 2011, *Mobilising Climate Finance: A Paper Prepared at the Request of G20 Finance Ministers*, World Bank Group, IMF, OECD & Regional Development Banks: Washington, DC, USA.
16 Huifeng, H & Huang, K 2015, 'China's emissions trading scheme to be a "game changer" . . . eventually, experts say,' *South China Morning Post*, 3 November, http://www.scmp.com/news/china/economy/article/1875125/chinas-emissions-trading-scheme-be-game-changer-eventually.
17 Nene, N 2015, '2015 budget speech of the Minister of Finance, Republic of South Africa,' 25 February, www.treasury.gov.za/documents/national%20budget/2015/speech/speech.pdf.
18 International Monetary Fund 2015, *How Large are Global Energy Subsidies?*, 29 June, www.imf.org/external/np/fad/subsidies/data/codata.xlsx.
19 Budya, H & Arofat, MY 2011, 'Providing cleaner energy access in Indonesia through the megaproject of kerosene conversion to LPG,' *Energy Policy*, vol. 39, pp. 7575–7586.
20 Andadari, RK, Nulder, P & Rietveld, P 2014, 'Energy poverty reduction by fuel switching: Impact evaluation of the LPG conversion program in Indonesia,' *Energy Policy*, vol. 66, pp. 436–449.
21 Including sovereign, currency, and credit risks, as well as the social risks at the project level, such as NIMBY-ism.

22 Global Commission on the Economy and Climate 2014, *Better Growth Better Climate: The New Climate Economy Report*, World Resources Institute: Washington, DC.

23 See Reserve Bank of India 2016, 'Priority sector lending,' www.rbi.org.in/Scripts/FAQView.aspx?Id=87.

24 International Renewable Energy Agency 2016, *Policies and Regulations for Private Sector Renewable Energy Mini-Grids*, IRENA: Abu Dhabi, United Arab Emirates, p. 62.

25 Following, for example, an approach called Sustainable Green Management System, see Mustapha, MA, Manan, ZA & Alwi, SRW 2017, 'Sustainable Green Management System (SGMS): An integrated approach towards organizational sustainability,' *Journal of Cleaner Production*, vol. 146, pp. 158–172.

26 Climate Bonds Initiative 2016, '2015 Green bond market roundup,' www.climatebonds.net/files/files/2015%20GB%20Market%20Roundup%2003A.pdf.

27 Ibid.

28 Gruic, B & Schrimpf, A 2014, 'Cross-border investments in global debt market since the crisis,' *Bank for International Settlements (BIS) Quarterly Review: International Banking and Financial Market Developments*, March, pp. 18–19.

29 Burrows, M 2014, 'Keynote speech: Investing in sustainable landscapes,' *Forests Asia Summit 2013*, video recording available at www.youtube.com/watch?v=PeVYJ1wC3iY.

30 Kidney, S 2015, 'Bonds and climate change,' *CFA Institute Conference Proceedings Quarterly*, vol. 32, pp. 44–53.

31 Kidney, S 2014, 'USD 2tn of investors back Green & Climate Bonds to tap USD 100tn bond market for climate solutions, call on corps & govts to deliver projects for finance,' 23 September, www.climatebonds.net/2014/09/usd2tn-investors-back-green-climate-bonds-tap-usd100tn-bond-market-climate-solutions-call.

32 Dai, W, Kidney, S & Sonerud, B 2016, *Roadmap for China: Scaling Up Green Bond Market Issuance*, Climate Bonds Initiative, www.climatebonds.net/files/files/CBI-IISD-Paper2-Final-01B_A4.pdf.

33 Exim Bank is one of the most powerful actors in terms of financial flows for Chinese hydropower, according to Tan-Mullins, M, Urban, F & Mang, G 2017, 'Evaluating the behavior of Chinese stakeholders engaged in large hydropower projects in Asia and Africa,' *The China Quarterly*, vol. 230, pp. 464–488.

34 Ibid., p. 7.

35 Delina, L 2016, *Strategies for Rapid Climate Mitigation: Wartime Mobilisation as Policy Model?*, Routledge-Earthscan: Abingdon, Oxon, UK & New York, USA.

36 See wheel.renewfund.com.

37 See cleanenergyfinancecorp.com.au.

38 Tongsopit, S, et al. 2016, 'Business models and financing options for a rapid scale-up of rooftop solar power systems in Thailand,' *Energy Policy*, vol. 95, pp. 447–457.

39 Delina, L 2017, 'Multilateral development banking in a fragmented climate finance system: Shifting priorities in energy finance at the Asian Development Bank,' *International Environmental Agreements: Politics, Law and Economics*, vol. 17, pp. 73–88.

40 Nakhooda, S 2008, 'Correcting the world's greatest market failure: Climate change and the multilateral development banks,' *WRI Issue Brief (June 2008)*, World Resources Institute: Washington, DC, http://www.wri.org/sites/default/files/pdf/correcting_the_worlds_greatest_market_failure.pdf.

41 See OECD 2016, 'DAC list of ODA recipients: Effective for reporting on 2014, 2015, and 2016 flows,' www.oecd.org/dac/stats/documentupload/DAC%20List%20of%20ODA%20Recipients%202014%20final.pdf.

42 OECD 2008, 'Official development assistance: Definition and coverage,' www.oecd.org/investment/stats/officialdevelopmentassistancedefinitionandcoverage.htm.

43 CICERO and Climate Policy Initiative 2015, *Background Report on Long-Term Climate Finance*, German Federal Ministry of the Environment: Eschborn, p. 37.

44 Ibid., pp. 37–38.

45 Delina, L 2017, 'Multilateral development banking in a fragmented climate finance system: Shifting priorities in energy finance at the Asian Development Bank,' *International Environmental Agreements: Politics, Law and Economics*, vol. 17, pp. 73–88.

46 Fenton, A, et al. 2014, 'Debt relief and financing climate change action,' *Nature Climate Change*, vol. 4, pp. 650–653.

47 Cassimon, D, Prowse, M & Essers, D 2011, 'The pitfalls and potential of debt-for-nature swaps: A US-Indonesian case study,' *Global Environmental Change*, vol. 21, pp. 93–102.

48 Doornbosh, R & Knight, ERW 2008, 'What role for public finance in international climate change mitigation,' *OECD Roundtable for Sustainable Development Discussion Paper No. SG/SD/RT (2008)3*, http://ssrn.com/abstract=1291763.

49 Fenton, A, et al. 2014, 'Debt relief and financing climate change action,' *Nature Climate Change*, vol. 4, pp. 650–653.

50 Delina, L 2011, 'Asian Development Bank's support for clean energy,' *Climate Policy*, vol. 11, pp. 1350–1366.

51 See United Nations Framework Convention on Climate Change 1992, Article 4(3); also see Articles 4(5) and 11(5).

52 Wagner, G, et al. 2009, 'Docking into a global carbon market: Clean Investment Budgets to finance low-carbon economic development,' in D Helm & C Hepburn (Eds.), *The Economics and Politics of Climate Change*, Oxford University Press: Oxford, UK, pp. 385–408.

53 UNEP DTU Partnership 2017, 'Number of CDM projects each month,' http://cdmpipeline.org/overview.htm#3.

54 See CDM Executive Board 2014, *Executive Board Annual Report: Clean Development Mechanism*, UNFCCC: Bonn, Germany.

55 UNEP-DTU Partnership 2016, 'CDM projects by host region,' www.cdmpipeline.org/cdm-projects-region.htm.

56 United Nations Framework Convention on Climate Change 2015, *Annual Report of the Executive Board of the Clean Development Mechanism to the Conference of Parties Serving as the Meeting of the Parties to the Kyoto Protocol*, FCCC/KP/CMP2015/5, http://unfccc.int/resource/docs/2015/cmp11/eng/05.pdf.

57 Newell, P 2014, 'The global political economy of the Clean Development Mechanism,' *Global Environmental Politics*, vol. 12, pp. 49–67.

58 See for example Kumar, S 2015, 'Green Climate Fund faces slew of criticism,' *Nature*, vol. 527, pp. 419–420.

59 United Nations Secretary General High-Level Advisory Group on Climate Change Financing 2010, *Report of the SecretaryGeneral's HighLevel Advisory Group on Climate Change Financing*, 5 November, www.un.org/wcm/webdav/site/climatechange/shared/Documents/AGF_reports/AGF_Final_Report.pdf.

60 Green Climate Fund 2017, 'Pledge tracker,' www.greenclimate.fund/documents/20182/24868/Status_of_Pledges.pdf/eef538d3-2987-4659-8c7c-5566ed6afd19, as of 3 March.

61 Paramati, SR, Apergis, N & Ummalla, M 2017, 'Financing clean energy projects through domestic and foreign capital: The role of political cooperation among the EU, the G20 and OECD countries,' *Energy Economics*, vol. 61, pp. 62–71.

62 Delina, L 2011, 'Asian Development Bank's support for clean energy,' *Climate Policy*, vol. 11, pp. 1350–1366.

63 The World Bank 2016, 'Depth of credit information,' http://data.worldbank.org/indicator/IC.CRD.INFO.XQ.

64 The World Bank 2016, 'Ease of doing business,' http://data.worldbank.org/indicator/IC.BUS.EASE.XQ.

65 Eberhard, A, et al. 2016, *Independent Power Projects in Sub-Saharan Africa: Lessons from Five Key Countries*, The World Bank Group: Washington, DC, Table A.2, p. 269.

66 Brautigam, D, Hwang, J & Wang, L 2015, 'Chinese-financed hydropower projects in Sub-Saharan Africa,' *Policy Brief No. 8*, The SAIS China-Africa Research Initiative at Johns Hopkins University: Washington, DC.
67 Gallagher, KP, Kamal, R & Wang, Y 2016, 'Fueling growth and financing risk: The benefits and risks of China's development finance in the global energy sector,' *Global Economic Governance Initiative Working Paper No. 2*, Boston University: Boston, Massachusetts.
68 Ibid.
69 Ibid., Table 3.
70 Ibid., Table 6.
71 Eberhard, A, et al. 2016, *Independent Power Projects in Sub-Saharan Africa: Lessons from Five Key Countries*, The World Bank Group: Washington, DC, Table D.1, pp. 280–281.
72 See eepmekong.org.
73 Cumming, D, Leboeuf, G & Schwienbacher, A 2017, 'Crowdfunding cleantech,' *Energy Economics*, vol. 65, pp. 292–303.
74 See Indiegogo 2016, 'Energy Access Practitioner Network,' www.indiegogo.com/partners/eapn.
75 See examples in Sovacool, BK 2013, 'Expanding renewable energy access with pro-poor public-private partnerships in the developing world,' *Energy Strategy Reviews*, vol. 1, pp. 181–192.
76 Banerjee, M, Rehman, IH & Tiwari, J 2017, 'Solar-based decentralized energy solution: A case of entrepreneur based model from rural India,' in W Yan & W Galloway (Eds.), *Rethinking Resilience, Adaptation and Transformation in a Time of Change*, Springer: Cham, Switzerland, pp. 341–356.
77 Srivastava, AK 2013, 'Solar minigrids in rural areas of Uttar Pradesh,' Ministry of New and Renewable Energy, Government of India, http://mnre.gov.in/file-manager/akshay-urja/ january-february-2013/EN/16–17.pdf.
78 International Renewable Energy Agency 2016, *Policies and Regulations for Private Sector Renewable Energy Mini-Grids*, IRENA: Abu Dhabi, United Arab Emirates, p. 62.
79 Sovacool, BK 2013, 'Expanding renewable energy access with pro-poor public-private partnerships in the developing world,' *Energy Strategy Reviews*, vol. 1, pp. 181–192.
80 United Nations Economic and Social Commission for Asia and the Pacific n.d., *5P Approach-Partnerships for a Resilient Energy Future*, ESCAP: Bangkok, http://css.escwa.org.lb/SDPD/3583/S4D3.pdf.
81 Streitferdt, V, Chirarattananon, S & Du Pont, P 2016, 'Lessons learned from studying initiatives to support energy efficiency finance in Thailand from 1992 to 2014,' *Energy Efficiency*, doi:10.1007/s12053–016–9492–1.
82 Lemaire, X 2009, 'Fee-for-service companies for rural electrification with photovoltaic systems: The case of Zambia,' *Energy for Sustainable Development*, vol. 13, pp. 18–23.
83 Sovacool, BK & Drupady, IM 2011, 'Summoning earth and fire: The energy development implications of Grameen Shakti (GS) in Bangladesh,' *Energy*, vol. 36, pp. 4445–4459; Scott, I 2017, 'A business model for success: Enterprises serving the base of the pyramid with off-grid solar lighting,' *Renewable and Sustainable Energy Reviews*, vol. 70, pp. 50–55.
84 Author's fieldwork in Thailand, November 2016 to January 2017.
85 Scott, I 2017, 'A business model for success: Enterprises serving the base of the pyramid with off-grid solar lighting,' *Renewable and Sustainable Energy Reviews*, vol. 70, pp. 50–55.
86 Rao, PSC, et al. 2009, 'Energy microfinance intervention for below poverty line households in India,' *Energy Policy*, vol. 37, pp. 1694–1712.
87 Author's fieldwork in Thailand, November 2016 to January 2017.

88 These interventions are obviously contested following these projects' impacts on societies and the environment, see for example Tan-Mullins, M, Urban, F & Mang, G 2017, 'Evaluating the behavior of Chinese stakeholders engaged in large hydropower projects in Asia and Africa,' *The China Quarterly*, vol. 230, pp. 464–488.
89 Pickering, J, Betzold, C & Skovgaard, J 2017, 'Special issue: Managing fragmentation and complexity in the emerging system of international climate finance,' *International Environmental Agreements: Politics, Law and Economics*, vol. 17, pp. 1–16.

7 Institutional turn

To accelerate sustainable energy transitions, many developing countries need to overcome a key challenge: their relatively weak and fragmented institutional arrangements. Developing countries need to create and sustain an institutional environment that leads to cohesive and effective coordination of many transition-related activities as they are produced across spaces by multiple actors and institutions. This requires an institutional turn in ways that institutions are currently arranged. Institutions – being normative and dynamic structures, socially constructed, unique, grounded in particular histories, and housed in distinctive cultures – need to be harnessed to the imperative of heterogeneously processed transitions.

Critical to the institutional turn necessary for accelerating the transitions in developing countries is the imperative to employ a variety of internally and externally driven approaches to trigger institutional change. Internally, institutions need to streamline their structures, activities and programs as well as strengthen the capacity of their workforce. Externally, institutions need to strengthen partnerships and other collaborative arrangements across a variety of transition actors that are contributing to a multitude of transition solutions and to systematically link them. To provide developing countries some guidance, this chapter describes how institutions involved in the transition could look like in the future (7.1), how these institutions could be harnessed and linked so that they produce better decisions, and how transition interventions ought to be delivered to reach higher level of success (7.2).

7.1. Imagined transition institutions

Transition institutions need to be flexible in their structural design and intervention approaches but key is to create explicit synergy between development goals and climate policy. These approaches include, but are not limited to, developing policy; instituting regulations; legislating the transition; opening up new markets; building new business models; promoting transition investment; financing; preparing the labor sector; enhancing the domestic manufacturing sector; connecting with other markets in a region; etc.[1]

The need for institutional flexibility stems from these heterogeneous processes,[2] as well as the diverse nature of transition activities. These approaches are produced across scales (e.g. at the household, local, community, organization, state, and national levels), by multiple actors (e.g. state and non-state actors and institutions, and increasingly in partnership, each with varying service needs), using a variety of approaches (e.g. information sharing, financing, bottom-up such as community oriented and cooperative-like systems), both traditional (e.g. using public funds through grants) and hybrid (e.g. financing mechanisms that involve both public and private resources) (see Table 7.1 for a broad illustration of this complexity).

Controversies are becoming common given that the institutions of the transitions can also be considered as an 'institutional complex.'[3] In this prism, the actors and institutions participating in the transition have different characteristics (whether an institution with established norms, or a newly set-up organization with informal rules), constituencies (whether public or private or hybrid), level of governance (determining spatial scope whether local, national, or international, as well as rural or urban), and subject matter (such as service needs, e.g. education (providing electricity to a school), agriculture (pumping irrigation water), small and medium size enterprise (efficient technologies), transport (better fuel efficiency), or industries (efficient heat generation).[4] Different decision-makers, therefore, will have different informational needs, will have different imaginaries of the futures of energy, and will have different approaches to particular challenges. Aligning and coordinating these multiplicities is one key challenge in the governance of transitions.[5] Using more plural approaches is imperative not only in bringing about multiple pathways for change but also in making visible the political pressures, inherent interests, and power dynamics.[6] Plurality is key for the design of more sophisticated transition institutions.

Welcoming heterogeneity bridges tensions and contestations, yet they need to be effectively managed and coordinated. This entails new forms and types of challenges that institutions have to systematically, reflexively, and inclusively negotiate. Building upon the previous chapters, which scoped and highlighted the heterogeneity of the hardware technology, policy, and financing approaches, this chapter attempts to envisage how institutions in developing countries can make sense of these arrangements, negotiate resulting tensions, and become successful in their interventions.

In developing countries, these approaches to new institutional arrangements will be dependent upon existing capacities, development levels, natural endowments, human and financial resources, the level of public engagement, and the quality and strength of interconnections between state and non-state actors, among others. Because these variables are also heterogeneous across countries, countries will develop and strengthen their transition institutions differently.[7] Even within a country itself, the transition will most likely be pursued in multiple directions and pathways across various levels of governance. For example, city-level institutions have different institutional needs compared to those at the national-level. These differences extend in terms of the ways in which capacities need to be developed and strengthened, tensions are to be negotiated and settled,

Table 7.1 A broad illustration of the institutional complexity of the energy transition architecture

Constituency	Level of governance		
	Local	*National*	*Regional and International*
Public	Local governments (e.g. City of Johannesburg)	Ministries (of Energy, of Environment, of Trade, of Finance) Regulators (e.g. Philippine Energy Regulatory Commission) National development banks (e.g. State Bank of India, China's Export-Import Bank) Bureaus and other streamlined agencies (e.g. India's Bureau of Energy Efficiency) National universities Research institutes	United Nations agencies (UNFCCC, Regional Commissions) International organizations (e.g. International Renewable Energy Agency) Regional energy centers (e.g. ASEAN Centre for Energy) Multilateral development banks (e.g. World Bank, African Development Bank, Asian Development Bank) European Union Green Climate Fund
Private	Households Community-based energy co-operatives Women's groups Microcredit groups Consumer groups Energy service companies (ESCOs)	Energy project developers Commercial banks Private development banks (e.g. Grameen Bank) Research institutes Private colleges and universities Federation of electricity co-operatives Independent power producers ESCOs	Multinational corporations International NGOs International philanthropy organizations (e.g. William and Belinda Gates Foundation) Crowdfunding platforms
Hybrid	Public-private partnerships	Public-private partnerships	Public-private partnerships

short and long-term objectives are to be bridged, and risks and trade-offs are to be recognized and understood.

There are similarities, however. In developing countries, the transition needs to revolve around human development: a better quality of life for all. The focus on the well-being of people as the transitions occur raises key questions such as: whose futures matter, who makes decisions for that futures, for whom these futures are designed, who wins and who loses with the choices that decision-makers use in designing and implementing these futures, what and whose capacity needs to be developed or strengthened. While these questions seem to be simple ones, their answers require thoughtful processes since it means that while a segment of the population benefits from the transitions, there are those who will be sidestepped and marginalized. Equity, justice, and fairness, therefore, are values that are inherent in the transitions and should be built-in the design and structures of transition institutions.

As transitions occur across multiple scales, these built-in mechanisms for facilitating stronger, effective and high-quality public engagement that link several actors of multiple transitions become more essential.[8] The level of engagement required for successful and accelerated sustainable energy transitions in developing countries requires that these processes and exercises go beyond mere public consultations. This means that actors of the transitions – especially end-users and recipients of development interventions in developing countries – have to be effectively mobilized and engaged in new institutional arrangements. Their engagement runs from the design of the project (including during the initial framing of the issue, during the identification of data and information needs,[9] during the discussions on risk, and uncertainty management) to its implementation (or construction) to its operations and management to its evaluation and, finally, to its decommissioning (if relevant).

Institutionalizing public engagement with the transitions, however, is not a simple affair. The multiplicity of actors involved in the energy production and consumption sectors, as well those between them (e.g. regulators, funders, etc.), means that transition institutions need to put a premium on the recognition that the transitions will involve people-to-people interactions.[10] As these processes occur, therefore, it is only prudent that new institutional arrangements have mechanisms to intelligently understand the underlying play of power and interests as they pan out in transition activities, exercises, and projects.[11] Such built-in mechanisms are vital since these various kinds of power dynamics have the potential to either realize or suppress the transitions.[12]

Power, nonetheless, is a contested and problematic concept in itself. Its definition goes beyond the colloquial meaning of the term to mean the exercise of some form of social control to one that has to be recognized and understood 'in a more nuanced and qualified guise: as 'asymmetrically structured agency.'[13] Here, agency refers to the various kinds of capacity involved in the shaping and performance of social action – instead of controlling it. Power, thus, is asymmetrically distributed, dynamic, and relational. In other words, it is multidimensional and complex. And as agency flows in the multiple contours of the transition landscapes, tensions and contestations occur: incumbents subverting change and niche actors progressively advancing the cause.[14] Future transition institutions inarguably need not only to understand and recognize these billows of power flows but also to transform what Andy Stirling calls the 'knowing and doing' of power itself.

In developing countries, the transformation of power is imperative in the institutional turn necessary for accelerating sustainable energy transitions. The most significant point of reference for doing this is to understand that the transition is really about human development: the quest for human-centered sustainable development for all. Future transition institutions, therefore, need to situate their decision-making efforts that centered on people's development needs, and not merely on technical resources. This way, decision-makers could uncover the multidimensionality that varied human experiences and attitudes have in shaping their own development pathways. This could eventually result in nudging every decision towards the most important objective of accelerating the transitions.

Future energy transition institutions, wherever they are located in the complex, multilevel governance system, need to be more culturally sensitive and attuned to allow for a thorough understanding of the organization and dynamics involving development choices. Broadly, these entail future institutions to recognize and understand: who are the relevant actors for a specific development intervention, policy, strategy, etc.? How could the decision-making process be opened up to avenues and platforms for engaging these networks of actors? Which relevant actors are typically (and/or historically) excluded from decision-making processes? How these habitually excluded actors can be included in the transition agenda? How could forces adverse to sustainable energy transitions be addressed? What are the relative values, preferences, lifestyles, interests, power, and influence of these actors? How could decisions-makers be provided with insights about the variety of lifestyles of multiple energy actors, their belief systems and routines, the qualities of their positions, and the possible resistance to changing them? How accurate are the processes of uncovering and understanding these multiple interests and values? Given these interests, power, and influence, what possible controversies and frictions may arise during these processes? How could these be negotiated or settled? What technologies or platforms can be used to ensure the engagement of these actors? How the process can be made sensitive to multiple expertise, cultural, and experiential backgrounds? How could the process be designed that would enable actors to make substantial, yet equal and fair, contributions? What criteria determine fair contributions?

Brought to fore when these questions are responded to and as transition institutions are focused on alleviating the human condition and in fulfilling capacities for meeting both sustainability and development agendas are elements of justice and equity, and of democracy and inclusiveness.

In developing countries, justice and equity can be considered in terms of its *processes*, which are related to emissions issues, and *outcomes*, which are related to vulnerabilities and impacts of change. Justice can also have distributive (i.e. the distribution of benefits and adverse impacts across societies) and procedural (i.e. to whom, and by whom the transition is made) forms.[15] Future institutions could contribute to the meaningful understanding of how the concept of justice and equity relate to transitions by asking themselves: how could concepts such as due process, transparency, and fairness be used to influence energy choices and practices? How could the transitions be designed such that its exercises, processes, and policies account for the sustainability of resources for future generations? How do the various energy system choices nurture or destroy the well-being of future generations? What are the implications of the various energy system choices on social justice? Do these options ensure fair distribution of the costs and benefits? What types of sustainable energy technologies and systems would empower those with less in life? What sustainable energy technologies and systems would address inequality, deprivation, and poverty in developing countries? What forms of fair, just, and non-paternalistic technology, financing, and capacity transfer can be designed? How could the decision-making process be structured so that the process itself opens up, includes, and engages habitually excluded actors, such as women and girls?

Inclusiveness – opening up processes and modes of engagement to wider public engagement – is also critical in future transition institutions. The institutional turn towards democratizing all aspects of the transition offers a number of co-benefits and should therefore be pursued. These include: increased public buy-in of the interventions; opportunities for collaborative learning; and the emergence of innovative ideas, useful analyses, and new information – all critical for learning and reflection, which are essential when scaling up. Opening up new avenues and bringing in multiple viewpoints to mingle within unruly arenas of civil society politics are both imperative in the institutional turn for accelerating sustainable energy transitions.[16]

Engaging multiple publics in this institutional turn – although time consuming and costly – can yield additional insights and may even include innovative solutions. Having access to this information is invaluable since decision-makers often differ in their degree of trade-off appreciation and the relative importance they place on uncertainties and risks. Future institutions need some structured guidance about what trade-offs and synergies to consider when facilitating the transitions, and these could include the following. How could institutions be altered and re-designed such that they enable the full participation and engagement from all relevant actors? What platforms could be established or strengthened to achieve greater level of public engagement? How could an environment and culture of epistemic respect and charity be fostered in these platforms? What democratic technologies can be used to effectively facilitate interactions among various forms of expertise in these engagement platforms? What are the risks and challenges of having weak or strong public engagement in a transition process, policy, initiative, or exercise? How could these be addressed?

The recognition of complexities and heterogeneities require that future institutions also have to be cognizant of the need to incorporate multiple insights in its mechanisms. Insightful comprehension of the complexities of transition challenges is imperative.[17] This entails welcoming expertise from several underpinning disciplines.[18] A trans-, inter- and multi-disciplinary approach to knowing is essential since a decision based only on one discipline risks missing the opportunities to have that discipline's weaknesses addressed by other competent fields of inquiry. An approach that revels on the multi-, inter- and transdisciplinarity of the transition architecture therefore is necessary to bring about a more coherent, integrated, and structured process. Future institutions need to understand the following: how could the research outputs of energy researchers be matched with the practical interests of policymakers, entrepreneurs, and other research end-users? What are the strengths and weaknesses of relevant disciplinary approaches? How do they complement each other? What are the disciplinary contradictions? How could insights outside the engineering and economic disciplines be included in the decision-making processes? How could decision-makers best couple quantitative and qualitative energy research insights? How could the often costly and complex qualitative energy researches be improved? What lay knowledge should be taken into account into the decision-making processes, and how this could be produced? How could these processes highlight, rather than erase, contributions from alternative epistemologies? How could these processes take advantage of comparable cases of successes and failures to shed light on the complex challenges of the transitions?

While there are no easy answers to these questions a normative institutional turn can be pushed and driven by making them better positioned and acclimatized to the new challenges of accelerating sustainable energy transitions.

7.2. Making better institutional arrangements

This section offers a normative design to make institutional arrangements for sustainable energy transitions expedient, coherent, and effective. Three sets of what could be called building blocks for achieving this purpose are described: the generation of transition tools (i.e. the hardware, financing, policy, initiatives, interventions, projects, programs); the manner by which these tools are delivered; and the processes and arrangements by which institutions deliver these tools. While an attempt has been made to cover as many essential elements and to provide these narratives, the list of criteria mentioned here is never comprehensive (see Table 7.2 for summary).

Table 7.2 Building blocks for making better institutional arrangements, their guiding principles, and criteria for evaluating them

Building blocks	Description	Guiding principle	Evaluation criteria
Tools generation and development	Tools refer to the resources for the transitions, including options for technological hardware, policy, and financing, and the capacity required to process them such as skills and knowledge transfers	Adequacy Predictability Equity Measurability	Scale Timeframe Level Source Contribution
Delivery	Options for delivering the transitions	Effectiveness Efficiency Equity Appropriateness	Engagement Theme Level
Institutions	Recognizing and understanding fragmentation and the need for coherence	Transparency Efficiency Effectiveness	Arrangements Coherence Level

Tools generation and development

The first block examines the range of tools that have been put forward to generate sustainable energy transitions. The tools of the transitions broadly refer to resources, capacity, and regulatory approaches. Resources include the technological hardware for meeting the access, efficiency, and renewable energy deployment objectives of the transition (as discussed in Chapter 3). It also includes technologies and systems for transmission and distribution (as discussed in Chapter 4), and the necessary policy push and financing support (as discussed in Chapters 5 and 6 respectively). Capacity includes the skills and knowledge transfers to individual and institutional actors to determine their hardware, deployment, policy, and financing options; recognize the trade-offs; understand the risks; design new systems; and implement, operate, and maintain them. Absorptive capacity, which refers to the capacity of actors to design, implement, monitor, and sustain transition activities, also falls under this ambit. For future institutions to maximize the potential use of these tools, some common principles can be used as guide: adequacy, predictability, equity, and measurability. To these ends, the various options can then be weighed according to some criteria, including scale, timeframe, level, source, and contribution.

The first step is understanding the extent to what tools will be needed that meet the principles earlier mentioned. The scale presents an estimate of how much of which type of tools will be required, as a whole and periodically, e.g. on an annual basis. The concept of scale is then linked to the questions of when the resource will become available and how predictable and sustainable it will be, especially for the longer term. How much new technology is needed? How much money will be raised? What new regulations are needed? How many people will be provided or trained with new skills? This criterion, in effect, addresses the adequacy principle.

Timeframe refers to the period when the tools required are likely to be made available and also responds to the adequacy principle. Depending on the timeframe of the development intervention, this can be short-term, medium-term, or long-term. The commitment periods under the Agenda 2030 (SDGs) (up to 2030) or the Paris Agreement may be used to distinguish them: medium-term (<2020) and long term (>2020). The availability of the transition tools over different timeframes is strongly related to their suitability. Certain activities such as capacity building, capacity strengthening, and pilot/demonstration projects will require upfront support in the short term, whereas other actions such as the implementation of national policies and measures for universal energy access or a full transition to higher penetration of renewables might not be required at scale after say 2020. In such cases, institutions may adopt a 'phased approach' concept where ambitions are stepped up following regular review and monitoring, which should happen frequently, say annually.[19]

Level describes whether the resources will be generated or developed locally, nationally, or internationally. This criterion addresses the predictability principle. Financial resources can be either generated or developed at the local level through local mobilization of local resources such as household contributions or from assistance from local governments. At the national level, these resources can be generated through national policy and frameworks such as a renewable energy target or emissions reduction target. At the international level, these resources can be produced using internationally agreed mechanisms such as the Green Climate Fund, technology transfers, bilateral and multilateral mechanisms, etc.

There are trade-offs that must be considered when examining the level criterion. In developing countries, local and national level resource generation is often considered to be unpredictable due largely to the competing concerns of other local and national interests and circumstances. Resources from the international level faces political challenges since contributing countries have historically preferred to maintain visibility and control over their contribution to international finance.

Source refers to the type of social, political, institutional, or economic instruments used to generate or develop the tools. This criterion also addresses the predictability principle since these instruments can be broadly grouped into categories, according to their varying predictability, sustainability, and adequacy. In funding the transition activity for example, both market (e.g. revenues from a carbon price) and non-market mechanisms (e.g. grants) should be considered. These instruments will face barriers and challenges since, among other reasons, they are governed by independent international organizations and national governments.

The contribution criterion describes 'who will pay' for the development intervention. These include actors who will provide the technology hardware, the financing, and the policy and regulations. This criterion responds to the principles of equity and measurability. Central to the design of international climate finance mechanisms, for instance, is the contribution or 'burden-sharing' of payments. There is a multitude of ways to interpret 'responsibility' and 'capability' under the United Nations Framework Convention on Climate Change (UNFCCC). Greenhouse gas emissions, both historical and current, and gross domestic product have been used as proxies for determining 'responsibility' and 'capability,' but the choice of application and weighing of these metrics will have implications for the distribution of commitments across countries, including high emission states in the global south.[20] In the absence of clear sources and mechanisms for the allocation of funds, it is prudent that developing countries also seek options other than those externally provided by international climate finance. This brings about the need to respond to the question of where these new contributions to transition finance can come from and how to tap them.

Delivery

The second block explores the options for delivering interventions that support sustainable energy transitions. How is the technological hardware delivered? How is finance delivered? How is knowledge or skills-strengthening delivered? Who will benefit? Which activities will be rewarded? As transition tools are made available, transition conduits and intended users will need to appropriate delivery instruments and mechanisms. An array of state and non-state delivery instruments and mechanisms are currently available.[21] The choice of delivery instruments will depend on how and why the resource is being generated or the capacity is being developed or strengthened.[22] These choices have to be clearly articulated. A set of common principles can be used as guide for future transition institutions in designing transition delivery instruments: effectiveness, efficiency, equity, and appropriateness. To analyze and understand the different options for the delivery of transition tools, three criteria can be derived from these principles: engagement, theme, and level.

The engagement criterion, which responds to the equity principle, aims to identify the types of countries, regions, localities, or communities that are most likely to benefit from a given intervention or support. The ability of end-users to receive support (or to repay or recoup it) is important in the design of the intervention itself.[23] In transition finance, for example, concessional loans require some level of capacity to manage repayments. Engaging end-users needs to be reconsidered as a multi-way process, not just the typical back-and-forth one. This entails appreciating and navigating public engagement on transition activities in terms of equity co-produced by a diverse cohort of actors producing turbulent and rhizoidal transitions.[24]

Theme describes transition activities or interventions that would be appropriate to receive development support – hence, responds to the appropriateness principle. Certain tools are more appropriate for different types of interventions than others. Some development interventions have very clear outcomes – for instance, a market approach is appropriate primarily for activities related to delivering measurable and verifiable development-mitigation outcomes. However, others are less definitive, and the appropriateness of support may be contingent on other factors. For example, the use of loans is unlikely to be appropriate for technology transfer or capacity / skill building / enhancement exercises but may apply across different interventions depending on a series of other factors such as financial returns likely associated with the intervention and the social, political, and economic contexts of end-users. The thematic balance chosen for transition activities will also determine equitable allocation of development interventions. The balance will influence which countries, regions, communities, or sectors are likely to receive support.

Support for transition activities can be delivered either at the project level at communities, the private sector, or local governments, or at the national level, or at the international level. This criterion responds to the principles of both effectiveness and efficiency. Project-based interventions are those where support is delivered to either public or private entities for the implementation of individual projects within a specific location and timeframe. Most access interventions fall in this type. Programmatic delivery of support, by contrast, is for longer-term coordinated planning, sector budget support, or general budget support. Large-scale access programs, industrial energy efficiency programs, and utility-scale solar PV are some examples.

Programmatic support typically involves the integration of transition tools – funding, skills, or technologies – into the institutional arrangements of end-users – their organizational structure, budgets, agencies, labor, or certain sectors or groups. The level at which these interventions are delivered will have important implication for both the effectiveness – in terms of scale achieved, reduced risk of leakage, ownership, and coordination with other transition activities – and the efficiency of the intervention or support itself. Often, programmatic support is more likely to achieve economies of scale and is often associated with reduced transaction costs and risks to both providers and end-users.

Nonetheless, project-based support has a number of key advantages. In case of transition finance, for example, contributing countries are often unwilling to deliver pooled funding because of concerns of fiduciary responsibilities and other risks related to larger scale funding in programmatic support – hence the allure of project-based finance. In many developing countries, project-level support may be more appropriate especially for end-users who lack the institutional capacity to apply programmatic-level of interventions to energy transition activities. Combining project-based with programmatic approaches can, nonetheless, be done through 'nested approach' interventions such as through working coalitions and public-private partnerships.

Institutions

The proliferation of institutions at the national and international levels could led to a fragmented, decentralized model in which developing countries will be presented with an array of uncoordinated activities, aims, and tools of and for the transitions. The plurality of institutions with different governance structures and approaches makes the management of development interventions complicated for recipient countries, especially for those with 'weak' or absent institutional arrangements to coordinate transition-related activities. In the absence of strong coordination mechanisms, fragmentation can lead to competing centers of authority – where institutions compete for funding and political attention – and further duplication of efforts. Synergizing agendas, explicitly delineating immediate outcomes, and identifying potential and concrete benefits of linkages need to be central in new institutional designs.[25] Some principles to address fragmentation include transparency, efficiency, and effectiveness. The following criteria can be used: arrangements, coherence, and level.

Creating new and/or strengthening existing institutional arrangements are options that depend upon the level of governance, capacities, and the boundaries of the transition agenda itself. A central argument for creating or reforming new institutions is that existing ones might represent contradicting views and competing interests with climate-and-development goals. This is particularly important since institutions and their contexts are decisive factors in deployment, especially those comprising complex and large-scale technologies whose formative and deployment phases need to be compressed to meet the speed requirement.[26] In the case of the time-bound energy transitions, having a unique institutional arrangement with strong mandate to aggressively pursue the accelerated transition objectives and coordinate the various activities of multiple actors is an essential step forward to achieve goals in time. This criterion addresses the transparency principle.

The extent by which there will be consolidation of resource contributions (e.g. in international climate finance, or between ministries of energy and environment in terms of policy and target-setting), channels of resources (e.g. the Green Climate Fund vis-à-vis multilateral development banks, national development banks vis-à-vis private banks, national-level departments vis-à-vis local governments), recipient institutions (e.g. public institutions vis-à-vis private sector vis-à-vis civil society organizations) are options that are also dependent upon specific circumstances and contexts. There must be coherence amongst institutions delivering heterogeneously produced transition activities through some forms of coordination, interconnection, or linkage mechanisms. This criterion addresses the principles of efficiency and effectiveness.

The level of coherence among transition institutions is a spectrum ranging from a fully consolidated institution at the international and national levels to a completely fragmented, plural architecture at the other. A fully amalgamated model would require that all resources be channeled and received through a single entity at both the conduit and the end-user nodes.[27] At the other end of this spectrum is a fragmented system that would involve disaggregated delivery of interventions.[28] A more likely option is a hybrid system, with more consolidation at the top (where coordination mechanisms can be situated), and more fragmentation at the bottom. It is key to understand here the resulting complexities and trade-offs of this institutional turn to a polycentric governance system. Stronger coordination and information exchanges among state agencies and non-state actors are imperatives in this institutional turn.[29]

Broadly, there are two ways at which decisions can be made: centralized or decentralized. At the international level, centralization means decisions can be made through an international body such as the Conference of Parties to the UNFCCC, or a representative high-level body, or a governing entity of a multilateral fund. At the national level, it can be through a central agency, often attached to the executive branch. Decentralization, which relieves international and national bodies of an otherwise unmanageable number of operational decisions related to the approval of interventions, for example, means individual actors can make decisions on how they wish to contribute to the transitions. This 'level' criterion addresses both efficiency and effectiveness principles.

Linkages between a central institution and the diversified and decentralized actors and institutions are imperative. Partnerships and working coalitions amongst actors from both state and non-state institutions, often working on public-private partnerships, have been demonstrated to work in practice, and hence need to be supported and scaled. Pro-poor public-private partnerships (or 5Ps), for example, can be used as a vehicle for meeting universal energy access as well as for harvesting energy efficiency potentials and deploying renewable energy.[30]

7.3.   Institutional turn approaches

The multiple dimensions of the necessary institutional turn to support the acceleration of sustainable energy transitions in developing countries described in the previous section require recognizing the diversity of the criteria to be considered, the polycentric nature of transition governance, and the heterogeneity of interests and power involved. There are several approaches to capture these nuances. This section broadly and briefly describes at least three of these approaches below.

Polycentrism

Accelerating the transitions in developing countries requires many linked things. It can be argued that the transitions occur in a polycentric environment, where transition initiatives spring from pockets of solutions across multiple scales and levels, driven and sustained by numerous individuals, groups, and organizations with varying goals and interests. Indeed, a number of transition initiatives have been occurring at the community level such as in cooperatives, community renewable energy, real-world laboratories, transition clubs, etc. for income generation, job creation, social cohesion, and learning purposes. At the same time, transition activities are also occurring in cities and local governments,[31] in states and provinces, and, of course, at the national level. Several actors are involved in these many processes, from development workers to small- and medium-sized entrepreneurs to rural and national development banks to multilateral development banks to private investors to policymakers to utilities to regulators. The first approach in the institutional turn requires that these transition initiatives and their key actors are networked and coordinated.[32]

The processes of linking heterogeneous initiatives by multiple actors with their own vested interests can be demanding in that these require meeting certain conditions in polycentricity to be deemed successful.[33] These conditions are: shared perception of a common resource (this can be the global climate system, etc.), which may be challenging to be agreed upon in a consensus; reliable information on the condition of the common resource; trust among key actors; social capital; good communication about the state of the resource; effective monitoring of one's behavior by those who access the resource; long time horizons; and linkages to individual benefits.[34] While acknowledging the polycentric nature of transition governance is imperative, the polycentric approach is not perfect.[35] It tends to ignore divisive politics, including issues of interests[36] and power[37] – hence the need for some innovative complementary approaches such as multi-criteria mapping and deliberative exercises.

Multi-criteria mapping

The multiplicity and diversity of criteria that needs to be accounted for when navigating the transition calls for a multi-criteria mapping approach. This approach aids actors to appreciate the multiple facets of the task ahead and understand the risks, trade-offs, benefits, and strategies. A multi-criteria mapping approach opens up assessment processes by mapping the practical implications of alternative options, their uncertainties and risks, their trade-offs and synergies, and the different perspectives and values inherent to multiple choices.[38]

As a method, multi-criteria mapping allows participants to define their own 'options' to address a particular aim. Bringing out these options ensures comparability across different perspectives. Using their own evaluative criteria, the participants then assess each option. Everyone is free to amend these criteria but has to provide reasoning behind the amendment. For sustainable energy transitions, these appraisal criteria diverge according to purpose (i.e. access, efficiency, or renewable energy deployment, or a combination), location (i.e. local, national, or international), scale (small, medium, large), and the availability of the transition tools.

Some example criteria – in addition to ones describe in the previous section – that can be considered when mapping options for transition include: costs, air pollution, water pollution, water consumption, health impacts, affordability, reliability, stability, climate change impact, public acceptability, land use, aesthetics, employment, income generation, community empowerment, democracy, inclusion, justice, etc. Each criterion is then assigned scores reflecting positive and negative views of conditions. In every option, participants make detailed notes on the reasons of their judgments. This allows for the development of a rich picture of the relevant risks and uncertainties, as well as their practical implications, especially synergies and benefits to end-users.[39] The process ends by assigning weights to express the relative subjective importance of the various criteria used. Decisions can then be made at the conclusion of this decision-making method.

Deliberative exercises

Deliberative exercises are inclusive and democratic ways that enable citizens to participate in processes that impact their own future.[40] Thus far, these exercises appear to be the most intensive form of public engagement approaches developed and practiced. The inclusiveness of this approach is in its aim to produce ranking options that could then be considered in actual decisions. Instead of one option, participants[41] in a deliberative exercise develop a list of options that are then ranked using multiple criteria, which is similar to multi-criteria mapping described above. Because participants do not work on one best option, the process results in more reflexivity[42] and, hence, diversity, which often include options that were not previously considered or thought about. For the rankings to be credible, however, they have to be normatively justified and empirically validated. In addition, balance and adequate representation of relevant actors in the exercise are also vital.

In gist, a deliberative exercise has to be authentic, inclusive, and consequential.[43] Authenticity entails that participants, under conditions of equality and fairness, can entertain and welcome various competing arguments and alternatives to an issue they are trying to provide solution to during the exercise.

Inclusivity ensures that participants are provided with ample opportunity to learn, participate, reflect, and engage in the pluralities of options presented before them. Consequentiality means that the results of the deliberative exercise are reflected in the decisions made.

Some advanced forms of deliberative techniques have gone beyond mapping multiple options towards making the final decision and implementing that decision. This far end of the public engagement spectrum has mostly been shown to work in micro-settings, such as at community or village level; there are, however, various cases showing its wider application in state or national settings (e.g. the post-9/11 Manhattan deliberation, the British Columbia deliberation on electoral system) making it a promising approach to democratize the transitions. To maximize impact, deliberative processes for transition-making, however, have to be scaled. This requires linking deliberative sites in a wider deliberative system[44] that includes multiple forms of public engagement across the broader transition system comprising activism, grassroots innovation, and real-world laboratories.[45] This turn needs some form of institutional design that not only connects these many sites together[46] but also opens up more avenues for learning and reflection[47] for citizens to engage widely with the transitions.

7.4.   Conclusion

The complexities, messiness, and plurality of the processes and pathways to achieve sustainable energy transitions arise from the multiple aspects that need to be considered and the multiple activities and interests of multiple actors and institutions involved. Such diversity entails the recognition and understanding of the issues around power and interest: who decides for whom, whose interests matter most, etc.

Given the heterogeneity of the many aspects of the transitions, developing interventions, making decisions, implementing solutions, and monitoring initiatives, regardless of level of governance, would remain highly contested – and one that should be welcomed for its ability to bring about multiple approaches that could lead to plausible pathways for meaningful change.[48] Coordinating these efforts as they are linked adds to that messiness.[49] Nevertheless, this can be mitigated through a structured approach to governing and facilitating the transitions through a substantial turn in institutional arrangements. This turn need to highlight flexibility, dynamism, and adaptability.[50] Such turn needs to be informed by all applicable epistemic traditions, not only from engineering (the technical), economics (the financial), but also from other social sciences.

Scoping all tools available, both real and imagined, allows for better appreciation of the options' own limitations and strengths, their risks and trade-offs thereby bringing to light key aspects to be considered. Analyzing the many options for delivering these tools and making new or innovating existing institutional arrangements are equally vital. An effective, coherent, and democratic approach to this process is required to ensure better outcomes, although, of course, success could never be guaranteed. The systematic method for evaluating options and understanding their risks and trade-offs provided by multi-criteria mapping offers an opportunity for negotiating the transitions. This approach considers multiple options, investigates the synergies and trade-offs among the options, and carefully assignes scores on those options. On a similar vein, deliberative exercises, where inclusivity and democracy are at its core, further provide new avenues in which public engagement can be strengthened.

Accelerating sustainable energy transitions in developing countries is a highly contested proposition. Tensions can be expected when it enters official policy nomenclature and new development pathways are determined. This is especially true in countries whose economy and society are highly dependent on fossil fuels. Transitions in these areas are more complicated to process. Yet, the need to do the transition shall prevail. Stronger mechanisms that open up opportunities for public engagement may address this dilemma. Although not a panacea, a built in and strong public engagement in new institutional arrangements, through deliberative exercises for example, is key element for ensuring greater public appreciation, transparency, and robustness of transition-related interventions. Multiple co-benefits arise from these exercises – not just stronger engagement.

In closing, this chapter imagines an institutional turn for accelerating the transitions. Politics is not to be marginalized; instead, understanding whose power and interests matter and whose do not is key. Also important is for future transition institutions to recognize and appreciate the heterogeneity of the processes and actors involved in knowledge-making, capacity building, institutional strengthening, and coherent decision-making. The messiness, complexities, and tensions arising from these arrangements entail holistic, inclusive, structured, systematic, and reflexive institution-making that needs to be framed around justice, equity, inclusiveness, and strong public engagement. People-centric institutions, ones that place human development at its core, are key in accelerating sustainable energy transitions in developing countries.

Notes

1 These can also be considered as motivations as to why institutions need to coordinate, facilitate, and navigate the transitions, see Dubash, NK, et al. 2013, 'Developments in national climate change mitigation legislation and strategy,' *Climate Policy*, vol. 13, pp. 649–664; and Moncel, R & van Asselt, H 2012, 'All hands on deck! Mobilizing climate change action beyond the UNFCCC,' *Review of European, Comparative & International Environmental Law*, vol. 21, pp. 163–176.
2 See discussion in Abbott, KW 2011, 'The transnational regime complex for climate change,' *Environmental Planning C*, vol. 30, pp. 571–590; and Abbott, KW 2014, 'Strengthening the transnational regime complex for climate change,' *Transnational Environmental Law*, vol. 3, pp. 57–88.
3 Zelli, F & van Asselt, H 2013, 'The institutional fragmentation of global environmental governance: Causes, consequences, and responses,' *Global Environmental Politics*, vol. 13, pp. 1–13; also see Abbott, K 2012, 'The transnational regime complex for climate change,' *Environment and Planning C: Politics and Space*, vol. 30, pp. 571–590.
4 Biermann, F, et al. 2009, 'The fragmentation of global governance architecture: A framework for analysis,' *Global Environmental Politics*, vol. 9, pp. 14–40.

5 Marquardt, citing examples from the Philippines and its development cooperation landscape in the field of renewable energy, found that the absence of coordination could easily lead to long-term failure of a development intervention, see Marquardt, J 2016, 'Diversification in practice: How fragmented aid affects renewable energy support in the Philippines,' in S Klingebiel, T Mahn & M Negre (Eds.), *The Fragmentation of Aid: Concepts, Measurements and Implications for Development Cooperation*, Palgrave Macmillan: London, UK, pp. 199–214.

6 Stirling, A 2010, 'Keep it complex,' *Nature*, vol. 468, pp. 1029–1031.

7 Lachapelle, E & Paterson, M 2013, 'Drivers of national climate policy,' *Climate Policy*, vol. 13, pp. 547–571.

8 Chilvers, J & Longhurst, N 2015, 'Participation in transition(s): Reconceiving public engagements in energy transitions as produced, emergent and diverse,' *Journal of Environmental Policy & Planning*, vol. 18, pp. 585–607.

9 The most essential of which is to identify real and aspirational demand, to understand capacity to pay, and to match and respond accordingly.

10 Bulkeley, H, et al. 2014, *Transnational Climate Change Governance*, Cambridge University Press: Cambridge, UK; Green, JF 2013, *Rethinking Private Authority: Agents and Entrepreneurs in Global Environmental Governance*, Princeton University Press: Princeton, NJ, USA.

11 Biesenbender, S & Tosun, J 2014, 'Domestic politics and the diffusion of international policy innovations: How does accommodation happen?,' *Global Environmental Change*, vol. 29, pp. 424–433.

12 Avelino, F & Rotmans, J 2009, 'Power in transition an interdisciplinary framework to study power in relation to structural change,' *European Journal of Social Theory*, vol. 12, pp. 543–569.

13 Stirling, A 2014, 'Transforming power: Social science and the politics of energy choices,' *Energy Research and Social Science*, vol. 1, pp. 83–95.

14 cf. Newell, P, et al. 2015, 'Governance traps in climate change politics: Re-framing the debate in terms of responsibilities and rights,' *WIREs Climate Change*, vol. 6, pp. 535–540.

15 Miller, N 1992, 'Distributive justice: What the people think,' *Ethics*, vol. 102, pp. 555–593; Anand, P 2001, 'Procedural fairness in economic and social choice: Evidence from a survey of voters,' *Journal of Economic Psychology*, vol. 22, pp. 247–270; Newell, P & Mulvaney, D 2013, 'The political economy of the "just transition",' *The Geographical Journal*, vol. 179, pp. 132–140; Goldthau, A & Sovacool, B 2012, 'The uniqueness of the energy security, justice and governance problem,' *Energy Policy*, vol. 41, pp. 232–240.

16 Shove, E & Walker, G 2007, 'CAUTION! Transitions ahead: Politics, practice and sustainable transition management,' *Environment and Planning A*, vol. 39, pp. 763–770.

17 Jordan, AJ, et al. 2015, 'Emergence of polycentric climate governance and its future prospects,' *Nature Climate Change*, vol. 5, pp. 977–982.

18 Wong-Parodi, G, et al. 2016, 'A decision science approach for integrating social science in climate and energy solutions,' *Nature Climate Change*, vol. 6, pp. 563–569; Jasanoff, S 2011, 'Cosmopolitan knowledge: Climate science and global civic epistemology,' in JS Dryzek, RB Norgaard & D Schlosberg (Eds.), *The Oxford Handbook of Climate Change and Society*, Oxford University Press: Oxford, UK, pp. 129–143.

19 See Horn-Phathanothai, L 2016, 'Commentary: Making the links real,' World Resources Institute: Washington, DC, http://www.wri.org/news/commentary-making-links-real; Auld, G, et al. 2014, 'Evaluating the effects of policy innovations: Lessons from a systematic review of policies promoting low-carbon technology,' *Global Environmental Change*, vol. 29, pp. 444–458.

20 Newell, P, et al. 2015, 'Governance traps in climate change politics: Re-framing the debate in terms of responsibilities and rights,' *WIREs Climate Change*, vol. 6, pp. 535–540.

21 Dubash, NK, et al. 2013, 'Developments in national climate change mitigation legislation and strategy,' *Climate Policy*, vol. 13, pp. 649–664; Lachapelle, E & Paterson, M 2013, 'Drivers of national climate policy,' *Climate Policy*, vol. 13, pp. 547–571.

22 Bulkeley, H, et al. 2012, 'Governing climate change transnationally: Assessing the evidence from a database of sixty initiatives,' *Environmental Planning C*, vol. 30, pp. 591–612.

23 Ostrom, E 2010, 'Polycentric systems for coping with collective action and global environmental change,' *Global Environmental Change*, vol. 20, pp. 550–557; Ostrom, E 2014, 'A polycentric approach for coping with climate change,' *Annals of Economics and Finance*, vol. 15, pp. 71–108.

24 Jasanoff, S (Ed.) 2004, *States of Knowledge: The Co-Production of Science and Social Order*, Routledge: London; Chilvers, J & Longhurst, N 2016, 'Participation in transition(s): Reconceiving public engagements in energy transitions as co-produced, emergent and diverse,' *Journal of Environmental Policy & Planning*, vol. 18, pp. 585–607.

25 Janetos, A, et al. 2012, 'Linking climate change and development goals: Framing, integrating, and measuring,' *Climate and Development*, vol. 4, pp. 141–156; Bäckstrand, K 2008, 'Accountability of networked climate governance: The rise of transnational climate partnerships,' *Global Environmental Politics*, vol. 8, pp. 74–102.

26 Delina, L 2016, *Strategies for Rapid Climate Mitigation: Wartime Mobilisation as a Model for Action?*, Routledge-Earthscan: Abingdon, Oxon, UK.

27 Delina, L 2012, 'Coherence in energy efficiency governance,' *Energy for Sustainable Development*, vol. 16, pp. 493–499.

28 See Delina, L 2017, 'Multilateral development banking in a fragmented climate finance system: Shifting priorities in energy finance at the Asian Development Bank,' *International Environmental Agreements: Politics, Law and Economics*, vol. 17, pp. 73–88.

29 Also see Horn-Phathanothai, L 2016, 'Commentary: Making the links real,' World Resources Institute: Washington, DC, http://www.wri.org/news/commentary-making-links-real; Marquardt, J, Steibacher, K & Shreurs, M 2016, 'Driving force or forced transition? The role of development cooperation in promoting energy transitions in the Philippines and Morocco,' *Journal of Cleaner Production*, vol. 128, pp. 22–33; Bulkeley, H, et al. 2012, 'Governing climate change transnationally: Assessing the evidence from a database of sixty initiatives,' *Environmental Planning C*, vol. 30, pp. 591–612.

30 Sovacool, BK 2013, 'Expanding renewable energy access with pro-poor public-private partnerships in the developing world,' *Energy Strategy Reviews*, vol. 1, pp. 181–192.

31 Bulkeley, H, et al. 2014, *Transnational Climate Change Governance*, Cambridge University Press: Cambridge, UK.

32 Mansbridge, J 2014, 'The role of the state in governing the commons,' *Environmental Science and Policy*, vol. 36, pp. 8–10; Aligic, PD 2014, *Institutional Diversity and Political Economy: The Ostroms and Beyond*, Oxford University Press: Oxford, UK.

33 Ostrom, E 2010, 'Polycentric systems for coping with collective action and global environmental change,' *Global Environmental Change*, vol. 20, pp. 550–557; Ostrom, E 2014, 'A polycentric approach for coping with climate change,' *Annals of Economics and Finance*, vol. 15, pp. 71–108.

34 Dryzek, J, Norgaard, R & Schlosberg, D 2013, *Climate Challenged Society*, Oxford University Press: New York.

35 Ostrom, E, Janssen, MA & Anderies, JM 2007, 'Going beyond panaceas,' *PNAS*, vol. 104, pp. 15176–15178.

36 Biesenbender, S & Tosun, J 2014, 'Domestic politics and the diffusion of international policy innovations: How does accommodation happen?,' *Global Environmental Change*, vol. 29, pp. 424–433.

37 Kellon, D & Arvai, J 2011, 'Five propositions for improving decision making about the environment in developing communities: Insights from the decision sciences,' *Journal of Environmental Management*, vol. 92, pp. 363–371.

38 Zhou, P, Ang, BW & Poh, KL 2006, 'Decision analysis in energy and environmental modeling: An update,' *Energy*, vol. 31, pp. 2604–2622.

39 Kellon, D & Arvai, J 2011, 'Five propositions for improving decision making about the environment in developing communities: Insights from the decision sciences,' *Journal of Environmental Management*, vol. 92, pp. 363–371.

40 Dryzek, J 2000, *Deliberative Democracy and Beyond: Liberals, Critics, Contestations*, Oxford University Press: New York.

41 Participants in a deliberative exercise are selected using a systematic and structured process that considers the heterogeneity of the public. The selected cohort, in deliberative democracy parlance, is called a 'mini-public.'

42 Dryzek, JS & Pickering, J 2017, 'Deliberation as a catalyst for reflexive environmental governance,' *Ecological Economics*, vol. 131, pp. 353–360.

43 Dryzek, J 2000, *Deliberative Democracy and Beyond: Liberals, Critics, Contestations*, Oxford University Press: New York.

44 Felicetti, A, Niemeyer, S & Curato, N 2016, 'Improving deliberative participation: Connecting mini-publics to deliberative systems,' *European Political Science Review*, vol. 8, pp. 427–448; Curato, N & Boker, M 2016, 'Linking mini-publics to the deliberative system: A research agenda,' *Policy Science*, vol. 49, pp. 173–190.

45 Chilvers, J & Longhurst, N 2015, 'Participation in transition(s): Reconceiving public engagements in energy transitions as produced, emergent and diverse,' *Journal of Environmental Policy & Planning*, vol. 18, pp. 585–607; Chilvers, J & Kearnes, M (Eds.) 2016, *Remaking Participation: Science, Environment, and Emergent Publics*, Routledge: Abingdon, Oxon, UK.

46 Hendriks, C 2016, 'Coupling citizens and elites in deliberative systems: The role of institutional design,' *European Journal of Political Research*, vol. 55, pp. 43–60.

47 Chilvers, J 2013, 'Reflexive engagement? Actors, learning, and reflexivity in public dialogue on science and technology,' *Science Communication*, vol. 35, pp. 283–310; Smith, A & Stirling, A 2007, 'Moving outside or inside? Objectification and reflexivity in the governance of socio-technical systems,' *Journal of Environmental Policy and Planning*, vol. 9, pp. 351–373.

48 Stirling, A 2010, 'Keep it complex,' *Nature*, vol. 468, pp. 1029–1031.

49 Jordan, AJ, et al. 2015, 'Emergence of polycentric climate governance and its future prospects,' *Nature Climate Change*, vol. 5, pp. 977–982; Janetos, A, et al. 2012, 'Linking climate change and development goals: Framing, integrating, and measuring,' *Climate and Development*, vol. 4, pp. 141–156; Bäckstrand, K 2008, 'Accountability of networked climate governance: The rise of transnational climate partnerships,' *Global Environmental Politics*, vol. 8, pp. 74–102.

50 Auld, G, et al. 2014, 'Evaluating the effects of policy innovations: Lessons from a systematic review of policies promoting low-carbon technology,' *Global Environmental Change*, vol. 29, pp. 444–458.

8   Conclusion

Accelerating sustainable energy transitions in developing countries needs to be institutionalized as a key global agenda. The transitions require tectonic shifts in the mobilization of necessary resources, both the technological hardware and the non-technical solutions. Most of the technologies required in the transitions are market ready – and will be, in the short term, more accessible and affordable for developing countries. The falling cost, the economies of scale, public preference over sustainable solutions, the associated benefits to health, education, the economy, and inclusiveness are among the many reasons why the transitions are necessary. Most importantly, however, the transitions are required to achieve universal energy access and the reduction of greenhouse gas emissions – both of which are key aspects of international norms on sustainable development and climate change action. Accelerating the transitions towards sustainable energy-powered societies in developing countries requires a focus on three key solutions: universal energy access, energy efficiency, and renewable energy. The underlying objective, of course, remains consistent with both the development and the climate ambitions: new renewable energy generation to compensate for the retirement of polluting energy systems without harming the development objectives of those in the global south, and doing this rapidly. Navigating this process is not an easy task. It requires simultaneous turns in the deployment of the transition hardware with key changes in policy, financing, and institutional arrangements. In many developing countries, such turns necessitate the strongest political will – and in the absence of one, the strongest means of activism and social action.

Developing countries are heterogeneous in a number of respects. Their development trajectories are as varied as their demography, cultures, capacities, and national endowments. The extent by which energy has been made accessible to the population also varies. In the countries studied for this book, there remains a wide gap between the energy rich and the energy poor, between rural and urban energy consumers, between communities far from the grid and those with ready access to the grid, and between those with vast natural endowments and those with less. The human condition, at least during the last 20 years or so, has appeared to be improving in many of these countries. However, as better quality of life is achieved, the magnitude and intensities of carbon emissions, particularly from the energy sector, are also rising fast. The number-one emitter in the world now is from among the countries in the global south. These carbon profiles, alongside continuing development challenges that developing countries face, present both present and future implications. Addressing environmental sustainability and human development at the same time should, therefore, become an imperative for these countries. Adding to these complexities is the need to address these two-pronged challenges not only simultaneously but also as fast as we can. Taking these aspects altogether, the greatest challenge in the global south will be how to accelerate the transition towards sustainable development that puts a premium towards meeting the needs of those living in the present while also respecting the needs of those who are yet to be born without jeopardizing their own development aspirations.

Many countries in the global south are already at different levels of their transition hardware deployments. Closing the gap towards universal energy access is fast becoming a reality. China and Thailand, among the study countries, for instance, have already achieved universal access. Yet, the need to address the challenge of transitioning from dirty cooking fuels towards modern forms of energy, including improved cookstoves remains in many parts of the developing world. Deploying improved cookstoves and solar home systems, the key hardware for closing this gap, needs to be scaled rapidly. Another opportunity that many developing countries are missing, thus far, is related to the full exploitation of energy efficiency potentials. While many economies have already started to register improvements in their energy intensity, a number of developing countries still lack the capacity to make their energy generation, distribution, and consumption processes efficient. Bringing energy efficiency to the core of transition policy, thus, is imperative. Another aspect of the transitions – which is key in the decarbonization agenda – pertains to the rapid deployment of renewable energy technologies. Developing countries need additional capacity in a number of areas to finally retire their dirty coal-fired or natural gas-fired power plants and replace them with environmentally benign energy systems, wind and solar in particular. In many developing countries, the potential to tap wind and solar, alongside other renewable energies such as geothermal and micro-hydro, is high, yet barriers to entry remain solid; thus, the share of new renewables in the energy mixes of these countries remains at a very low level. While the key technologies to tap renewable energy potentials are already commercially available, with their cost fast decreasing, the transitions towards the greater use of renewables still need strong policy support to open up new markets, facilitate investment, and provide some form of guarantees. Policy, financing, and institutional turns therefore are necessary for accelerating the transitions.

The obvious variability and intermittency of the replacement technologies also calls for some form of hardware support. The hardware challenges, therefore, are no longer towards these technologies, but on the way they are and could be integrated. Integration is key. Yet in many developing countries, visions of how to process integration in the future remain absent. Every country and utility in the global south is different, and each will need to customize its own portfolio of integration solutions.

A turn in policy requires innovative, stronger, credible, predictable, and coherent policy to transmit new signals of support to investors and the public at large. The greater the degree of commitment on the part of government means the louder the signal. In many developing countries, however, this, at present, registers a key challenge. Many state policies are either fragmented as is clearly shown, for example, in the weak correspondence between energy and climate policy. Coherence of policy frames is important in the long term since this contributes to more predictable policy direction.

A turn in financing requires a strategic and portfolio approach to provide capital for the transitions. Mobilizing transition finance in developing countries has to simultaneously occur across multiple scales using public, private, and hybrid financing streams. Accessible, affordable, flexible, stable, and reliable finance remains necessary to support transition-related activities. In many developing countries, this requires ready access to capital, which entails flexibility in lending terms such as zero to minimal collateral requirement, staged repayment terms, reduced interest rates, and preferential treatment, among others. Ensuring the financial sustainability of transition-related hardware and systems, especially post-deployment, is also essential. Although the availability of finance is important, efforts to remove key financing barriers are equally necessary. Many developing countries will need additional support to strengthen the capacity of institutions: public, private, non-state, and financial intermediaries, as well as that of end-users. The goal is to develop sound planning mechanisms to facilitate capital-intensive investments, backed by appropriate risk mitigation instruments in terms that funders and end-users can clearly understand.

An institutional turn is necessary in response to the complexities of the processes and pathways to achieve sustainable energy transitions. The diversity of actors involved, as well as of their power and interests, entails the recognition and understanding that the transitions will be governed in a polycentric arrangement. Coordinating the many efforts as they happen across many pockets of governance requires a structured and systematic approach to governing and facilitating the transition. This institutional turn needs to highlight flexibility, dynamism, and adaptability informed by all applicable epistemic traditions, not only from engineering (the technical) and economics (the financial) but also from other social sciences. This turn also entails scoping all tools available to better appreciate the options' own limitations and strengths, their risks and trade-offs. An effective, coherent, and democratic approach to this process is essential to ensure public buy-in and better outcomes, although, of course, success could never be guaranteed. The systematic method for evaluating options and understanding their risks and trade-offs provided by multi-criteria mapping and deliberative exercises needs to be incorporated in future institutional arrangements. Scaling up the transitions and accelerating them would require linking innovative institutional arrangements through working coalitions, partnerships, and networks.

Index

rebate 93, 105, 107–108, 110, 115–116
rebound 46, 91
reflexivity 13, 94, 152, 164, 166, 169
refrigeration 2, 3, 8, 45–46, 59, 62, 70, 104
regulation xiii, 7, 11–12, 15, 49, 57, 71–73, 75–76, 79, 85, 88, 91–94, 99, 102–103, 105, 107, 109, 113, 115, 118, 124–125, 127, 130, 133, 140, 151, 153–154, 158–159, 163
regulatory approach *see* regulation
REIPPP *see* Renewable Energy Independent Power Procurement Program
reliability xiii, 2–4, 8, 10, 25–26, 31–32, 42, 44–45, 49, 58, 63, 74–75, 77, 80, 82, 88, 100–101, 114–115, 126, 133, 145–146, 164
Renewable Energy Independent Power Procurement Program 114, 116, 118
Reserve Bank of India 130, 147
resilience 23, 149
revolution xiv, 6
Rousseff, Dilma 94
Russia xix, 142

SDG7 *see* Sustainable Development Goal 7
SDGs *see* Sustainable Development Goals
SE4All *see* Sustainable Energy for All
Shaanxi Green Energy 62
Shandong 64, 92
Shengshan Island 64
shipping 2
small and medium enterprise 15, 45, 73, 125–126, 143, 149, 152
small-scale public-private partnership 143; *see also* 5Ps
smart grid 75, 83–85, 99
SME *see* small and medium enterprise
Smil, Vaclav 11, 18–20
social action 7, 18, 154, 170; *see also* activism
sociotechnical system 6–7, 12, 87
solar energy xi, 46, 49, 58–61, 63, 79–80, 93, 97–98, 111, 123
solar lantern 3, 132, 144
Solar Lantern Project 144
Sorsogon 62

South Africa xix, xxii, 16, 18, 21, 23–36, 38, 47–50, 53, 56, 59–60, 63, 79, 89, 91, 93, 96, 98, 102–103, 105–106, 111, 113–114, 116–118, 127–128, 132, 137, 140, 146
South America 63
South Asia 21, 84, 142
Southeast Asia 15, 21, 39, 57, 118
south-to-south 16, 120
Sovacool, Benjamin 12–13, 17–20, 42–43, 65–66, 73, 79, 85–86, 109, 118, 149, 167–168
state development bank *see* national development bank
Stirling, Andy 18, 154, 167, 169
stockpiling 9
storage 11, 49–50, 52, 59–61, 66, 70, 73, 82–85, 99, 111
stranded assets 12, 44
Sub-Saharan Africa xii, 3, 140–141, 148–149
subsidy xii, xiv, 12, 43, 72–73, 85, 90, 105, 108–109, 114–116, 118, 126, 128–129, 138, 146
sugarcane bagasse 53, 112
Sumatra 62
SunSawang 144
supply side management *see* energy efficiency
Sustainable Development Goal 7 xx, 2–3, 6, 8, 11, 17, 26, 30
Sustainable Development Goals xiii, xiv, xx, 2, 5, 11, 14, 16–17, 30, 72, 151, 158, 161, 168–169
Sustainable Energy for All xiii, xv, xx, 2, 17, 25, 31, 53–54, 56, 59, 61, 143
Suzlon Group 58
Swedish International Development Agency 144
synergy 69, 151, 156, 161, 164, 166

tax xii, 72, 91, 104–108, 111, 115–116, 118, 124, 126–128, 138
technology transfer 159–160
Thailand xvii, 15, 16, 21–34, 36, 47–48, 50, 53, 54, 56–57, 59, 61–62, 67, 72, 79, 91, 93, 96, 98–99, 105–106, 109, 112, 117, 128, 133, 137, 140, 144, 147, 149, 171

For Product Safety Concerns and Information please contact our EU
representative GPSR@taylorandfrancis.com
Taylor & Francis Verlag GmbH, Kaufingerstraße 24, 80331 München, Germany